Process Facilitation in Psychoanalysis, Psychotherapy and Social Work

Process Facilitation in Psychoanalysis, Psychotherapy and Social Work elaborates a differential theory of therapeutic engagement with full reference not only to psychoanalysis and to psychotherapy but also – surprisingly – to social work. When contemporary social work with the marginalised achieves mutual constructive collaboration, social workers characteristically notice an unfolding process. Could this correspond to the 'analytic process' of psychoanalysis?

Sylvia O'Neill seeks to explain theoretically, and to illustrate clearly in practice, just how a quasi-autonomous therapeutic process becomes established. The theory underpinning the book is Jean-Luc Donnet's conceptualisation of the establishment of the analytic process in psychoanalysis through introjection of the analytic setting. Donnet designates the psychoanalytic setting as the analytic 'site'. O'Neill proceeds to trace, by means of detailed clinical discussion, the analogous process by which a viable therapeutic process can become established through created/found discovery and introjection of the relevant 'site' or setting in psychoanalytic psychotherapy and in social work. Amongst the most important elements are the practitioner's internalised theoretical principles.

The book demonstrates that unconscious introjection figures more importantly in effective therapeutic engagement than a conscious therapeutic alliance. An important corollary for social work is that, contrary to popular myth, no prior psychological-mindedness is required. The differential theory of *Process Facilitation in Psychoanalysis, Psychotherapy and Social Work* is equally relevant to psychodynamic counselling.

Sylvia O'Neill is a psychoanalytic psychotherapist practising privately in Edinburgh and in the NHS in Glasgow. She trained in psychotherapy at the Tavistock Clinic after practising social work in Melbourne and London. Her published research interests include therapeutic engagement, autistic pathology, male anorexia and professional cultures.

Process Facilitation in Psychoanalysis, Psychotherapy and Social Work

Sylvia O'Neill

Routledge
Taylor & Francis Group

LONDON AND NEW YORK

First published 2019
by Routledge
2 Park Square, Milton Park, Abingdon, Oxon OX14 4RN

and by Routledge
711 Third Avenue, New York, NY 10017

Routledge is an imprint of the Taylor & Francis Group, an informa business

British Library Cataloguing in Publication Data
A catalogue record for this book is available from the British Library

Library of Congress Cataloging in Publication Data
Names: O'Neill, Sylvia, 1946- author.
Title: Process facilitation in psychoanalysis, psychotherapy and social
    work / Sylvia O'Neill.
Description: New York : Routledge, 2018. | Includes bibliographical
    references and index.
Identifiers: LCCN 2018004796 (print) | LCCN 2018013381 (ebook) |
    ISBN 9780429490651 (Master) | ISBN 9780429955556 (Web PDF) |
    ISBN 9780429955549 (ePub) | ISBN 9780429955532 (Mobipocket/
    Kindle) | ISBN 9781138591080 (hardback : alk. paper) |
    ISBN 9781138591097 (pbk. : alk. paper)
Subjects: LCSH: Psychotherapy. | Psychoanalysis. | Social case work.
Classification: LCC RC465.5 (ebook) | LCC RC465.5 .O54 2018 (print)
    | DDC 616.89/14—dc23
LC record available at https://lccn.loc.gov/2018004796

ISBN: 978-1-138-59108-0 (hbk)
ISBN: 978-1-138-59109-7 (pbk)
ISBN: 978-0-429-49065-1 (ebk)

Typeset in Times New Roman
by Swales & Willis Ltd, Exeter, Devon, UK

To Fionnuala
who believed in a book not yet written

Contents

Acknowledgements

My thanks are due in a number of quarters.

Some parts of this book make use of previously published material, which is reproduced here by kind permission from the copyright holders:

Chapter 3 was originally published in *European Psychotherapy* in 2008 as follows: O'Neill, Sylvia, 'The psychotherapy site: towards a differential theory of therapeutic engagement'. It is reprinted here, with revision, by kind permission of the publisher, CIP-Medien Verlag.

Chapter 4 first appeared in 2015 as O'Neill, Sylvia, 'The facilitating function of the setting' in the *British Journal of Psychotherapy*, pp. 463–475, volume 31, issue 4, November 2015, published by Artesian Books Ltd. It is featured in revised form in this book by permission of John Wiley & Sons, Inc.

Chapters 10 and 11 were originally published in the *Journal of Social Work Practice* in 2001 and 2003 respectively as linked papers as follows: O'Neill, Sylvia, 'Michael, part one: a boy in conflict with the school authorities', pp. 205–213, volume 15, issue 2, 2001 and O'Neill, Sylvia, 'Michael, part two: conflict and resolution in the transference', pp. 25–34, volume 17, issue 1, 2003, copyright © GAPS. They are reprinted here in revised form by permission of Taylor & Francis, LLC (www.tandfonline.com) on behalf of GAPS.

In addition, I am grateful to Sandie Meyer for the informal permission she gave me, many years ago, to avail myself of the very coherent account she gave of the work described in Chapters 10 and 11.

Chapter 12 includes passages from an article that appeared 2007 in *Psychoanalytic Psychotherapy* as follows: O'Neill, Sylvia, 'The introjected psychodynamic site: a theory of the therapeutic process in psychodynamic practice', pp. 197–215, volume 21, issue 3, 2007 © Copyright Informa UK Limited, reproduced here by permission of Taylor & Francis Ltd (www.tandfonline.com).

Chapter 7 and a brief passage in Chapter 1 draw on O'Neill, Sylvia, 'Psychoanalytic application and psychoanalytic integrity', pp. 125–146, volume 86, issue 1, February 2005, from the *International Journal of Psychoanalysis.* Reprinted by permission of John Wiley & Sons, Inc.

I would like to express my thanks to the staff of the National Library of Scotland for their courtesy and helpfulness over a period of years.

Since a book such as this attempts to pass on certain traditions, I should like to place on record the names of some of my one-time teachers – some, sadly, no longer living – who have been an abiding influence: at the University of Melbourne, Leonard Tierney and Louise Arnold; at the Family Welfare Association, Jane Knight; at the Tavistock Clinic, David Malan and John Steiner. While I wish to pay high tribute to their inspiration and influence, they cannot of course be held responsible if what I have made of their teaching has strayed from what they would wish to represent.

I owe an immense debt of gratitude to the patient, loyal and discerning work of five people who undertook the labour of reading the manuscript in its draft form, and offered helpful comments on it: to Anne Amos, Anne Gilchrist, Mark Cohen, Brian O'Neill and Fionnuala O'Neill Tonning. My grateful thanks to them for this labour of friendship and love.

Finally, I would like to pay tribute to the courage and humanity of all those who have been a companion to me, down all the years, in the work of different kinds about which this book is written, as each discovered the 'site' at which the work took place to be transformed in time into a 'functioning situation' in which we were fellow labourers.

Introduction

The first stirrings of life that would one day grow into this book took place when, as a young social worker, I found myself absorbed in listening every week to a woman talking, apparently prosaically, about ordinary matters such as the repairs that were being done to her flat. It might have sounded utterly banal: and yet I was enthralled. It was possible to sense, however dimly, that for this working class woman with a congenital learning disability, a process of psychosocial repair was happening. She herself could sense it, and so could I.

This book proposes that such a discernible social work process is analogous to the process in a psychoanalytic treatment first mentioned by Freud (1913) and known subsequently as the analytic process, the appearance of which marks the analysand's full engagement in his analysis. Freud noticed that establishment of the analytic process appeared to be facilitated by certain features of the psychoanalytic treatment setting. His observation provides the basis for a differential theory that is this book's central theme.

It is to Jean-Luc Donnet that we are indebted for developing Freud's observation into a conceptualisation of how an analytic process in psychoanalysis gets established: namely, through the introjection (taking in) of the analytic setting (Donnet, 2001, 2009). Donnet designates the psychoanalytic setting in its broadest sense as the analytic 'site', composed of 'elements' that can potentially be discovered and introjected, one by one, until the analysand's transformative discovery that he is in a functioning 'analysing situation'. By this point, an analytic process is in train.

One of the beauties of Donnet's theory of discoverable site elements is that it lends itself to the fully differentiated application that this book sets out to elaborate. The theory has the potential for generalised application across widely differing spheres of practice, in that eventual introjection of the setting effects an established therapeutic process. Yet each of the settings (whether psychoanalysis, psychotherapy or social work) has its own site that comprises a unique set of elements proper to that particular sphere of professional practice, as the book spells out. The theory applies equally to counselling; however, thinking the theory through in relation to the parameters of counselling is left to the interested reader.

The thesis of this book is therefore a psychoanalytic one, and at the same time its differential character accords full recognition to the integrity of a given sphere of practice. The process of engagement has an irreducibly unconscious dimension with two aspects to it. Introjection itself is an *unconscious* fantasy of taking into the inside of ourselves something from the outside. In addition, as the book repeatedly illustrates in both a psychotherapy and a social work context, the gradual discovery in a meaningful way of that which may be taken in has a paradoxical created/found aspect (Winnicott, 1974) that reveals an unconscious aspect to the process of piecemeal discovery of elements of the site.

Because the establishment of viable engagement in the work is a product of introjection of elements of the site, it follows that full therapeutic engagement is *not* conditional on ready-made psychological-mindedness. Pre-existing psychological-mindedness is sometimes held to be essential if a patient is to be offered psychotherapy, yet there is actually no need to expect it of the patient. In Chapters 3 and 5 we will meet Juliana and Velia, whose need at the outset of their therapy to restrict themselves to sterile, repetitive ruminations gave no hint that later, when there had been opportunity to encounter and to introject aspects of the psychotherapy site, they would immerse themselves with absorbed interest in their treatment with a wealth of free associative flow.

A grasp of this issue is even more vital in the field of social work, where the necessary theory has been wanting. This book can claim to be the first to demonstrate on clear theoretical grounds, as well as to illustrate in practice, that collaborative social work engagement depends simply on the client being able to encounter in the social work 'site', in a meaningful way that he can introject (take in), the ordinary social work frame of reference (rather than an imitation of psychotherapy). Failure to understand this largely accounts for social work's widespread disillusion with psychodynamic theory and practice, a misunderstanding which this book sets out to counter.

The gap in social work theory has been a serious one. On the one hand, modern textbooks perpetuate the myth that psychodynamic practice has little to offer the working class client beset with concrete practical problems (e.g. Payne, 2014). Several chapters in this book demonstrate otherwise, and Chapters 7 and 12 do so particularly clearly. On the other hand, there is already a literature, mostly from Israel, showing that in populations of families who have previously been despaired of, certain social workers have found that constructive, mutual collaboration has after all been achieved with the families concerned: and where this collaboration has been achieved, the social workers are apt to mention their sense of a *process* (Knei-Paz, 2009). I call that phenomenon the social work process, by analogy with the analytic process of psychoanalysis; it is traced in detail in Chapters 7 and 12, and aspects of it are analysed in the whole section comprising Chapters 7 to 13. It is clear then that social workers working effectively with the very deprived and marginalised have sometimes sensed that a quasi-autonomous process was in train, but they have had no coherent theory to demonstrate it or to validate their way of working. The concept of the introjected social work site supplies the theory that was wanting.

The wider context

These professional issues imply a particular approach to civic life. Since the early 1990s, public and corporate life has been dominated by the New Public Management, an approach to running public service organisations using methods derived from the business world with the intention of improving efficiency. These methods include the handing over of power to senior management executives, the identification and setting of targets (preferably numerically quantifiable ones), and the continuous monitoring of performance using audits, benchmarks and performance evaluation. The hegemony of the New Public Management over the public sector reflects an assumption that human concerns are to be solved by transmissible prescription. This prescriptiveness can burgeon, as can be seen in the field of child protection in Britain. *The Munro Review of Child Protection* (2011) drew attention to the massive proliferation of prescriptive statutory guidelines on child protection in England and Wales (for example, 'Working together to safeguard children' was 55 times longer in 2010 than in 1974!)

Yet there is an alternative conception of professional method, which regards it not as a set of prescriptions to be disseminated, but rather as the facilitation of a process. Donnet makes this point in relation to psychoanalysis (Donnet, 2009). Silvia Fargion's research into diametrically opposite social work cultures in Italy brings out this second conception very clearly:

> Work here is very often associated with following and participating in the natural evolution of the situation, rather than taking control of it . . . [T]he work is portrayed as creating the conditions for things to happen and develop, rather than as determining what should happen and how things should develop
> (Fargion, 2014, p. 30)

This conception of professional method as process facilitation was implicit in *The Munro Review of Child Protection*'s recommendation of major reforms to restore British social work's scope and capacity for professional judgement, and because the wide-ranging review had itself had been commissioned by a Secretary of State, it seemed that social work in Britain stood on the brink of really major reform. Yet by 2015 the Social Work Reform Board, which was to see through this reforming of the profession, was abolished, and the immensely important *Munro Review* itself side-lined.

The findings and fate of *The Munro Review of Child Protection*, as well as the continued dominance of the New Public Management, demonstrate the need for a concept of professional method as process facilitation, rather than as transmissible prescription, to be robustly articulated across a variety of professions.

A demonstration of process facilitation entails the tracing of sequential changes. The clinical material or case discussion on offer in this book consists mostly, though not solely, of a small selection of very detailed illustrations; sometimes a whole chapter is devoted to a single example. The subject of the book demands it, if depiction of a complex process is to be meaningfully illustrated. Donnet's theory of analytic site and analysing situation deserves to be far better known outside France and is now available in English translation: but its abstract presentation and minimal clinical illustration has meant that it has not yet caught the imagination of psychoanalysts and psychotherapists in the English-speaking world. I hope that the psychoanalytical psychotherapy illustrations in this book may kindle a wider interest in Donnet's work. Meanwhile, in recent social work literature there have been almost no accounts of social work practice that depict processes of significant change over time. The social work section of this book will trace such processes, showing that where effective engagement of the social work client took place it was because the client took in, or introjected, parameters that were specifically social work ones.

The differential theory of the introjected site therefore offers to social work an original theory of effective engagement: but evidently, insofar as this book deals with social work, it is relevant to only a part of the field, not to the whole of it. Because social work has always been responsible to intervene at a macroscopic societal structural level as well as at the microscopic level of the individual and the family, it has always needed to draw on other disciplines and on a variety of knowledge and expertise (Brekke, 2014). The life work of the late Tony Atkinson on the economics of inequality is one example of some crucial equipment that is needed to lobby for a redress of the structural causes of poverty; the work of critical theorists on power relations is another (Atkinson, 2015; Northdufter & Lorenz, 2010). Again, the recent massive influx into European countries of refugees in urgent need of provision calls for expertise in social administration, social planning and the collaborative facilitation of neighbourhood networks. No single source of interdisciplinary knowledge, including psychodynamic knowledge, is sufficient for social work: and this book makes no claim that it is otherwise.

That said, psychoanalytic and psychodynamic practice are sometimes thought unsympathetic to critical theory, which been addressing issues of power and societal structural change ever since its beginnings in the Frankfurt school of philosophy and sociology (Horkheimer & Adorno, 1987). This book aims to offer an interdisciplinary contribution to this discourse by way of the question of subjective agency. One important function of the secure introjection of the analytic site is subjectivisation, the process by which the analysand becomes a subject in a fuller way than before (Donnet, 2001). This issue, vital for psychoanalysis and psychotherapy, has always been considered vital also within critical theory.

It is just as important for social work. In an article applying the thought of the critical theorist Adorno to social work, Aila-Leena Matthies (2009) argues that Adorno's critical theory concerns the process of becoming a subject – meaning an autonomous, thinking citizen as opposed to a manipulated, systems-functioning one – and that the subjectivisation of those who use social work services is indispensable if the social work is to *work*. One aim of this book is to illustrate processes of gradual subjectivisation that are set in train as a product of introjection of the site (or setting). It does so with particular explicitness in Chapter 5 (in psychotherapy) and Chapter 7 (in social work). Chapter 13 points out that such subjectivisation is consonant with the empowerment that is central to much modern social work discourse and aligns postmodern social work theory with the theory of the introjected site.

An overview

The book is structured as follows: Part I is devoted to psychoanalysis, Part II to psychotherapy and Part III to social work. Part IV draws some threads together in a conclusion. The book is framed by Freud's address 100 years ago to the 1918 International Congress of Psycho-Analysis, with its well-known reference to an 'alloy' with the 'pure gold of analysis' (Freud, 1919): reference to the vision in this speech, in which Freud predicted that psychoanalysis would in the future be freely offered to the poor, begins and ends the book.

Chapter 1 offers a new reading of Freud's 1918 Congress address, drawing attention to an ambiguity as to whether the psychoanalysis for the people that he envisaged was the modified form of psychoanalysis that we call psychotherapy, or a practice fundamentally different in kind that would come to be called psychodynamic social work and that is comparable to psychoanalysis only by way of analogy. The twin possibilities of psychotherapy and social work structure the main part of the book. Chapter 2 forms the book's theoretical bedrock. It presents Donnet's theory of how a patient's psychoanalysis is effectively set in motion by discovery and introjection of elements of the analytic setting in its widest sense, until a metamorphosis occurs whereby the patient discovers that he is in a functioning 'analysing situation'.

In the psychotherapy section in Chapters 3, 4 and 5 we meet Carl, Juliana and Velia, and discover what it can be like to find oneself in the situation that is psychotherapy (once a week, or twice a week or, in the case of Velia, three times a week on the couch). With each of them in turn, we follow the process of gradual discovery and introjection of elements of the psychotherapy 'site', until the point where they realised that the psychotherapy situation was one that worked for them – they had got the hang of it, so to speak, and a discernible psychotherapeutic process was in motion.

Chapter 6 provides a bridge to the section of the book that deals with social work, where there is a different and very direct relation to external reality. Sometimes, in a psychotherapy, external reality can burst upon the scene in such a way that it seems to hijack all the available thinking space and leave little room for continuing to reflect on psychic reality. Chapter 6 describes a three times weekly psychotherapy in which, in the manner described by Andre Green, an unconscious fantasy was enacted on the stage of external reality (Green, 1986).

Part III is devoted to social work, which is charged by society with direct responsibility for dealing with social breakdown. This section of the book examines the nature of a specifically social work site that can potentially be introjected. It begins with Chapter 7, which introduces the idea of the social work site in an alive way by plunging the reader at once into the world of Miss M, the woman referred to in the opening words of this Introduction, bearing witness to the bleakness of her material life, her suffering and sadness, as also to the process of recovery and renewed hope. It then points to evidence of Miss M's evolving perception of the social work site, as well as to the establishment of a social work process. The chapters that follow study further some elements of the social work site, and in particular construct the concept of the social work frame of reference, one of the essential elements of the social work site. Chapter 8 adduces it from effective 21st century social work with the marginalised. Chapter 9 looks at the negative consequence of an impaired social work frame of reference, in contrast to Chapters 10 and 11 which, taken together, discuss a single case of school behaviour problems that illustrate very clearly the fivefold character of the social work frame of reference that clients can sense. Chapter 11 focuses on the relationship with the social worker as touchstone, reference to it allowing sense to be made of apparent chaos and a series of crises to be resolved. Chapter 12 traces in detail the gradual encounter and introjection of elements of the social work site in a case of non-accidental injury to a child, from my own former social work practice. Chapter 13 looks at modern social work discourse, including anti-oppressive practice, and proposes that there is a real potential for dialogue and rapprochement between initiatives such as the Jerusalem Family Aid project, or ideas such as postmodern reflexivity in the work of Jan Fook, and the theory (with its illustrations in practice) of the introjected social work site that is one part of this book's thesis.

Chapter 14 concludes that a viable therapeutic process can be established in the widely different fields of psychoanalysis, psychotherapy, counselling and social work where there is adequate encounter with, and consequent introjection of, the site (or setting, in its widest sense) proper to the relevant field.

References

Atkinson, A. B. (2015) *Inequality: What Can Be Done?* London, England and Cambridge, Massachusetts, Harvard University Press.

Brekke, J. S. (2014) A science of social work, and social work as an integrative scientific discipline: Have we gone too far, or not far enough? *Research on Social Work Practice.* 24 (5), pp. 517–523. Available from: https://doi.org/10.1177/1049731513511994.

Donnet, J.-L. (2001) From the fundamental rule to the analysing situation. *International Journal of Psychoanalysis* 82 (1), pp. 129–140. Available from: DOI: 10.1516/3FUH-9WTT-E68B-WF70.

Donnet, J.-L. (2009) *The Analyzing Situation.* A. Weller (trans.). London, Karnac. Originally published in French as *La Situation Analysante.* Presses Universitaires de France, 2005.

Fargion, S. (2014) Synergies and tensions in child protection and parent support: Policy lines and practitioners' cultures. *Child & Family Social Work* 19 (1), pp. 24–33.

Freud, S. (1913) On beginning the treatment (further recommendations on the technique of psycho-analysis. In: J. Strachey (ed. and trans.), *The Standard Edition of the Complete Psychological Works of Sigmund Freud* (Vol. 12), pp. 121–144. London, Hogarth Press.

Freud, S. (1919) Lines of advance in psycho-analytic therapy. In: J. Strachey (ed. and trans.), *The Standard Edition of the Complete Psychological Works of Sigmund Freud* (Vol. 17), pp. 157–168. London, Hogarth Press.

Green, A. (1986) The dead mother. K. Aubertin (trans.). In: A. Green, *On Private Madness*, pp. 142–173. London, Hogarth Press.

Horkheimer, M. & Adorno, T. (1987) *Dialectic of Enlightenment (Cultural Memory in the Present)*. G. Schmid Noerr (ed.). Frankfurt, S. Fischer Verlag.

Knei-Paz, C. (2009) The central role of the therapeutic bond in a social agency setting. *Journal of Social Work* 9 (2), pp. 178–198. Available from: http://journals.sagepub.com/doi/abs/10.1177/1468017308101821.

Matthies, A.-L. (2009) The concept of subjectivisation by Adorno – applied in social work. *European Journal of Social Work* 12 (3), pp. 319–332. Available from: DOI: 10.1111/cfs.12061.

Munro, E. (2011) *The Munro Review of Child Protection. Final Report: A Child-Centred System*. London, Department for Education. Available from: www.gov.uk/government/uploads/system/uploads/attachment_data/file/175391/Munro-Review.pdf.

Payne, M. (2014) *Modern Social Work Theory*. 4th edition. Basingstoke, Palgrave Macmillan.

Winnicott, D. (1974) Transitional objects and transitional phenomena. In: D. Winnicott, *Playing and Reality*, Chapter 1, pp. 1–30. Harmondsworth, Pelican Books.

Part I

'Lines of advance in psychoanalytic therapies'

Lines of advance, then and now

Continuum, or radical break?

Freud addresses an international congress

The Fifth Congress of the International Psycho-Analytical Association was held in Budapest on 28th and 29th September 1918. Many psychoanalysts who would otherwise have attended (such as Freud's future biographer, Ernest Jones from England), faced insurmountable barriers to international travel because the world was still at war. Consequently, of the 42 delegates, almost all (the exceptions being two Dutch, one Polish and three German participants) came from the Austro-Hungarian Empire (Jones, 1974). Many of them had enlisted as army psychiatrists and wore their army uniform to the conference. In an unprecedented act of recognition of psychoanalysis within official channels, the representatives of three governments – Austria, Germany and Hungary – attended this conference, attracted ironically enough by the promise of contributions on the subject of 'war neuroses'. The traditional attitude to shell-shocked soldiers had been to regard them as malingerers, but official interest had been growing in the work done by Ernst Simmel in a German military hospital using psychoanalytically derived ideas to treat war-traumatised soldiers, and as a part of the Congress there was a symposium on the subject of war neurosis for which Simmel, Karl Abraham and Sándor Ferenczi had all prepared papers (Gay, 1988). Simmel explained that, pragmatically, he did his best to reduce the number of treatment sessions to two or three. Ferenczi had meanwhile written a paper on his development of an 'active technique' in the treatment of a female patient for which he had solicited Freud's keen attention and to which Freud's speech to the Congress would refer (Ferenczi, 1919; Freud, 1919). Evidently, the adaptation of psychoanalytic treatment to meet the exigencies of circumstance and of time, cost and manpower had already begun (as had also the potential threat of its being harnessed for exploitative purposes, exemplified by the official interest in making soldiers well enough for return to the battlefront).

Freud's choice of a subject for his own address to the Congress concerned the lines along which he thought that psychoanalysis, from that juncture, should progress and develop. In a departure from his usual practice of speaking without notes, and to the disapproval of his son Ernst and daughter Anna, who were guests at the Congress, he read the paper – which suggests that he had considered very carefully indeed what he had chosen to say (Jones, 1974). The paper bore the title 'Lines of advance in psycho-analytic therapy', and would be published the following year (Freud, 1919).

The Congress paper contained Freud's famous remark that, in the modified psychoanalytic therapy that he was proposing, the 'gold' of analysis would have to be alloyed freely with the 'copper' of direct suggestion. That observation has often been quoted in discussions that juxtapose psychotherapy with psychoanalysis. However, it was not until well into the 21st century that attention was drawn to history's surprising neglect of Freud's bold claim on that occasion – Max Eitington was to call it half prophecy and half challenge – that psychoanalysis could in future be extended on a large scale to the mass of the people too poor to be able to afford to pay a fee for psychoanalysis. In *Freud's Free Clinics*, Elizabeth Danto has documented in detail the way that several of the members of Freud's audience rose to that challenge during the 1920s and 1930s and established clinics offering free psychoanalytic treatment in several European cities (Danto, 2005). Thus, Eitington and Simmel opened the Berlin Poliklinik in 1920, Eduard Hitschmann started the Vienna Ambulatorium in 1922 and Ferenczi established a free clinic in Budapest in 1929. Four other members of the audience – Melanie Klein, Hanns Sachs, Sándor Radó and Karl Abraham – were all to play an important part in the work of the Berlin Poliklinik. Jones, not present, would open the London Clinic of Psycho-Analysis in 1926. Danto has restored a chapter that had gone missing from the history of psychoanalysis, and her book's point of departure is Freud's address to the 1918 Congress in Budapest.

Yet an important if subtle feature of Freud's Congress paper remains overlooked. The paper oscillates, implicitly, between two basic standpoints. There is a discernible antinomy in it that suggests Freud's intuitive sense of an inherent and problematic tension between two ways of conceiving of the potential future practice that he was sketching. One conception is that of psychoanalysis (albeit with some modification) extended to the poor. The other conception is that of the poor having extended to them a practice so far modified in its essentials that it amounts to something fundamentally different in kind from the psychoanalysis inspiring it – so different as to constitute not psychotherapy but something that would come to be called psychodynamic social work, a practice comparable with psychoanalysis only by way of analogy.

A close reading of Freud's Congress paper reveals the antinomy at its heart.

A reading of 'Lines of advance in psycho-analytic therapy': the prominence of analogy

New influences were in the air when Freud wrote 'Lines of advance in psychoanalytic therapy'. Particular pathologies were posing challenges in the consulting-room, notably phobias, obsessional neuroses and certain kinds of treatment-resistant hysteria, and in the light of this challenge Freud was interested in weighing up the merits of the 'active technique' about which Ferenczi had recently written a paper which would be published the following year (Ferenczi, 1919; Freud, 1919). Strachey's editorial commentary on Freud's Congress paper states that it consists chiefly of a discussion of Ferenczi's active technique (Strachey, 1955). Certainly, that is a central part of Freud's paper.

However, the other major 'line of advance' proposed by Freud in his Congress address was that psychotherapy, as a modified version of psychoanalysis, might make a psychoanalytic therapy available to whole populations then excluded from it by poverty, social class and associated deprivations. A second influence was at work here. Freud wrote the paper in July 1918 while he was a guest in the house of Anton von Freund (Strachey, 1955). Von Freund had been in analysis with Freud the previous year after consulting him about post-operative depression following apparently successful surgery for testicular cancer, and was now himself training to be a psychoanalyst. The son of a wealthy industrialist, von Freund had obtained a PhD but had then laid aside his wish to become a teacher and had instead entered the family brewing business. This however left unsatisfied his wish to advance knowledge and social justice (Freud, 1920). After his analysis with Freud he not only set himself to train as a psychoanalyst – Freud would refer to him after his untimely death from the cancer, which returned and killed him in 1920, as one of the brightest hopes of psychoanalysis – but he also believed passionately that psychoanalysis should be far more widely available than just to those who like himself could afford to pay for it. He conceived a plan not only to endow a psychoanalytic publishing house but also to set up outpatient clinics, funded by his private fortune, which would train a large number of personnel in psychoanalysis and in which psychoanalysis would be freely available to the poor (Freud, 1920). He handed over a substantial sum of money to the municipal authorities in Budapest for this purpose. This project of making analysis as freely available to the poor as to the wealthy was something he valued very highly and was very near to von Freund's heart. It was also one with which the political landscape would soon be in tune, in cities like Vienna (to be declared a republic on 11th November), after the imminent end of the First World War and with it the collapse of the Austro-Hungarian Empire and a move in some of its former cities towards social democracy (Clark, 1980; Danto, 2005). Freud, who had previously recorded his belief that psychoanalytic treatment does not work if a fee is not charged, evidently listened keenly to von Freund's ideas about making psychoanalysis freely available to the people (Freud, 1913). The Congress paper demonstrates that, characteristically, he also went on thinking.

In the context of Freud's call at the end of his Congress address for a psychotherapy for the mass of the people, the opening of the paper shows itself to be part of a fascinating sub-text. Freud's opening point comprises a systematic discussion of the use and limitations of *analogy*. He first points out that the term 'analysis' in psycho-analysis refers to the psychoanalyst's work of identifying the particular constituent elements of compound mental manifestations, and that the analogy is, in that sense, to chemical analysis – that is, to the laboratory chemist's work of separating out the constituent elements of chemical compounds. He then takes issue with those who were proceeding to advocate that the new lines of advance in psychoanalysis should entail a shift at a certain point in the treatment from psycho-analysis to psycho-*synthesis*, just as the chemist sets out to synthesise, in new ways, the elements that he has isolated. According to Jones, the chief advocate of this idea was one Bezzola (Jones, 1974). Freud had also taken issue with Pfister concerning the same idea in a letter to him the previous year: 'In the technique of psycho-analysis there is no need of any special synthetic work; the individual does that for himself better than we can' (Meng & Freud, 1963, p. 62). Freud reasons in his Congress paper that the idea of psycho-synthesis is based on a false analogy. He spells out the nature and limitations of analogy: 'the two objects compared need only coincide at a single point and may be entirely different from each other in everything else' (Freud, 1919, p. 161). It is utterly meaningless to push a comparison beyond such a point of coincidence. 'What is psychical is something so unique and peculiar to itself that no one comparison can reflect its nature' (Freud, 1919, p. 161). With regard to the particular point in dispute, Freud points out that the neurotic patient's mind is actually torn, divided by resistances, and as the resistances are analysed the ego itself achieves a psycho-synthesis during analytic treatment 'without the analyst's intervention, automatically and inevitably' (Freud, 1919, p. 161). In a footnote, Freud adds that a more apt analogy than to the chemist's labour of synthesis is to the kind of chemical synthesis that comes about not through the chemist's intentional manipulation but spontaneously:

> After all, something very similar occurs in chemical analysis. Simultaneously with the isolation of the various elements induced by the chemist, syntheses which are no part of his intention come about, owing to the liberation of the elective affinities of the substances concerned.
>
> (Freud, 1919, footnote, p. 161)

Now, this discussion of analogy takes up fully three pages of a paper that is only nine pages long and that ends with Freud's thoughts about the desirability of establishing institutions and clinics offering free psychoanalytic therapy to the poor. Immediately after this last suggestion, the final paragraph of the paper begins: 'We shall then be faced by the task of adapting our technique to the new conditions' (Freud, 1919, p. 167). This suggests that even at this point of simply sketching the outlines of a bold new idea, Freud may have had an intuition that such a therapy might sometimes turn out to be so unlike the psychoanalysis inspiring it that it might qualify for a definition as a clinical activity merely *analogous* to psychoanalysis – in short, a species of what nowadays we call psychoanalytic application – rather than being even the modified version of psychoanalysis that we call psychotherapy.

For what are the modifications that Freud proposes? Explicitly or implicitly, there are five; *four* of them entail fundamental variations of the parameters of psychoanalysis. The one that does not is simply sensible advice that, in working with uneducated patients, 'we shall need to look for the simplest and most easily intelligible ways of expressing our theoretical doctrines' (Freud, 1919, p. 167). A second explicit suggestion, however, is the oft-quoted variation prompted by the sheer scale of what Freud is envisaging: 'the large-scale application of our therapy will compel us to alloy the pure gold of analysis freely with the copper of direct suggestion' (Freud, 1919, p. 168). This is usually understood to distinguish from psychoanalysis proper Freud's concept of psychotherapy, envisaged as potentially less time-consuming, from psychoanalysis. The third of Freud's explicit proposals, however, is rarely cited by psychoanalysts, yet it is highly significant: *'Often, perhaps, we may only be able to achieve anything by combining mental assistance with some material support, in the manner of the Emperor Joseph'* (Freud, 1919, p. 167; italics mine). Here we might begin to suspect that we have left the realm of psychoanalysis far behind and have entered a quite different one, that of the 'applied' sphere of what was to become psychodynamic or relationship-based social work. Indeed, after the establishment of the Berlin Poliklinik two years later, members of the new profession of social work along with others in psychiatry and child guidance were to flock to the Poliklinik from a number of countries – the USA, France and Egypt among them – for training purposes (Danto, 2005). What is more, we might notice how Freud's appreciation that the work might need to begin with material support accords with the most enlightened 21st century social work approaches to helping multiply burdened families (Knei-Paz, 2009; Mason, 2012; Charles, Jones & Guo, 2014).

Two additional fundamental variations were already implicit in Freud's very suggestion of free clinics. The first of these is the absence of the fee. Only five years earlier, in 'On beginning the treatment' (1913), Freud had explicitly declared the requirement of the payment of a fee to be in itself an essential feature of the psychoanalytic treatment set-up. Danto suggests that this earlier attitude to the fee constitutes a view of the psychoanalyst as medical entrepreneur, an attitude from which she regards Freud as having been converted (Danto, 2005). I think we need, rather, to be careful to note the reason why Freud had stated, in 1913, that he regarded the fee as essential. This was on the basis of the disappointing failure of his own experimental attempts, over a ten year period, to conduct certain psychoanalyses in which he waived the fee: and he concluded that the fee functioned to ground the analysis in the world of reality, and thereby performed an important regulating function (Freud, 1913). It was an astute observation, and since history and contemporary experience demonstrate that free psychoanalytic psychotherapy can work very well, it raises the interesting question of what it might be in successful non-fee paying treatments that performs a regulating function corresponding to that of the fee. That question will be explored in Chapter 3 of this book.

The second variation implicit in the idea of a free clinic is that the treatment would be conducted not in a private practice setting, but within an institution, eventually to be established and funded, Freud suggested, by the state. This raises the issue of whether an institutional or agency setting, in itself, marks a fundamental difference in kind between the clinical practice of psychoanalysis and that of social work. Richard Titmuss would certainly think so: in years to come he was to argue that the institutional setting is one of the irreducibly defining features of social work practice, because social work is a societal concern (Titmuss, 1954).

Could Freud's creative intuition have been on the way to apprehending the fundamental difference in kind of some of the provision he was envisaging, an intuition contributing to his lecturing his audience so firmly, at the start of his paper, on the nature and limitations of analogy? What can certainly be stated is that in this paper on therapeutic advances in psychoanalysis, the subject of analogy occupies a very prominent place.

Psychoanalytic application: a form of analogy

This subject of analogy that Freud was at such pains to clarify invites further reflection. Psychoanalytic application, as it is misleadingly called, is a form of analogy. The term psychoanalytic application is so well established that it is evidently here to stay, but it is misleading because one cannot simply apply – in the sense of copying – a principle, technique or item of knowledge from psychoanalysis without clearly specifying in what sense, to what degree and to what extent it is applicable in a different field. I have previously defined psychoanalytic application as the endeavour to break new conceptual ground in some field of knowledge, whereby the new idea is conceived and articulated with the aid of reference to some analogous phenomenon in psychoanalysis (O'Neill, 2005). In a given field of study or endeavour, familiarity with psychoanalytic thinking may *facilitate the noticing* of some hitherto unremarked phenomenon, configuration or method. Freud was to imply this when he spoke once more of analogies in *Moses and Monotheism*, published 20 years after the paper we have been considering:

> Here I am not using the term 'repressed' in its proper sense. What is in question is something in a people's life which is past, lost to view, superseded and which we venture to compare with what is repressed in the mental life of an individual . . . For the moment . . . we will make shift with the use of analogies.
>
> (Freud, 1939, p. 132)

Discussing his own use of analogy for 'applied' purposes on another occasion, Freud again enjoins caution: 'we are dealing with analogies and . . . it is dangerous, not only with men but also with concepts to tear them from the sphere in which they have originated and been evolved' (Freud, 1930, p. 144). This implies that, in a valid and useful analogy, the point of similarity or correspondence must be understood in relation to relevant differences between the applied field and psychoanalysis, which entails competent understanding of the 'applied' field and of the psychoanalytic sphere as well as aptness in the particular analogy.

Social work practice is such an applied sphere – that is to say, a sphere in which new understanding of *some* (and only some) aspects of the work can be arrived at with the aid of reference to an analogous phenomenon in psychoanalysis. It can hardly be emphasised too much that only some aspects of social work can be illuminated by an analogy with some part of psychoanalysis, and also that the nature and the limitations of the analogy need to be carefully worked out so that the integrity of social work as a sphere of practice in its own right is not compromised.

'Psychoanalytic therapy': an inherent ambiguity

Psychoanalytic therapy for all: Freud's speech to the 1918 Congress reflected the inspiration and the challenge that von Freund had evidently conveyed to him, and the impetus of that inspiration and enthusiasm is reflected in the busy work that went on in the free clinics that were soon to be established (Danto, 2005). Freud's paper merely sketched an outline of the future: some of the working out would have to come later, as the inherent ambiguity in the term 'psychoanalytic therapy' started to pose problems insofar as it went unrecognised. Did it mean the practice of psychoanalysis as constituted by the carefully considered technique papers that Freud had published, relatively recently (Freud, 1911, 1912a, 1912b, 1913, 1914, 1915)? Did it mean a somewhat modified version of that practice that would come to be called 'psychoanalytic psychotherapy' in contradistinction to 'psychoanalysis'? Or did it include practice(s) with a potential to benefit greatly from a familiarity with psychoanalysis but fundamentally different in kind from psychoanalysis and psychotherapy – at least one of which would become known as psychodynamically influenced social work practice?

I have suggested that the prominent place accorded by Freud to a discussion of analogy indicates his intuitive awareness that these distinctions would, in time, have to be thought about. This book contributes to that discourse.

'You sits and you listens: that's all I can say': psychotherapy and social work

The distinctions that have just been noted form the organising principle of this book. Part I sets out a theory of the way that a patient in psychoanalysis becomes effectively involved in his own psychoanalytic treatment, beginning from when the patient first finds himself in the psychoanalytic situation at the start of his analysis. According to this theory, the critically important factor is the patient's gradual discovery, through experiencing them, of different aspects of the psychoanalytic set-up, ranging from concrete aspects (such as the couch) to other, non-concrete aspects that he can sense, over time, such as the analyst's relationship to his theoretical principles (Donnet, 2001). As a result of gradually discovering multiple aspects of the psychoanalytic set-up, the patient mentally takes in the psychoanalytic situation. Psychoanalysts give to this process of 'taking in' the name of introjection, which means an unconscious fantasy of taking into the inside of ourselves something from the outside of ourselves. It is as a result of taking in aspects of the psychoanalytic situation that the patient eventually gets a sense of how the psychoanalytic situation works: he 'gets the hang of it' as we say. Having reached this point, he is fully engaged in his analysis.

Part II considers a comparable issue in psychoanalytic psychotherapy: it considers the psychotherapy patient's engagement in his therapy, and his discovery of the therapeutic situation as one that functions for him, as a product of his encounter with the parameters of psychoanalytic psychotherapy and his unconscious taking in of them.

Part III considers the entirely different situation that pertains to social work. It puts the case that a comparable analogy still holds for some parts of social work practice. That is, it argues that in relationship-based social work with the poor and/or the marginalised, there is a critical issue of the encounter with the parameters of the set-up specific to social work, and an unconscious taking in of those specifically social work parameters, leading in time to a discovery of being in a situation that really is effectively working.

In a study that we will come back to, this last was most movingly illustrated by a client who was part of a project in a London Social Services Department, one of a group of clientele who had been the most worrying, the most time-consuming and the focus of the greatest despair on the part of the Social Services Department's regular social work staff (Mattinson & Sinclair, 1979). After a falling-out and reconciliation with her project worker, this client was asked why she felt it important that the project social worker continue to visit. She pondered and answered hesitantly: 'You sits.' Two months later, she amended this to: 'You sits and you listens: that's all I can say.' Months later again, evidently having gone on thinking about it, she herself raised the subject: 'I've got it, why you have to keep on coming. You sits and you listens: and when you do that, then I don't feel so silly anymore' (Mattinson & Sinclair, 1979, pp. 190–191). Her words imply that the social worker's listening to her gave her a gradually dawning sense that her thoughts, feelings and reactions about her situation were being rendered intelligible to herself and thereby open to reflection – rather than remaining unintelligible and vulnerable to ridicule or dismissal ('silly'). This illustrates what is meant by the social work client discovering herself to be in a social work situation that functions therapeutically – analogous to the 'analysing situation' of psychoanalysis (Donnet, 2001, 2009; O'Neill, 2005). The parameters that the social work client needs to have encountered and taken in and that are felt to make sense differ radically, of course, from those of psychoanalysis, and are explored in detail in the chapters in Part III of the book.

Donnet's theory of the analytic site and the analysing situation, which forms the theoretical bedrock of this book, is presented in the next chapter.

References

Charles, P., Jones, A. & Guo, S. (2014) Treatment effects of a relationship-strengthening intervention for economically disadvantaged new parents. *Research on Social Work Practice* 24 (3), pp. 321–338.

Clark, R. W. (1980) *Freud: The Man and the Cause*, pp. 387–389. London, Jonathan Cape and Weidenfeld & Nicolson.

Danto, E. A. (2005) *Freud's Free Clinics: Psychoanalysis and Social Justice, 1918–1938*. New York, Columbia University Press.

Donnet, J.-L. (2001) From the fundamental rule to the analysing situation. *International Journal of Psychoanalysis* 82 (1), pp. 129–140. Available from: DOI: 10.1516/3FUH-9WTT-E68B-WF70.

Donnet, J.-L. (2009) *The Analyzing Situation*. A. Weller (trans.). London, Karnac. Originally published in French as *La Situation Analysante*. Presses Universitaires de France, 2005.

Ferenczi, S. (1919) Technical difficulties in the analysis of a case of hysteria. In: Ferenczi, S. *Further Contributions to the Theory and Technique of Psycho-Analysis*, pp. 189–197. J. I. Suttie (trans. from German). London, Hogarth Press, 1926, Originally published in German in *Zeitschrift*, 1919.

Freud, S, (1911) The handling of dream-interpretation in psycho-analysis. In: J. Strachey (ed. and trans.), *The Standard Edition of the Complete Psychological Works of Sigmund Freud* (Vol. 12), pp. 89–96. London, Hogarth Press.

Freud, S. (1912a) The dynamics of transference. In: J. Strachey (ed. and trans.), *The Standard Edition of the Complete Psychological Works of Sigmund Freud* (Vol. 12), pp. 97–108. London, Hogarth Press.

Freud, S. (1912b) Recommendations to physicians practising psycho-analysis. In: J. Strachey (ed. and trans.), *The Standard Edition of the Complete Psychological Works of Sigmund Freud* (Vol. 12), pp. 109–120. London, Hogarth Press.

Freud, S. (1913) On beginning the treatment (further recommendations on the technique of psycho-analysis I). In: J. Strachey (ed. and trans.), *The Standard Edition of the Complete Psychological Works of Sigmund Freud* (Vol. 12), pp. 121–144. London, Hogarth Press.

Freud, S. (1914) Remembering, repeating and working-through (further recommendations on the technique of psycho-analysis II). In: J. Strachey (ed. and trans.), *The Standard Edition of the Complete Psychological Works of Sigmund Freud* (Vol. 12), pp. 145–156. London, Hogarth Press.

Freud, S. (1915) Observations on transference-love (further recommendations on the technique of psycho-analysis III). In: J. Strachey (ed. and trans.), *The Standard Edition of the Complete Psychological Works of Sigmund Freud* (Vol. 12), pp. 157–171. London, Hogarth Press.

Freud, S. (1919) Lines of advance in psycho-analytic therapy. In: J. Strachey (ed. and trans.), *The Standard Edition of the Complete Psychological Works of Sigmund Freud* (Vol. 17), pp. 157–168. London, Hogarth Press.

Freud, S. (1920) Dr Anton von Freund. In: J. Strachey (ed. and trans.), *The Standard Edition of the Complete Psychological Works of Sigmund Freud* (Vol. 18), pp. 267–268. London, Hogarth Press.

Freud, S. (1930) Civilization and its discontents. In: J. Strachey (ed. and trans.), *The Standard Edition of the Complete Psychological Works of Sigmund Freud* (Vol. 21), pp. 57–145. London, Hogarth Press.

Freud, S. (1939) Moses and monotheism: Three essays. In: J. Strachey (ed. and trans.), *The Standard Edition of the Complete Psychological Works of Sigmund Freud* (Vol. 23), pp. 1–137. London, Hogarth Press.

Gay, P. (1988) *Freud: A Life for Our Time*. London, J. M. Dent & Sons.

Jones, E. (1974) *Years of Maturity 1901–1919, Vol II of Sigmund Freud: Life and Work.* 2nd edition. London, Hogarth.

Knei-Paz, C. (2009) The central role of the therapeutic bond in a social agency setting. *Journal of Social Work* 9 (2), pp. 178–198.

Mason, C. (2012) Social work the 'art of relationship': Parents' perspectives on an intensive family support project. *Child & Family Social Work* 17 (3), pp. 368–377.

Mattinson J. & Sinclair, I. (1979) *Mate and Stalemate: Working with Marital Problems in a Social Services Department.* Oxford, Blackwell.

Meng, H. & Freud, E. (eds.) (1963) *Psycho-Analysis and Faith: The Letters of Sigmund Freud and Oskar Pfister*, p. 62 (Freud to Pfister 9.10.1918). E. Mosbacher (trans.), No. 59 in J. Sutherland (ed.), The International Psycho-Analytical Library. London, Hogarth Press and Institute of Psycho-Analysis.

O'Neill, S. (2005) Psychoanalytic application and psychoanalytic integrity. *International Journal of Psychoanalysis* 86 (1), pp. 125–146.

Strachey, J. (1955) Editorial introduction to S. Freud, Lines of advance in psycho-analytic therapy. In: J. Strachey (ed. and trans.), *The Standard Edition of the Complete Psychological Works of Sigmund Freud* (Vol. 17), p. 158. London, Hogarth Press.

Titmuss, R. (1954) The administrative setting of social service. *Case Conference* 1 (1), pp. 5–11.

Chapter 2

Donnet's concept of the analytic site or ensemble

This chapter looks at a theory of how formal psychoanalysis, as a going concern clinically, is set in motion. That theory is the conceptual bedrock of this whole book, illuminating as it does the possibilities of thinking, by analogy, how clinical practice is also set in motion in domains other than psychoanalysis. On the basis of the theory in this chapter, Part II of the book will conceptualise how a therapeutic process in psychotherapy is established, and the establishment in an analogous way of a viable social work process will be theorised in Part III.

Modell and Donnet: the role of the psychoanalytic setting

Arnold Modell, in America, and Jean-Luc Donnet, in France, have independently developed theories of how psychoanalysis works. James Strachey had previously put forward a classical theory that change in psychoanalysis comes about as an effect of the analyst's interpretations (Strachey, 1934). Where interest has been more specifically directed at the question of whether and how the psychoanalysis of a given patient becomes effectively launched, the factor that has been traditionally emphasised has been that of the patient's capacity to enter into a therapeutic alliance (Etchegoyan, 1991). Donald Winnicott, while not primarily aiming to set out a formal theory of how psychoanalysis gets established, has drawn attention to the immense importance of the psychoanalytic setting (Winnicott, 1978). Modell and Donnet similarly take the psychoanalytic setting to be crucial, and indeed they consider the opportunities inherent in the psychoanalytic setting to be the fundamentally important factor in therapeutic engagement (Modell, 1990; Donnet, 2001, 2002).

It is to Donnet's work and its relation to that of Winnicott that I am going to refer: but readers who are more familiar with Modell's work may care to notice significant resemblances. The conceptualisation of the setting undertaken by all three of these authors rests on a thoughtful reading of Freud's technique papers (Freud 1911, 1912a, 1912b, 1913, 1914, 1915). They all write also of the irreducible importance of paradox. Donnet and Modell refer centrally, in this connection, to the clinical theories of Winnicott (1974a, 1974b, 1978) and to those of the Argentinian analyst Jose Bleger (1967).

Before considering Donnet's thoughts on the analytic process, let us remind ourselves of Freud's.

Freud and the noble game of chess

Freud opened his paper 'On beginning the treatment' (1913) with an analogy with chess. 'Anyone who hopes to learn the noble game of chess from books,' he began, 'will soon discover that only the openings and end-games admit of an exhaustive systematic presentation and that the infinite variety of moves which develop after the opening defy any such description.' So, despite the infinity of possibilities afterwards, one *can* study openings: and by the analogous openings in a psychoanalysis Freud means his recommendations for the setting up of the treatment. He discusses six such opening moves. They are:

1   a fixed daily hour (less ten minutes and a rest day);
2   an agreed fee (without which, Freud insisted at this time from experience, the treatment fails);
3   duration established as open-ended;
4   use of the couch;
5   explicit enunciation to the patient of the 'fundamental rule' that he is to say everything that comes into his mind;
6   a forbearing interpretative reticence towards the developing transference.

Freud offered a detailed discussion of each of these recommendations in turn. (This included a clear discussion of his view at that time of the importance of charging a fee, the omission of which he had found from experience was problematic – probably because, he concluded, the fee functioned to ground the patient in the world of reality.) What is the reason for such very careful, studied attention to each of these details of the set-up? Freud observed, as in chess, the general principle that each of these particular opening moves derives its importance from its relation to the general plan of the game. Quite simply, he found that these opening moves appeared to be the conditions in which a particular phenomenon could establish itself. Here is what Freud wrote about that singular phenomenon whose arrival he noticed in the course of his work, and that has become known as the *analytic process*. The psychoanalyst, he wrote:

> sets in motion a process . . . He can supervise this process, further it, remove obstacles in its way, and he can undoubtedly vitiate much of it. But on the whole, once begun, it goes its own way, and does not allow either the direction it takes or the order in which it picks up its points to be prescribed for it.
>
> (Freud, 1913, p. 130)

Donnet: from analytic site to analysing situation

Freud noticed, then, that the conditions in which such an analytic process could become established were those of a treatment that is set up in a particular way. Donnet has further developed these ideas of Freud's, by theorising *how* it is that the details of the set-up recommended by Freud can facilitate the establishment of this analytic process.

In extrapolating from Freud's technique papers a theory of the way psycho-analysis works, Donnet accepts as fundamental the psychoanalyst's treatment set-up or frame. He refers to the work of the Argentinian psychoanalyst Jose Bleger, who had proposed that the patient in psychoanalysis develops, unnoticed, a symbiotic relation to the psychoanalytic frame – by which he meant the agreed structure of time, place and fee arrangement which merely *frames* the treatment process, is taken for granted, and seems not to count (Bleger, 1967; Donnet, 2002). Bleger draws a comparison with the child's taking his parents' presence for granted; unless a separation makes the child aware of the issue of their presence/absence, they are for the child 'just there' in a way that does not seem to him particularly to count. Bleger considered the patient's unnoticed symbiosis to the frame to be phase-appropriate in the early and middle phases of the analysis (just as early parent/child symbiosis supports at first the child's development) and usually to require analysis only late in the treatment.

Winnicott had already drawn attention quite explicitly to the importance of the treatment set-up as recommended by Freud (Winnicott, 1978; Abram, 2007). Winnicott regards the setting as so important that he proposes a division of Freud's work into two parts, the first being that of technique (the work of understanding the patient's material and interpreting it to the patient) and the second being the setting in which the work is conducted, which mirrors the very early environment of the baby as provided by its mother:

> Freud takes for granted the early mothering situation and my contention is that *it turned up in his provision of a setting for his work*, almost without his being aware of what he was doing.
>
> (Winnicott, 1978, p. 284; italics in original)

Winnicott enumerates 12 aspects of the clinical setting as devised by Freud. They include lying on a comfortable couch in a comfortably warm room quietly free from disturbance and noise but with background household sounds, the analyst's reliable punctuality and physical presence ('on time, alive, breathing') and availability to be preoccupied with the patient for the whole of the daily analytic hour, and various aspects of the principles of neutrality and of abstinence not always to be relied on in people in ordinary life such as 'absence of the talion reaction', and non-intrusiveness whether of moral judgements or of the analyst's personal life and ideas or of temper tantrums or of compulsive falling in love. Winnicott also specified the method of objective observation, the aim of understanding the material presented and communicating this understanding in words, the distinction between fact and fantasy 'so that the analyst is not hurt by an aggressive dream', the analyst's survival, and the following observation: 'The analyst expressed love by the positive interest taken, and hate in the strict start and finish and in the matter of fees. Love and hate were honestly expressed, that is to say not denied by the analyst' (Winnicott, 1978, p. 285). He saw in all these things (availability, reliability, non-intrusiveness, attentiveness, objective observation and all the rest) a marked similarity with the ordinary task of parents, and in some respects with the task of the mother at the very beginning of her baby's life. In a footnote, he observes that Freud mostly treated patients with neurotic rather than psychotic difficulties 'when it is possible to take for granted the work done by the mother and by the early environmental adaptation in the individual patient's past history' (Winnicott, 1978, pp. 284–285). Although the main focus of the article in which this discussion of the Freudian setting appears is to discuss a need for therapeutic regression in those patients for whom there has been a failure of maternal adaptation in early infancy, Winnicott's thought is close to Bleger's in thinking that where early environmental provision has been adequate, its being repeated (in a virtual way) in the psychoanalytic setting simply gets taken for granted by the patient, important though it is, without the patient noticing it. Presently we will consider Winnicott's view of the immense importance of the original environmental provision for the development of a secure subjective sense of self, and its parallel in Donnet's thought.

Although his explicit reference to Winnicott is confined to the particular concept of created/found (to be discussed below), Donnet's thought about the setting is along similar lines to those of Winnicott as he, through a thoughtful reading of Freud's technique papers, develops and greatly expands Bleger's idea about the patient's relation to the frame. Borrowing a term from theoretical geography, Donnet calls the psychoanalyst's set-up or frame at the start of treatment the analytic site. At the start, in Donnet's conception, the patient who has been given the fundamental rule of free association just finds himself at the place, or site, where psychoanalysis is beginning. Donnet's thesis is that the patient has to undergo a transformation in which he metamorphoses from passive patient to participating analysand (a metamorphosis to be elaborated later in this chapter), in what has only then become, *effectively*, the analysing situation: 'the transformation of the patient into analysand implies the functional introjection of the various elements contained by the analytic site' (Donnet, 2001, p. 129).

What does this very condensed statement mean? In geographical theory, Donnet tells us, a site is a configuration, which furnishes its human occupying establishment with the local elements of its material life, these same local elements also representing inherent possibilities of expansion (Donnet, 2002). By analogy, the analytic site furnishes the patient with the necessary local elements, or resources, for his analysis and for its development.

The local elements of the analytic site are multitudinous, and range from the most concrete, such as details of session times and of the consulting room and of its environs and features of the analyst's person, to the most virtual, such as the analyst's particular theoretical principles and even his countertransferential position. Crucial theoretical principles are to be found in Freud's technique papers, such as the principle of listening with 'evenly suspended attention' (Freud, 1912b, pp. 111–112), and the principles of neutrality (Freud, 1912b, pp. 118–119 & 1915, pp. 163–164) and of abstinence from action, for example in the face of pleas from a patient for demonstrations of love (Freud, 1915, pp. 165–167). We have seen Winnicott's gloss on these principles: Winnicott's summary version was his remark that 'the whole thing adds up to the fact that the analyst *behaves* himself . . . simply because of being a relatively mature person', and that this was as important in Freud's work as Freud's cleverness with accurate interpretations (Winnicott, 1978, p. 286). Theoretically, an inventory could be taken of the elements of the analytic site: they are all there. But they await the patient's discovery and exploitation of them, in a way that can potentially transform him from being just a patient into an analysand – at which point the analytic site is discovered by the patient to have been transformed into the analysing situation.

How does the patient discover the elements within the analytic site? The order in which he does so is highly individual, since it is determined by his unconscious options, in a paradoxical manner that Donnet thinks can only be described by Winnicott's idea of created/found.

The important idea of created/found calls for explanation. Winnicott's concept of the paradox of created/found is an essential part of his complex theory of transitional objects and transitional phenomena. According to this theory, an illusion of omnipotence develops in the very young baby when the mother, at first, necessarily adapts herself almost entirely to the baby's needs. 'The mother, at the beginning, by an almost 100-per-cent adaptation affords the infant the opportunity for the *illusion* that her breast is part of the infant' (Winnicott, 1974a, pp. 12–13). This happens because, right from the very beginning of life, when the baby is in a state of instinctual tension the ordinarily responsive mother supplies the breast or its equivalent: 'The mother places the actual breast just where the baby is ready to create, and at the right moment' (Winnicott, 1974a, p. 13). As this happens repeatedly, with the aid of memory traces the baby develops an idea of the breast and for a while believes that he can summon it by hallucinatory wish-fulfilment, supported by the mother's supplying the actual breast almost as soon as it is wanted. In Winnicott's view, the opportunity for the baby's early illusion that he has created and can summon the breast at will is essential for the development of a secure sense of self. The mother's eventual task, as formulated by Winnicott, is to disillusion the baby, gradually and tactfully, 'but she has no hope of success unless at first she has been able to give sufficient opportunity for illusion.' As a consequence of this gradual process of disillusionment, the baby eventually comes to recognise that the breast and the mother herself are not part of him but are outside, separate and not under his control. It is on the way to this real-isation that the baby makes use of what Winnicott calls the transitional object – that is, the piece of blanket or cloth and later the teddy bear or other such object to which the baby becomes attached and of which he makes use when going to sleep or at times of anxiety. Winnicott defines this transitional object as the baby's first 'not-me' possession: it stands for the breast or for the mother herself, but it is transitional in that it is also recognised as not being her, although under the baby's control: 'In relation to the transitional object the infant passes from (magical) omnipotent control to control by manipulation (involving muscle ero-tism and coordination pleasure)' (Winnicott, 1974a, p. 10). Winnicott considered that the most important feature of the transitional object is its paradoxical character. It is *found* by the baby in that he recognises it as something that has an actual existence in the outside world and is not part of himself, yet in another way it is *created* by the baby as something which stands for a breast or mother he can have as his own possession, so it represents his connection with his mother. The para-dox of created/found, in Winnicott's view, has value as something whose ambigu-ity is allowed to stand unquestioned and unresolved: 'We agree never to make the challenge to the baby: did you create this object, or did you find it conveniently lying around?' (Winnicott, 1974c, p. 113).

To return to the discovery of the elements in the analytic site: Donnet considers that Winnicott's notion of created/found is present in Freud's technique papers in a virtual way, partly in Freud's vivid description of the transference as like a real fire breaking out during a theatrical performance (Freud, 1915, p. 162), and also in Freud's fundamental principle that the analysis is to proceed by the patient say-ing everything that comes into his mind (Freud, 1913, pp. 134–135). In Donnet's view, the enunciation of this 'fundamental rule' of psychoanalysis establishes the treatment as a *tabula rasa* that the patient will write on, a pristine terrain in which, as the patient sets foot in it for the first time he paradoxically finds/creates, in Winnicott's sense, his own analysis. It is the opportunity for the patient to utilise the analytic situation that is all-important (Donnet, 2002, pp. 35–36).

With the important caveat that *if* the patient's encounter with the site is – in Donnet's terms – 'sufficiently adequate', the patient introjects, one by one, the elements that he discovers there. This goes on, element by element, to the point of a cumulative introjection of a critical proportion of the elements – a critical proportion that brings about a tipping point. This amounts to a metamorphosis: through introjecting the site, the patient acquires a sense of it as an *analysing situation* having its own logic, ethics and specificity constituting, for psycho-analysis, the 'rules of the game'. Donnet's implicit reference here is to Freud's 'noble game of chess' analogy. Donnet suggest that the analyst's relationship to and respect for the 'rules of the game' has a helpful triangulating function, an early manifestation of which is that the patient often develops an attachment to the site itself (to the logic, ethics and specificity constituting the 'rules of the game') that is independent of his attachment to the person of the analyst. This move from a sense of being in a two-term situation (patient and analyst) to a three-term situation (patient, analyst and a site to which the analyst can be seen to relate and to which the patient, too, learns to relate) becomes generalisable to the world at large. Donnet refers to this as 'thirdness', a concept which will be briefly discussed below, and which will be met with on numerous occasions throughout this book in discussion of clinical examples.

The eventual transformative introjection of the site as a whole marks the metamorphosis of patient into analysand, and is the point at which the analytic process has become securely established and proceeds thereafter in a quasi-autonomous fashion.

Overcoming the obstacles to understanding Donnet

Donnet's ideas, which were and remain highly respected in France, were presented to an international audience at the Psychoanalytic Congress of the International Psychoanalytic Association in Nice in the year 2000, but were largely met with incomprehension, as he was later to note with regret (Donnet, 2009, pp. 3–6). Since the presentation of the 2000 Congress paper Karnac's publication of *The Analyzing Situation* in 2009 has made Donnet's thought available in English translation. However, his ideas are still not well known outside France.

The geographical analogy of the site can initially seem bewildering, but it has a very precise meaning. We can recall that in geographical theory a site is a con-figuration, the resources of which make available to the human beings there the local elements that they can exploit for their material life. Perhaps the easiest way to grasp Donnet's theory is to notice that when he refers to the analytic site he is drawing attention to *what is available and placed at the disposal* of the patient who is starting psychoanalysis. The patient is respected as the active agent whose opportunity is to start to notice and to explore the site, while the analyst remains attentive and available but without intruding. This respectful and forbear-ing attentiveness to what the patient may initiate is very close to Winnicott's ideas about playing (Winnicott, 1974b, 1974c). That which is available and placed at the patient's disposal consists of disparate elements that exist in a latent state until, in piecemeal fashion and in an order dictated by what the patient unconsciously needs to find out, the patient begins to encounter them. If the encounter with a given element is adequate, the patient takes it in or introjects it.

The concept of introjection is itself familiar to psychoanalysts, although it may be less so to the general reader. Freud noticed early that bodily processes to do with feeding and elimination offer images for early ego development to be mod-elled on. Introjection is an unconscious fantasy of taking something into the inside of ourselves, into the interior of our mind in the way that food is taken into the body. (It is the counterpart of projection, an unconscious fantasy – modelled on bodily elimination of waste – of the ridding ourselves of something unwanted by expelling it from inside ourselves to the outside.) Donnet's specific idea is that an adequate encounter with an element of the analytic site can result in the patient's 'taking in' or introjection of that element, and that this can happen repeatedly and cumulatively, until the accumulation of introjected elements reaches a critical level that effects a transformation.

It is the all-important process of unconscious introjection that differentiates the concept of the therapeutic alliance from Donnet's theory of an analysing situation that is discoverable by the patient. In Donnet's view, the concept of the therapeutic alliance lays a disproportionate emphasis on the patient's conscious cooperation. According to his theory, it is through the unconscious process of gradual and cumulative introjection that a transformation is effected, whereby the patient finds himself to be in an analysing situation which has a logic and an efficacy that he can sense. By this point, he himself has undergone a metamorphosis from patient (passive sufferer) to analysand, and the analytic process has been set in motion. His sense of subjective agency will have been enhanced, allowing him to exploit the resources of the analysing situation in his own unique fashion.

We can notice how far Donnet's respect for the patient's created/found exploration, and care that it should not be hindered, parallels Winnicott's theory that the healthy development of a subjective sense of self depends in the first instance on the new-born infant's being allowed the illusion, through his mother's highly attuned adaptation to him, that he has created the breast, and secondly on parental respect for his use of a transitional object as he begins to manage the perception of his mother as separate from himself.

The possibility of the patient's having an adequate encounter with what is placed at his disposal does imply care on the analyst's part over what is made available, together with respect for the patient's exploration of it. Particularly crucial is the analyst's relationship to his psychoanalytic and ethical principles: it is largely this relationship, if it is adequate, that is sensed at some level by the patient and eventually introjected.

Thirdness and the third position

Donnet's comment on thirdness requires a few words of explanation. The issue is regarded as important in both British and French psychoanalysis, but it is approached from different standpoints.

In British psychoanalysis the 'third position' has usually been discussed in oedipal terms as the child's capacity or incapacity to tolerate the sexual relationship between the parents, from which the child is perforce excluded. Acceptance of the parents' relationship to each other, and the adult analysand's acceptance of its symbolic equivalent in respect of his psychoanalyst, is known as the third position. If the child can accept observing the parental couple, he can also envisage his own relationship with one parent (entailing two bodies and hence two positions) being observed and thought about by the other parent in a third position (Padel, 1986; Britton, 1989). Failure in this area has important consequences for the capacity to think. The twosome which has no room for the parent to occupy the third position resembles a merged, symbiotic state in which reflective thought is impossible because no separateness is possible; as a developmental stage to be negotiated, achievement of a capacity to tolerate awareness of a third position is therefore crucial.

Donnet's reference in this regard is to André Green's development of the idea of thirdness, originally in a lecture in Paris in 1989, drawing on the work of the 19th century philosopher C. S. Peirce (Donnet, 2002; Green, 2002, 2016; Houser & Kloesel, 1992). The French idea of thirdness therefore has its roots in philosophy, but Green did then link it up with developmental theory. In terms of early development, Green revised Winnicott's statement that there is no such thing as a baby (that is, there is only a mother-and-baby unit) – to suggest that there is also no such thing as a mother-and-baby, but rather a baby-and-mother with an Other (usually, the father) in the mother's mind. Green considered the issue of thirdness to be the 'other of the mother' – that is, from birth, the presence or absence of the nursing mother's love for the father (as well as love for the baby) transmits itself to the baby before the father is recognised as a person. It is crucial since, if the mother has no room in her mind for the father, this has pathogenic consequences for the child (Green, 2016; c.f. McDougall, 1989). In his lecture on thirdness, Green insists on the distinction between Freud's *psychische Repräsentanz* (the psychical representative of the drive, which is a state of bodily tension in search of something but without having any external reference) and Freud's *Vorstellungrepräsentanz* (the ideational representative, where memory traces allow an evocation of the breast or of any of its qualities). It is the first of these that allows the illusion of primary creativity as described by Winnicott, the baby 'conceiving the idea of something that would meet the growing need that arises out of instinctual tension. The infant cannot be said to know at first what is to be created' (Winnicott, 1974a, p. 13).

For both Green and Donnet, the potential for thirdness is represented by the analytic setting itself. Donnet observes that the patient can develop an attachment to the analytic site itself that is independent of his attachment to the analyst, and that when he senses the analyst's relation to the site and to the principles contained in it, this assists the patient to develop a thirdness that can then be generalised to the world at large (Donnet, 2001). The first of several illustrations of such an acquisition of thirdness is soon to be met with, in Chapter 3.

Discovering an element in the analytic site: a clinical vignette

Let us move from the abstract statement of the theory of the introjected site to consideration of an example, taken from a psychoanalytic treatment of my own, of a patient's early encounter with at least one element of the analytic site.

A patient, who had had various kinds of treatment before, remarked during the third week of his psychoanalytic treatment that he had noticed that his sessions began punctually, and expressed his appreciation of this. He added earnestly that he would, however, entirely understand if, someday, his session started half an hour late because another patient had been very distressed and had needed to be given extra time to deal with this. He elaborated his understanding of such a potential situation, and how he would not mind at all.

What was at issue?

I interpreted, gently, that the patient had noticed that his sessions begin on time, and that while one of his reactions was to appreciate this reliability, he seemed to have at the same time a different reaction. Although our agreement was for 50-minute sessions, he seemed to find it impossible to believe that I could be hard-hearted enough to end a session on time if a patient were acutely distressed, whether that be someone else or the patient himself. He seemed to have believed that the agreement over times would not hold should a session prove particularly distressing, and he could not bring himself to believe that I could be as hard and cruel, in such a situation, as to hold to the time boundary.

Various unconscious aspects of the patient's opening communication might be inferred, such as his denial of potential hurt and jealousy should his session time be encroached on for another patient's sake, his projection of the needy, distressed aspect of himself into another patient while he aligned himself with me as the two wise, understanding ones, and possibly his wish (through the invitation to exploit his putative tolerance) for some kind of excitement in the face of the (so far) invariant frame. I thought, however, that there would be ample opportunity for all such issues to re-surface, *provided that the analytic set-up itself was adequately constructed* – a burning issue since there was an implicit warning that the patient's distress might erupt someday right at the end of the session, threatening him with the re-enactment of a trauma (given his implied belief that such an eruption of distress would gain him extra time, and the further implication that he would be severely shocked in such circumstances to have the session end on time). The interpretation, therefore, addressed the patient's implicit exploration of the time boundary. Implicitly, it offered him ego support, since the further confirmation that sessions do end on time gave him some preparation for their doing so, along with an acknowledgement of the painful disappointment of his longing (in one respect) for it to be otherwise.

This vignette illustrates also the paradox of the created/found encounter. The time boundary had always been present in the set-up, since the 50-minute length of the sessions was part of our original arrangement. The patient had already begun to encounter its actuality in his attendances so far (he said that he had noticed, and appreciated, that the sessions did start on time). Yet, through his remark about a potential delay construed as understandable, the patient unconsciously created a new and meaningful further encounter with the element of the time boundary, as well as an encounter with my way of listening to him. This encounter gave him, too, an early encounter with the function of the invariant time frame in its capacity to act as a projective screen (on to which can be projected his wish/fear that the boundary might not hold, together with the individually unique degree of specificity of his own fantasy about it, and so on).

The term 'ensemble' as an alternative to 'site'

Donnet appears to have noticed that, outside France, there has often been a bewildered reaction to his extrapolation of the concept of the site from abstract geographical theory. In his later writing, Donnet employed a different term, the 'ensemble' of the treatment set-up that is put at the patient's disposal (Donnet, 2009).

By ensemble Donnet means much more than the treatment frame as described by Bleger, who was referring to the arrangements of fixed time, place and fee for the psychoanalysis. I do not know whether Donnet knew of Winnicott's 12-point commentary on the psychoanalytic setting, but both seem to have gleaned from Freud's technique papers a similar sense of the setting and its fundamental importance. For Donnet, the ensemble of the treatment set-up means everything that he had described as the elements of the site, and that are placed at the patient's disposal: the concrete aspects of the session times and the open-ended duration and the fee and the consulting-room including its couch, yes, but all else that the patient can meet with, from the most concrete to the most virtual, including the operation in practice of the analyst's theoretical principles and even his counter-transferential position. Needless to say, these last are not expounded to the patient: rather, the patient comes to sense this or that aspect of them in the course of his exploration of the situation he finds himself in.

Summary

Freud discovered the possibility of setting in motion, in his psychoanalysis of a given patient, 'a process . . . [that], once begun . . . goes its own way and does not allow either the direction it takes or the order in which it picks up its points to be prescribed for it' (Freud, 1913). This singular but recognisable phenomenon has been known since then as the analytic process. Freud's six recommendations concerning the setting up of a psychoanalysis were, he indicated, pragmatic: along with an initial interpretive reticence towards the transference, the daily fixed hour, open-ended duration, use of the couch, the 'fundamental rule' of free association and the fee were, taken together, the conditions under which he found, from experience, such an analytic process was most likely to become established.

Donnet's theory of how that establishment actually comes about postulates a process of introjection of various elements of the analytic set-up itself, where the set-up includes the analyst's theoretical and ethical principles. Donnet's thesis is that a sufficiently adequate encounter with that set-up, or analytic site, allows a paradoxical created/found discovery and piecemeal introjection of its elements, revealing the 'rules of the game' that the treatment's logic, ethics and specificity comprise. One patient's created/found encounter with at least one element of the site (the time boundary of the session) has been illustrated.

Eventual introjection of a critical proportion of the elements amounts, in Donnet's conceptualisation, to a transformational introjection of the analytic site, allowing metamorphosis of the site (in the patient's experience of it) into an analysing situation. This is the point at which the analytic process has become established. Thereafter, the patient demonstrates himself to have become an analysand who can make a subjectivised use of the site through his own singular configuration of its resources. This assists him to develop 'thirdness', an important aspect of an adequate relation to reality.

It is important to notice the limitations of the clinical vignette in this chapter, which merely illustrates an early encounter with one element of the analytic site, when it was not yet clear whether the encounter with that element was introjected by the patient. This chapter has not illustrated the point of transformation, the point at which the introjection of a critical mass of those elements brings about the metamorphosis that ushers in the analytic process.

However, detailed illustration is presented in the next three chapters of a comparable process in psychoanalytic psychotherapy. I will discuss the similarities and differences of the psychotherapy site from the analytic site, and with reference to three psychotherapy treatments, at different frequencies, will show how the acquisition of a critical mass of introjected elements results in a transformation and ushers in a discernible therapeutic process.

References

Abram, J. (2007) *The Language of Winnicott: A Dictionary of Winnicott's Use of Words*. 2nd edition. London, Karnac.

Bleger, J. (1967) Psycho-analysis of the psycho-analytic frame. *International Journal of Psychoanalysis* 48 (4), pp. 511–519.

Britton, R. (1989) The missing link: parental sexuality in the Oedipus complex. In: J. Steiner (ed.), *The Oedipus Complex Today: Clinical Implications*, Chapter 2, pp. 83–101. London, Karnac.

Donnet, J.-L. (2001) From the fundamental rule to the analysing situation. *International Journal of Psychoanalysis* 82 (1), pp. 129–140. Available from: DOI: 10.1516/3FUH-9WTT-E68B-WF70.

Donnet, J.-L. (2002) *Le Divan Bien Tempéré* [*The Well-Tempered Couch*]. 2nd edition. Paris, Presses Universitaires de France.

Donnet, J.-L. (2009) *The Analyzing Situation*. A. Weller (trans.). London, Karnac. Originally published in French as *La Situation Analysante*. Paris, Presses Universitaires de France, 2005.

Etchegoyan, H. (1991) *The Fundamentals of Psychoanalytic Technique*. London, Karnac.

Freud, S. (1911) The handling of dream-interpretation in psycho-analysis. In: J. Strachey (ed. and trans.), *The Standard Edition of the Complete Psychological Works of Sigmund Freud* (Vol. 12), pp. 89–96. London, Hogarth Press.

Freud, S. (1912a) The dynamics of transference. In: J. Strachey (ed. and trans.), *The Standard Edition of the Complete Psychological Works of Sigmund Freud* (Vol. 12), pp. 97–108. London, Hogarth Press.

Freud, S. (1912b) Recommendations to physicians practising psycho-analysis. In: J. Strachey (ed. and trans.), *The Standard Edition of the Complete Psychological Works of Sigmund Freud* (Vol. 12), pp. 109–120. London, Hogarth Press.

Freud, S. (1913) On beginning the treatment (further recommendations on the technique of psycho-analysis. In: J. Strachey (ed. and trans.), *The Standard Edition of the Complete Psychological Works of Sigmund Freud* (Vol. 12), pp. 121–144. London, Hogarth Press.

Freud, S. (1914) Remembering, repeating and working-through (further recommendations on the technique of psycho-analysis II). In: J. Strachey (ed. and trans.), *The Standard Edition of the Complete Psychological Works of Sigmund Freud* (Vol. 12), pp. 145–156. London, Hogarth Press.

Freud, S. (1915) Observations on transference-love (further recommendations on the technique of psycho-analysis III). In: J. Strachey (ed. and trans.), *The Standard Edition of the Complete Psychological Works of Sigmund Freud* (Vol. 12), pp. 157–171. London, Hogarth Press.

Green, A. (2002) De la tiercéité. In: A. Green, *La Pensée Clinique*, pp. 259–308. Paris, Éditions Odile Jacob.

Green, A. (2016) On thirdness. In: J. Abram (ed.), *André Green at the Squiggle Foundation*, pp. 39–68. 2nd edition. London, Karnac, for the Squiggle Foundation.

Houser, N. & Kloesel, C. (eds.) (1992) *The Essential Peirce, Selected Philosophical Writings, Volume 1 (1867–1893)*. Bloomington, Indiana University Press.

McDougall, J. (1989) The dead father: On early psychic trauma and its relation to disturbance in sexual identity and creative activity. *International Journal of Psychoanalysis* 70 (2), pp. 205–219.

Modell, A. (1990) *Other Times, Other Realities: Toward a Theory of Psychoanalytic Treatment*. Cambridge, Massachusetts, Harvard University Press.

Padel, J. (1986) Ego in current thinking. In: G. Kohon (ed.), *The British School of Psychoanalysis: The Independent Tradition*, pp. 154–172. London, Free Association Books.

Strachey, J. (1934) The nature of the therapeutic action of psycho-analysis. *International Journal of Psycho-analysis* 15, pp. 127–159.

Winnicott, D. (1974a) Transitional objects and transitional phenomena. In: Winnicott, D. *Playing and Reality*, Chapter 1, pp. 1–30. Harmondsworth, Pelican Books.

Winnicott, D. (1974b) Playing: A theoretical statement. In: D. Winnicott, *Playing and Reality*, Chapter 3, pp. 44–61. Harmondsworth, Pelican Books.

Winnicott, D. (1974c) The location of cultural experience. In: D. Winnicott, *Playing and Reality*, Chapter 7, pp. 112–121. Harmondsworth, Pelican Books.

Winnicott, D. (1978) Metapsychological and clinical aspects of regression within the psycho-analytical set-up. In: D. Winnicott, *Through Paediatrics to Psycho-Analysis*, Chapter 22, pp. 278–294. London, Hogarth Press and the Institute of Psycho-Analysis.

The site in psychoanalytic psychotherapy

Chapter 3

Juliana and her faithless boyfriend

The psychotherapy site in a twice weekly psychotherapy

Donnet's theory of the analytic site, which was introduced in the previous chapter, sheds a brilliant shaft of light not only on psychoanalysis but on other clinical practice too, as Donnet himself came to recognise that it might do (Donnet, 2009, pp. 8–9). This chapter and the two that follow will each look in detail at a clinical example of psychotherapy, in the light of the idea that there is in psychotherapy a 'site' or ensemble that is comparable to the analytic site and that has a comparable potential for a transformative introjection that ushers in a working therapeutic process.

The case to be discussed in this chapter was one of formal psychotherapy in a British National Health Service setting, which required no fee from the patient. In at least two respects the setting resembled that of psychoanalysis, in that it was:

- of open-ended duration;
- the fundamental rule of free association was enunciated to the patient.

However, it was:

- without fee to the patient, in a British National Health Service clinic;
- face to face;
- there were two sessions per week.

The above features can be numbered amongst the 'elements' (in Donnet's terms) of the psychotherapy site. The last three elements mark out the difference of that site from the analytic site of psychoanalysis. The absence of a fee raises an intriguing issue. In public sector psychoanalytic psychotherapy, *is there an analogy to the element of the fee?*

The 'psychotherapy site' in psychoanalytic psychotherapy: the case of Juliana

Pre-history: encountering elements of the site at the pre-treatment stage

Through cancellations at the consultation/assessment stage, a patient who will be called Juliana was investigating – unconsciously, and in the created/found mode to which Donnet has drawn attention – the nature of the object (or person) potentially to be found in the clinic's psychotherapy site. A re-arranged appointment was cancelled and yet another requested; it was only on receiving a letter containing the mildly firm words, '*I can offer you one more appointment*' – in other words, on encountering limit-setting – that Juliana first managed to attend. She created/found further encounters at this consultation/assessment stage – as when she casually mentioned, just as her request for a treatment arrangement was being accepted, that she was about to spend a year abroad. She was initially dismayed to hear that psychotherapy meant arranging to be in one place for an indefinite period. When at length referred to me for treatment, *she had already made the above preliminary encounters with elements of the psychotherapy site.*

Juliana's next unconscious investigation of the psychotherapy site occurred in the preliminary meeting to set up treatment. She conveyed a problem of being helplessly trapped, serially, with an exploitative object (a boyfriend); yet she held up to me, as an ideal, a picture of a patient/therapist couple in which her former private therapist had given extra sessions, free, whenever she thought Juliana really needed them. Interpreting Juliana's problem about allowing adequately realistic planning for her needs, I proposed twice weekly clinic sessions. After initial agreement she reverted to a preference for one session a week, adding politely: '... *if that's all right with you.*' I drew attention to Juliana's assumption of my compliance with an arrangement insufficient for her therapeutic needs, although her rider, 'if that's all right with you', hinted at some question about this in her mind. Taken aback, she seemed to feel that I was taking her seriously. This illustrates an encounter with the site's *ethics*, for example, in the hint that I might *not* be prepared to engage her in a treatment structure that on the evidence of her own account would have been an insufficient one, and illustrates, too, her meeting the *logic* and *specificity* with which, for example, her apparently throwaway rider was heard as a serious though unconscious question.

Treatment: unpromising beginnings?

These early encounters with elements of the site allowed Juliana to attend faithfully and always very early, once her twice weekly treatment began. She produced however an unpromising series of sterile, repetitive, ruminative monologues about her boyfriend Bertrand's possible/probable unfaithfulness and her longing for reassurance that he loved her, all the while parading evidence of his sexual unfaithfulness and, as he gambled away his own and her money, his cynical exploitation of her. She spoke of the relentlessly constant parental rows of her childhood over her father's infidelities, suspected by her mother and known to a younger sibling but not, apparently, to Juliana, who had once screamed above the parental marital row, 'Get a divorce!'

At this stage, a preparedness to be reticent was probably crucial. My few comments usually focussed on Juliana's traumatised state – for example, I remarked that the relentless din of her parents' rows had left her feeling intruded on and insufficiently protected, making it difficult for her to listen or think. Through regular attendance Juliana discovered an accumulating experience of the reliable regularity of the sessions and of the reliable presence of the therapist. The approach of the first interruption, a two week Christmas holiday break, stimulated further created/found encounters in that Juliana's anxiety about the interruption came to be represented in her sessional material from early December onwards. Under this stimulus, therefore, she discovered the site as a place where her unconscious anxieties could be represented, understood and interpreted. This afforded her considerable relief, and was the beginning of a discovery that the site might be a place where her inner fantasy life could be represented and elaborated.

After two months of therapy a qualitative change – a sense that a *process* was now unfolding – became manifest when sessions resumed after the Christmas break. It might be described as 'Stage one' of Juliana's introjection of the psychotherapy site as a whole. The atmosphere of sterile, circular ruminations modulated into one in which Juliana seemed more fully engaged in what she was saying, and in a way which recruited my genuine interest. New representations were appearing, depicting both halves of a split representation of the parental couple. In parallel with a description of a really vicious, violent physical fight with Bertrand, there appeared a new, harmonious representation of a (parental) sexual couple when Juliana described a companionable drinking of early morning tea during a Christmas stay with her father and stepmother, herself perched on the edge of their bed after the stepmother had called to her to join them.

Thirdness

As we saw in the last chapter, Donnet (2001, 2009) suggests that the analysand comes to sense the analyst's relationship to and respect for the 'rules of the game', and that through this the patient too can develop an attachment to the analytic site itself, with its 'rules of the game'. This can assist in the development of 'thirdness' (an evolved capacity to appreciate three-term relations).

It is equally true that in psychotherapy also, the patient's sense of the therapist's relation to her theoretical principles, which constitutes so large a part of the psychotherapy site, helps the patient, too, to develop a relationship to the site. This in turn assists the capacity for three-term relations and a firmer sense of subjective agency. For example, Juliana reported a tempting offer from her workplace of some (temporary) extra hours of work, which would clash, however, with one of her psychotherapy sessions: could I alter it? I said I could not. Previously, faced with such a dilemma, Juliana seemed helplessly to see only a *two-term* situation of herself and the other person, and the sense was of her total capitulation unless the other capitulated to her. She surprised me by returning, with a newly purposeful air, having calculated the realities: by accepting the hours and travelling in a taxi to her session, she realised that despite the taxi fare she would be financially better off *and* able to oblige them at the workplace. I infer that through her internalised experience in psychotherapy of the three terms of therapist, patient and the third term of the site, she could now think in terms of a three-term situation consisting of therapist, patient and an external reality. Her new 'capacity for thirdness' amounted to a new capacity to register, reflect on and deal effectively with reality. This also entailed a new sense of agency, in contrast to her previous sense of being manipulated by events or by another person or other persons.

The decisive encounter with the element corresponding to the fee

Yet a more dramatic, lasting transformation of Juliana as patient would occur a few months later. It awaited her discovery of an element in the National Health Service psychotherapy site that *corresponded* to an important element in the analytic site: that of the fee.

It is instructive to notice, in Freud's early discussion of the psychoanalytic set-up, the indispensable function of the fee. In his 1913 paper 'On beginning the treatment', he mentions several disappointingly unsuccessful attempts over a ten year period to treat patients without charging them a fee, under the misapprehension that resistance connected to resentment of the fee could thereby be avoided. He concludes that the fee performs a necessary regulating function, by keeping the patient anchored in the world of reality.

Now, it has been my repeated experience, when conducting free clinic psychotherapy treatments *of the open-ended kind*, that a point comes when the patient presents the therapist with a problem of therapeutic management having to do with the wasting of sessions in the sense of not attending them. I have come to believe that what the patient is thereby investigating (unconsciously) is whether an element in the psychotherapy site exists *which grounds the treatment in the world of reality*. It corresponds, therefore, to the fee. It has also been my repeated experience that a sufficiently adequate encounter with this corresponding element in the site – often at least a year into the treatment – performs a visibly regulating function for the patient, and often 'clinches' the transformational introjection of the site, signalling a new seriousness thereafter in the level of the patient's involvement in the treatment.

Let me illustrate with two consecutive, critically important sessions in Juliana's therapy at the seven month point. She had twice left her boyfriend and returned to him since beginning treatment with me.

Looking at me urgently on entering, Juliana said that a lot had been happening with a lot of issues. She recounted, circumstantially, the lovelessness of the last days during that week with Bertrand, and the cold, hate-filled finality of the way in which they had parted for good. She moved to a description of the recourse she had then impulsively and helplessly tried to have to various sources of succour, ineffectively, until she stopped and *thought* (a result, she surprised me by observing, of 'coming here') that perhaps she could ring her stepmother. She did so and told her, in abbreviated form, everything: the years of entanglement, preoccupation and misery of the cohabitation with Bertrand, which she had kept secret, and its miserable ending. Her stepmother was responsive, and telephoned back after speaking with the patient's father, with a warm invitation to the patient to join them in a forthcoming five month stay abroad. The patient had spoken to her usually evasive father, who told her that he loved her and that she had a special importance to him from having saved his life, years before, when he had been suicidal. 'I have never in my life had such a conversation with my father!' The rest of the session concerned her vacillations over whether to accept the invitation to spend some months abroad. '*But – what if it's the one chance in my life to learn what my father really feels about me?*' I had not spoken at all this session, and simply said it was time to stop.

During the following day's session, I introduced a link to Juliana's first therapist, to whom she had paid a fee. Juliana replied animatedly that it was odd that I should mention her, as the former therapist had flashed into her mind only yesterday, she didn't know why. I observed that it was she who had given Juliana her sessions for free, when Juliana's money was being poured out on the perennially destitute Bertrand, who kept gambling his own money away. I went on: 'Perhaps you have wondered if I would keep your sessions open if you went abroad for several months, *because what you need to find out is whether I know more than you or your previous therapist do, about how to manage when someone who is extremely needy makes you feel that you cannot say "No"*.'

What was at stake here? Open-endedness is one of the fundamental elements in the analytic site, and it is important to be aware that when we do not place it on offer in psychoanalytic psychotherapy, we render unavailable to the patient an important resource that assists free associative flow. But in a treatment that is free to the patient, open-endedness appears sooner or later to stimulate fantasies of narcissistic omnipotent control, represented by proposed or actual wasting of sessions (often on a large scale), as though the patient is acting on a belief that he possesses an infinitude of sessions and can attend just if and when he likes. When the patient proposes or practises such non-attendance, he is creating a means of finding out whether the psychotherapy, together with the therapist's conception of it, is grounded in the world of reality.

The details of the unconscious meaning are always highly specific to the patient. By telling me that the father she had longed all her life to be close to had seconded his wife's warm invitation, Juliana tacitly invited me to authorise some months of unused sessions. In this wonderful instance of created/found investigation,

I was being invited to ignore the reality that, in a free clinic treatment, the sessions *are* being paid for by someone (although not by the patient), and I was thereby invited to act out in a way that would have paralleled Juliana's inability to refuse money to her compulsively gambling boyfriend, to which the former therapist's ad hoc free sessions seem in turn to have corresponded. It seemed to me that Juliana needed to know whether the site of her psychotherapy with me differed, in this dimension, from the site of her previous psychotherapy. For this reason, I framed my interpretation (above) in terms of *what Juliana needed to find out.*

Consequences of introjection of the site: Juliana confronts her oedipal illusion

The introjection of the site as a whole, metamorphosing it for Juliana into a working psychotherapeutic situation possessing inherent 'rules of the game' with characteristic logic, ethics and specificity, now reached its full accomplishment as a result of the encounter, precipitated by her, with that additional element of the site. What had made the encounter with *this* particular element so decisively transformative for Juliana? Faced with abandoning her psychotherapy for the sake of visiting her father, she had cried out her anguished question: '*What if it's the one chance in my life to learn what my father really feels about me?*' Evidently, she interpreted the issue as one of receiving parental love and support at a juncture where this was crucially needed. And yet, unconsciously, the 'it's' of her question was paradoxically ambiguous: would concretely paying a long visit to her father constitute her once-in-a-lifetime chance that she could learn 'what her father really felt about [her]', or, rather, might continuing with her psychotherapy constitute, owing to the site's inherent logic, that possibly once-in-a-lifetime chance?

In response to the interpretation on the day following this question, Juliana renounced the long visit to her father in order to continue her treatment. An aspect of her preoccupation about her father's feelings for her *would* be understood through her therapy. Perhaps she dimly sensed this potentiality, through her accomplishment at this point in time of the transformational introjection of the psychotherapy site, which sustained her in the decision to forgo the longed-for visit to her father. For Juliana's central difficulty was bound up with her inability to acknowledge, and to face, a conflict about whether to go on investing hope in an oedipal illusion. By this I mean an illusion, at the level of unconscious fantasy, that she would one day be revealed as the cherished chosen one of her father – chosen over, and supplanting, her mother. This illusion could be inferred from her compulsive, voyeuristic preoccupation with Bertrand's secret sexual relations with another woman, as well from the difficulty she had with allowing herself fulfilment as a wife and mother. Understanding this had to wait on the prior elaboration of Juliana's unconscious anxieties about what this secretly harboured illusion implied for her relations with her mother.

These anxieties were given representative form by means of what she spoke of in her sessions, which included a particularly vivid description of a cyst in her breast that she had believed was cancer. It had felt like an arrow transfixing her breast (which appeared to condense an unconscious fantasy that she had attacked her mother's breast and a fantasy that the cyst amounted to a punishment for the fantasied attack). Through her internalised sense that the psychotherapy site made this possible, Juliana continued, in this way, to elaborate her unconscious fantasies.

Thus, she began one session with her despair at age 11 about facing the '11+' (an examination qualifying for entrance to grammar school education, which Juliana would fail). She mentioned her father's liking for intellectual women; meanwhile, her dramatic mimicking of her mother's sneeringly envious and bitter reference to such women suggested projection of her angry, defeated sense of rivalry towards me in the transference. Then she feelingly described reviewing a novel whose protagonist's mother died when he was two and a half. Growing up in an ill-treated, unloved, unhappy state he turned for comfort to nature (as the patient once vividly described herself doing as a child.) Sibling rival figures appeared. The novel's focal point concerned the protagonist growing into a young man.

Juliana had been utterly absorbed in all that she had been telling me. I interpreted that she is very, very identified with the protagonist of the novel. The focal point, the threshold of growing up, is where she began today, with the '11+'. Turning to nature to assuage a sense of neglect and unhappiness seems to have symbolised, for the novel's character, something lost that he had once possessed – his mother, before he lost her at two and a half; and Juliana's own profound, loving union with nature, which she has sometimes described, seems to symbolise her own sense of having once had, but irretrievably lost, a loving union with her mother *before the time she can consciously remember*, before she was three, when her mother gave birth to another baby. Juliana feels that she has been left, since then, with only a bitterly rivalrous relation to her mother.

The faithful, vivid specificity of Juliana's account, which functioned to give representative form to a central part of her unconscious conflict, indicates how far she had introjected, and come to trust, the psychotherapy site with its implicit logic. Subsequent sessions worked further on the anxiety about the survival of the once loving relation with her mother in the face of her envious rivalry and rage, an anxiety worked out in parallel in the transference relationship with the therapist.

Juliana terminated her treatment after 21 months, in order to re-locate to a new job. She said, 'I feel I can love my mother now – and my father. It's as though something has lifted. I suppose I knew, before, that they're real people – but now I can feel it. A door has opened.' She added, 'It's as though – I've been through doors – and I've been through one, into a new room . . . and I've closed the door behind me. And my childhood can stay behind that door now, I know those things happened, but I don't need to stay there.'

Just before her therapy ended, we clarified at last Juliana's lifelong prevarication over her oedipal illusion. In a resistant atmosphere, she had been ruminating about untrustworthiness in all males and in Bertrand; but eventually she spoke of her father's extra-marital affairs and her search for reassurance that he loved her. This led me to say:

'You used to believe that you knew nothing of your father's unfaithfulness to your mother. More probably, you have always kept the knowledge in a separate part of your mind, fuelling an excited hope that *you* would one day turn out to be the person your father was supremely in love with. Growing up, it was hard to let go of this secretly cherished illusion, to face the difference between your father *loving you as a daughter* and his *being in love with you as his chosen one*. Your blindness to the signs that Andrew (her last boyfriend but one) had a wife and family suggest that you were re-creating the situation with your father – excitedly noticing the signs that he was interested in someone other than you, while another part of your mind maintained the illusion of noticing nothing. Similarly, your capacity to judge Bertrand as unlikely to be faithful to you was impaired because you were re-creating the same scenario in your mind about your father.'

Juliana said soberly, 'I think that's probably right.'

Her penultimate session described a weekend visit from father and stepmother, during which Juliana concretely enacted a conflict-ridden bid for, yet renunciation of, her father. She ended her account with a vehement account of her father's inconsiderateness on a former occasion: 'I *wanted* to go to that funeral!' I interpreted that she was telling me that she wanted to go to the funeral of the illusory hopes she had cherished for so long, in relation to her father, which she felt all but ready to lay to rest, but against some opposition still, which she felt emanated from her father.

Conclusion

Donnet's idea of the introjected site, when differentially considered by way of analogy, can shed theoretical light on the therapeutic action of formal psychotherapy. By the analytic site is meant what is available to the patient starting psychoanalysis; by the psychotherapy site is meant what is available to the patient starting psychotherapy. Respectively for these different kinds of treatment, conceptualisation in terms of an introjected site does justice to the integrity of the treatment concerned – to its unique logic, ethics and specificity.

Conceptualisation in these terms does justice also to the clinical reality of the *unconscious* dimension of the patient's collaboration in his treatment. This implies recognition that the psychological-mindedness which eventually characterises the patient's engagement in the treatment need not come ready-made. The case of Juliana demonstrates a series of correspondences between the analytic site and the psychotherapy site. In particular, it shows that that Juliana's successful engagement in a therapeutic process, after unpromising beginnings, was far from being a function of any pre-existing psychological-mindedness but was, rather, a product of her gradually achieved introjection of the psychotherapy site. The encounter with various elements of the site has been illustrated. The episode of Juliana's reported indecision over whether to absent herself for many weeks from her publicly funded treatment illustrated her created/found discovery of her psychotherapy as a working situation in which she could find a fresh re-presentation of previous scenarios dramatising her presenting problem (the boyfriend who had exploited her with his apparent helplessness, Juliana's former therapist who had succumbed to Juliana's apparent helplessness, and the question of whether I would succumb to it too).

The site of psychoanalytic psychotherapy differs from the analytic site of psychoanalysis. The analytic site is uniquely characterised by having available for the analysand's introjection those elements that constitute Freud's 'opening moves' (Freud, 1913), as well as principles set out in his technique papers such as those of analytic neutrality and of abstinence from any actions other than those of listening and analysing. Arguably, alteration of any one element in Freud's set-up constitutes the treatment not as psychoanalysis but as psychotherapy, and its site as the psychotherapy site.

The degree of its difference from the analytic site depends to a large extent on how many of Freud's 'opening moves' have been jettisoned. A time-limited once weekly psychotherapy, embarked on without enunciation of the fundamental rule, differs more widely from psychoanalysis than a three times weekly open-ended psychotherapy on the couch in a private practice setting. The next two chapters will further illustrate this.

Where the patient pays no fee, the element in an open-ended treatment that corresponds to the fee usually concerns proposed or actual non-attendance of the sessions that the patient has originally contracted for. Handling this issue is analogous to handling problems over payment of the fee, both entailing an issue of the treatment's rootedness in the real world.

References

Donnet, J.-L. (2001) From the fundamental rule to the analysing situation. *International Journal of Psychoanalysis* 82, pp. 129–140. Available from: DOI: 10.1516/3FUH-9WTT-E68B-WF70.

Donnet J.-L. (2002) *Le Divan Bien Tempéré* [*The Well-Tempered Couch*]. 2nd edition. Paris, Presses Universitaires de France.

Freud, S. (1913) On beginning the treatment (further recommendations on the technique of psycho-analysis I). In: J. Strachey (ed. and trans.), *The Standard Edition of the Complete Psychological Works of Sigmund Freud* (Vol. 12), pp. 121–144. London, Hogarth Press.

Chapter 4

The psychotherapy site in a once weekly therapy

The dark world of incest

Chapter 3 employed illustration from a twice weekly psychotherapy to show that a psychotherapeutic process comes about through a 'sufficiently adequate' encounter with elements of what I have called the psychoanalytical psychotherapy site and through the eventual introjection of that site.

This chapter illustrates that process in a once weekly psychotherapy.

Carl: early discovery of some elements of the psychoanalytical psychotherapy site

In a preliminary interview with Carl to set up treatment, we agreed a regular weekly time. I explained that he would be asked, as far as he wished and felt able, to put into words whatever he was thinking and feeling. Carl asked whether, during his sessions, it would be possible for the wall clock to be removed, or moved at least from his visual field. In a previous psychotherapy the loudly ticking desk clock, which had disturbed him, had been obligingly shut away by the therapist in the desk. Now, my clock was about to be moved! I told Carl that my clock was actually about to be moved to the wall adjacent to him, but that perhaps in the course of his treatment we might be able to enquire into, and possibly come to understand, what was so disturbing for him about it. He was visibly taken aback by this reply, which seems to have represented an element in the psychotherapy set-up – or site, to use Donnet's term – that was new to him.

In the first treatment session, we can already detect evidence that the patient's encounter with that new element has had an effect on him.

Carl's first treatment session began very slowly, with a reference to his psychiatrist having remarked that not all therapists have quite the same approach. He was nervous about the silences in the session, and said so, though he did not know why . . . Later he remembered the silences of his childhood at night, in bed . . . it felt as if something bad was going to happen. He lay awake and listened . . . and listened . . . to hear if someone would come . . . and sometimes . . . someone *did* come. I said, 'I'm not sure if you want me to know what happened when they came.' He looked at me and said that two members of his family had sexually abused him over very many years.

I said, 'So something bad *did* happen.'

Carl exclaimed, 'I didn't know I was going to find that out!' and seemed *immensely* surprised. He then described having had to pay a duty visit the previous week to the house of one of these incestuous abusers . . . it was set back from the road, a very quiet house, unoccupied during his visit, and the silence so disturbed and finally terrified him that he had been obliged to hurry away, his business not concluded and held over for another visit . . .

Let us think about this in terms of the effect of the set-up on the process. This patient seems to have listened with unusual acuteness to my reply to his original request about the clock. He registered its implicit suggestion that in the site of the therapy that was soon to start, he might encounter, instead of the requested action, an enquiring attitude towards himself that might lead him to new knowledge. And indeed this happened. In that very first session, Carl discovered *for himself* all three dimensions of the transference: the sinister silence within the session had contained within itself the silence in childhood that had been the prelude to the nocturnal incestuous visits, and the silence that week of the incestuous abuser's house. By saying 'I didn't know I was going to find that out!' Carl showed that he registered his discovery. Was it pre-existent in the site, this element of the psychotherapy site that allowed him to *find* a meaningful conjunction of his past life, his current life outside, and his immediate experience within the session? Or, through having the courage to speak his free associations aloud, did the patient *create* that astonishing conjunction of meanings? Winnicott, referring to the baby and the teddy bear or other transitional object that stands for the mother, advises us not to ask the question 'found *or* created?' (Winnicott, 1974a). Winnicott also compares psychotherapy to playing, and observes that 'the significant moment is that at which *the child surprises himself or herself.* It is not the moment of my clever interpretation that is significant' (Winnicott, 1974b, p. 51). Donnet says similarly that the site is put at the disposal of the patient, and that in relation to the paradoxical process of created/found discovery, the analyst's most important role is not to hinder it (Donnet, 2001). Similarly, we place the psychotherapy set-up, which I call the psychoanalytical psychotherapy site, at the disposal of the psychotherapy patient: and our principal business is not to hinder the patient's process of created/found discovery.

That is often, of course, by no means easy! The manner in which the patient goes on investigating the elements in the psychotherapy site can sometimes place the therapist in a technical dilemma. One example can be that of a personal question. Here Freud's governing principle is helpful: that it is the general plan of chess that determines its particular rules. This makes technique subservient to the overall task of the whole treatment project – to what Donnet calls method as opposed to technique.

In my current practice, I tend to take a relaxed and friendly approach when faced with personal questions. I might acknowledge that while it can feel strange not to be answered in the way that one expects, it can be helpful just to register the question and any thoughts surrounding it, so that we might in time come to understand something about it. In the anecdote that follows, I wish that it had occurred to me that in some such fashion the patient might have been spared discomfort. The incident to be described was uncomfortable for the patient, but it does nevertheless illustrate the patient's encounter with the principle of holding the psychotherapy situation constant so that the patient's difficulties can be thrown up against it in sharp relief.

The following happened in Carl's second treatment session.

It had been snowing. As he removed his jacket, Carl asked me if I had had trouble driving here, too. When I simply returned a quizzical look, he repeated his question in a very clear voice. I said, 'Were you wondering about that?' Visibly disturbed, Carl explained that there was nothing in his question at all, except to wonder whether the snow had made it difficult for me, too, to get here, adding with a smilingly expectant look: 'Did you drive here today?'

Evidently the patient expected, as an ordinary common courtesy which it would be unthinkably rude and unfriendly to refuse, a brief answer to his question. It can be argued that he should have been given one, on the grounds that is important not to re-traumatise an already traumatised patient. I thought, however, that something else was at stake. This profoundly traumatised patient had come asking for psychotherapy, and my paramount duty to him was to maintain my role as his psychoanalytic psychotherapist. When he asked me for the third time whether I had driven to work that snowy day, I therefore simply waited.

Your sympathies are likely to be with the patient, who was understandably appalled. He explained hurriedly and in acute distress that his question, which in itself meant nothing at all, was simply his way of trying to deal with the awkwardness of the start of the session. Freud draws attention, by the way, to this common attempt to partition the treatment into a formal part that is felt to count, and a tiny informal part at the start or at the end, which the patient does not think is really part of the treatment: and his advice in 'On beginning the treatment' is not to accept the division, or not for long. (Freud, 1913, p. 139). Carl now began to speak of something else. It was only later in the session that he could, with considerable courage, speak of his sense of humiliation by and reproach of me, and have me acknowledge this.

So, what was the point of my original response? Carl's question represented, I believe, a very proper attempt to investigate the psychoanalytical psychotherapy site and its potential to be of use to him. My response (although I now think it could and certainly should have included a friendly acknowledgement that it can feel strange in psychotherapy not necessarily to receive the answer that you are expecting) reflected my view of his question *as a communication to be listened to and thought about.*

Michael Parsons puts it like this:

> Psychoanalysis involves a stillness, an apparently passive attentiveness in the analyst, which depends on a framework set up expressly to make things possible that cannot happen in an ordinary relationship. Responsiveness at the level of ordinary reality is subordinated to an intensity of response at the level of psychic reality.

> (Parsons, 2000, p. 27)

This is just as true of psychoanalytic psychotherapy. Here let me describe my countertransference to Carl's question. At the time, I had felt an irresistible coercion to answer a personal question, which I was going to *have* to answer . . . *and* a simultaneous sense that the integrity of my role was lost if I capitulated. I then thought, and still think, that my first duty to Carl was to maintain that role: to maintain the integrity of the frame. It was only after the session that thinking about the countertransference reminded me of Carl's description of the first occasion on which, as a very young boy, a parent had abused him. With a comfortable air that conveyed that nothing at all untoward was happening, this parent had taken out Carl's penis and had begun to stimulate it. There had seemed no room for Carl's bewildered sense that his personal boundaries were being insistently invaded, because the parent conveyed such an atmosphere that nothing in particular was happening (and therefore there was nothing to object to or resist). This suggested to me that Carl's most compelling and urgent question to me concerned my competence to help him, and that the implicit question was this: *if you are faced, as I was in childhood, with inexorable pressure by an insistently invasive object to disavow your perception that an invasion of personal boundaries is being mounted* . . . are you as helpless to deal with this as I?

With so grave an issue at stake, a reply about my driving would *not* have been adequate for him as an answer.

The incident of Carl's question about driving in the snow represented, I conclude, the second stage of an encounter with the 'fundamental rule' of psychoanalytically oriented treatments, that the work proceeds by free association. The patient had heard it articulated at the outset, when I told him that he was asked to put into words whatever he was thinking and feeling, and he now encountered it as a lived experience. That is, he now found that his question was simply received *as one of his communications in words*, for listening to and reflecting on. Despite my failure to mediate this more kindly – which at the time, under the pressure of the moment, I could not think how to do – I infer Carl's probable introjection of this element of the site from the fact that the sessions that followed this one were marked by a deepening of rapport. He was able to specify some details of his truly horrific sexual abuse, and told me how, as a little boy of ten, reading about the Nazi concentration camps had helped him to feel less wholly humanly isolated.

Further discoveries of elements of the psychotherapy site

Carl went on to encounter some more of the elements of the psychotherapy site. One element was that sessions really are the length he had been told they would be. This invariance of the time frame allows the patient to discover, gradually, that his conflicts about it can become visible against its neutral background, and so accessible for reflection, and this remains the paramount reason for holding it constant (Bleger, 1967). I often felt that this was going to be impossible. I was acutely aware of Carl's vulnerability to hurt and frustration, as well as his slowly emerging murderous rage, and frequently he brought an urgent question which erupted right at the end of the session. But I also knew that I must not fail to end the session on time. It can be helpful to remember that however much the inexorable ending on time of the session represents to the patient an occasion for intense hurt and fury, it also represents a crucial ethic of the site, that it is expectable and reliable, whatever the forces opposing this: and, most especially for a patient such as Carl, it represents the ethic that the therapist does not seduce and is not to be seduced. As such, it may come to represent something hated but also reassuring.

Another of Carl's encounters with a crucial element of the psychotherapy site came about through his hints that he was preoccupied with a vivid image of a sexual practice to which he had been subjected which was almost unimaginably perverse, and which had left him with a bestial self-image. He conveyed intense suffering through the intrusive presence of this shameful self-image, which I knew about only in general outline. In response to this, I clarified that I wished neither to coerce him nor to forbid him to let me know more precisely what this image was, and that he was free simply to think about this. This startled him: he thanked me, and returned the following week describing this as having been 'right on the button', as he put it, and that it had left him feeling very shaken. I infer that he had discovered therapist neutrality but had also discovered that the psychoanalytical psychotherapy site has startling potentialities, and really was placed freely at his disposal, as Donnet puts it.

On the brink of metamorphosis: two decisive encounters

During the following weeks, Carl continued to encounter, and to integrate, various other elements of the psychotherapy site. His decisive encounter with two of them heralded his telling me that he now felt a new opportunity to go deeper in his therapy – from which I inferred his transformational introjection, at last, of the site as a whole.

Of these two elements, one was open-endedness. Carl discovered it as follows. He returned from the first break in the treatment in a precarious state, barely managing to function. He made casual reference to the two years of a previous psychotherapy, which he had always described as very long, and I suggested that he was wondering how long his treatment with me might be available. He agreed. I told him that I would expect to negotiate that with him. I clarified that the two year span of his previous therapy was in my view not necessarily to be regarded as very long, that I would wish to be available for as short or as long a time as necessary, and currently knew of no reason why I could not be available for quite a long time. He confirmed that he had been worried that the treatment might be too short, and said that this was an immense thing that I was saying to him.

This enabled us to reflect on his mention, earlier in that same session, that one of his two daughters had been in a car accident: she was being taken to hospital with abrasions and shock, and asked Carl to come and collect her. Because of his precarious mental state Carl was not yet dressed, and got into a panicky, agitated and procrastinating state, feeling hopelessly daunted over not knowing where this hospital was and feeling unable to find his way to it, so that when his daughter finally telephoned again he had not even set out, and the daughter had to take a taxi home.

I now began to realise that in telling me earlier about his daughter, on whose behalf I had silently felt very shocked, Carl had at a deeper level been representing himself. I interpreted that the daughter's sense of being disappointed and let down is also Carl's, because no-one has ever known the way to meet him and find him. I suggested too that what was now in the air, through the new thought about his treatment as now open-ended in duration, was a sense of an uncharted terrain, a question of whether I will know how to find my way to somewhere I may not ever have been to before, to find him and help him.

This encounter was to prove critical. On returning the following week Carl said again that what had been said about the time was something immense for him, and then he said it felt as though, *now*, there was a new beginning.

At this critical point, on the very brink of metamorphosis, Carl had to be sure of one more element in the site. He created an encounter, forthwith, with that very element, which I would call a respect for thirdness (Donnet, 2001; and see above, Chapter 2). Unusually, Carl arrived at his very next session four minutes late, with a glance at the wall clock and with an exclamation. One daughter had said the car clock was six minutes fast, and the other had said it was five minutes fast – and he had been in the parked car all the time! He spoke of the sense of a whole new beginning opening out in the treatment, referred briefly to his psychiatrist, and then spoke of his elder daughter. She was recovering from the accident, but was irritable. Carl said he has always felt guilty about his daughters growing up without the presence of their mother, but told me in rather pious tones that he has always brought them up to be decent, that he was conscious this week of the elder one as a young woman in the house, and he hopes she will not turn into a flirt and a slut.

I suggested that Carl's uneasy awareness of his daughter in the household with himself there, but no wife, recalls his childhood situation where one parent and a sibling actively abused him, while the other parent failed to hold a different standpoint which ought to have regulated the two abusers and so rescued him. He might be anxious that in embarking with me on what feels like a new beginning in his therapy, he could be similarly vulnerable to there being no external regulating reference point. The car clock situation felt similarly perplexing because one daughter had said it was six minutes fast and the other had said it was five minutes fast: but my clock said something different again! Theoretically, he *could* have checked with the radio or the telephone. Listening intently, Carl remarked here, 'Yes, I could, couldn't I?' I replied, 'The fact that it did not occur to you dramatises for us the situation that you have always felt yourself to be in – one *without* an external reference point. Yet you mentioned your psychiatrist today. He represents that external reference point that must regulate the situation here between you and me, just as your wife, although absent, might potentially represent it between you and each of your daughters, and just as the parent who was not actively abusing you *ought* to have represented it in coming to your rescue, but actually failed to do.'

Early in the next session, I inferred that a culminating introjection of a critical proportion of the elements of the psychotherapy site had been achieved, transforming the 'site' into a 'working situation', when Carl said: 'You have taken me seriously. I have always schooled myself never to have any expectations of anyone, but *now* I feel a whole new possibility of going deeper.'

A new flow of associations began, ushered in by Carl's telling me that he had passed, when walking his dog in the park, the boulders on which he used to play as a child. He stopped to look at them and tangibly touch them, and looked down the long vista which led to the street of the house that had been his childhood home. He stood there for a long time. As is so often the case when a treatment gets securely established, the beginnings of a shift towards a greater capacity for symbolic representation was already discernible here.

Creativity and the 'rules of the game'

Discourses on creativity have often been stimulated by the establishment of spontaneous flow that marks the establishment of an analytic or psychotherapeutic process, and by the concomitant acquisition or enhancement of the patient's capacity for symbolic representation of psychic experience. An important corollary of Donnet's theory is that to conceive of creativity as an attribute of the analyst or therapist is likely to miss the point and to stray into a narcissistically omnipotent state of mind which can only mislead.

The regulating external reference point at issue in Carl's session – that is, the presence between patient and therapist of a third party to whom both can refer – exists also in the ethics and logic of the psychotherapy site itself. It exists, that is, in what Freud and Donnet both call (on the basis of Freud's analogy between psychoanalysis and chess) the rules of the game, which the psychotherapist, like the psychoanalyst, is bound to respect. It is this that gives an alternative to the model of technique as interpretation – a two-term model of patient and interpreting psychotherapist that easily lends itself in turn to an erroneous conception of creativity (the creatively interpreting psychotherapist). A proper balance is inherent in a three-term model: the patient, the therapist and something outside and beyond them both to which the therapist is subject, the *third* term of the frame or site, with its ethics, logic and specificity (Donnet, 2001; O'Neill, 2005, 2007, 2008).

Modality and setting (site): supporting the patient's unconscious collaboration in his treatment

Notwithstanding fundamental differences in kind between the three treatment modalities of psychoanalysis, psychotherapy and psychodynamic social casework (the latter to be defined below), careful attention to the construction of the relevant treatment set-up supports the patient's potential *unconscious* collaboration in his treatment. It is the unconscious dimension of his collaboration – his introjection gradually of the elements of the relevant 'site' to the point of transformational introjection of that site as a whole – that establishes the creative spontaneous flow of the analytic or therapeutic process, as well as being the source of symbolisation. This implies care and consistency in the construction of the relevant treatment set-up, where the set of elements must be uniquely appropriate to the modality concerned and consistently maintained within it.

The analytic site of psychoanalysis is uniquely constituted by having available for the analysand's introjection those elements comprised by Freud's 'opening moves' (Freud, 1913). We can remind ourselves that they are:

1   within a fixed place, a fixed daily hour (less ten minutes and a rest day);
2   an agreed fee;
3   duration established as open-ended;
4   use of the couch;
5   explicit enunciation to the patient of the 'fundamental rule' that he is to say everything that comes into his mind;
6   a forbearing interpretive reticence towards the developing transference.

In his five other papers on technique, Freud specified other essential features of the analytic setting, such as the analyst's neutrality, his manner of listening with evenly suspended attention (now usually called free-floating listening), and his abstinence from all activity except analysing (Freud, 1911, 1912a, 1912b, 1914, 1915).

The degree to which the site of psychoanalytic psychotherapy differs from that of psychoanalysis depends largely on how many of Freud's 'opening moves' have been jettisoned. Thus, a time-limited once weekly psychotherapy, embarked on without enunciation of the fundamental rule, differs more widely from psychoanalysis than does a three times weekly open-ended psychotherapy on the couch in private practice.

Carl's once weekly psychotherapy was therefore very different from a psychoanalysis: the site differs from the analytic site. Yet Freud's recommendations concerning the set-up for psychoanalysis repay careful study by the psychotherapist no less than by the psychoanalyst. Enunciation of a version of the fundamental rule, for example, was one of the elements present in Carl's psychotherapy site; and Carl encountered it as a lived experience (albeit one that should have been more kindly mediated) on meeting my response to his asking whether I had driven to work. The invariance of the time frame, and therapist neutrality, were two further elements whose importance has been learned from psychoanalysis. Carl's encounter with all three of these elements has been explicitly illustrated. The manner of such an encounter and the discoveries it leads to are always highly specific to the patient – as when Carl discovered, in the frightening silence of his first session, the sinister silence heralding the nocturnal incestuous abuse of childhood and the equally sinister silence of his recent visit to the abuser's house.

The deepening of rapport following the encounter with each element of the site indicates their gradual introjection: and the transformative point of which Donnet writes, whereby introjection of a critical proportion of elements of the site marks the introjection of the site as a whole, was discernible in the two sessions where Carl spoke of there being at last a new beginning, and of a whole new opportunity to go deeper. The 'going deeper' was already beginning, as he spoke of the vista down which he looked, in the park, towards his childhood home.

References

Bleger, J. (1967) Psycho-analysis of the psycho-analytic frame. *International Journal of Psychoanalysis* 48, pp. 511–519.

Donnet, J.-L. (2001) From the fundamental rule to the analysing situation. *International Journal of Psychoanalysis* 82 (1), pp. 129–140. Available from: DOI: 10.1516/3FUH-9WTT-E68B-WF70.

Donnet, J.-L. (2002) Le site analytique et la situation analysante [The analytic site and the analysing situation]. In: *Le Divan Bien Tempéré* [*The Well-Tempered Couch*]. 2nd edition, pp. 7–47. Paris, Presses Universitaires de France.

Donnet, J.-L. (2009) *The Analyzing Situation*. A Weller (trans.). London, Karnac. Originally published in French as *La Situation Analysante*. Paris, Presses Universitaires de France, 2005.

Freud, S. (1911) The handling of dream-interpretation in psycho-analysis. In: J. Strachey (ed. and trans.), *The Standard Edition of the Complete Psychological Works of Sigmund Freud* (Vol. 12), pp. 89–96. London, Hogarth Press.

Freud, S. (1912a) The dynamics of transference. In: J. Strachey (ed. and trans.), *The Standard Edition of the Complete Psychological Works of Sigmund Freud* (Vol. 12), pp. 97–108. London, Hogarth Press.

Freud, S. (1912b) Recommendations to physicians practising psycho-analysis. In: J. Strachey (ed. and trans.), *The Standard Edition of the Complete Psychological Works of Sigmund Freud* (Vol. 12), pp. 109–120. London, Hogarth Press.

Freud, S. (1913) On beginning the treatment (further recommendations on the technique of psycho-analysis I). In: J. Strachey (ed. and trans.), *The Standard Edition of the Complete Psychological Works of Sigmund Freud* (Vol. 12), pp. 121–144. London, Hogarth Press.

Freud, S. (1914) Remembering, repeating and working-through (further recommendations on the technique of psycho-analysis II) In: J. Strachey (ed. and trans.), *The Standard Edition of the Complete Psychological Works of Sigmund Freud* (Vol. 12), pp. 145–156. London, Hogarth Press.

Freud, S. (1915) Observations on transference-love (further recommendations on the technique of psycho-analysis III). In: J. Strachey (ed. and trans.), *The Standard Edition of the Complete Psychological Works of Sigmund Freud* (Vol. 12), pp. 157–171. London, Hogarth Press.

O'Neill, S. (2005) Psychoanalytic application and psychoanalytic integrity. *International Journal of Psychoanalysis* 86, pp. 125–146.

O'Neill, S. (2007) The introjected psychodynamic site. A theory of the therapeutic process in psychodynamic practice. *Psychoanalytic Psychotherapy* 21 (3), pp. 197–215.

O'Neill, S. (2008) The psychotherapy site. Towards a differential theory of therapeutic engagement. *European Psychotherapy* 8, pp. 53–68.

Parsons, M. (2000) *The Dove That Returns, The Dove That Vanishes: Paradox and Creativity in Psycho-Analysis*. London and Philadelphia, Routledge.

Winnicott, D. (1974a) Transitional objects and transitional phenomena. In: D. Winnicott, *Playing and Reality*, Chapter 1, pp. 1–30. Harmondsworth, Pelican Books.

Winnicott, D. (1974b) Playing: A theoretical statement. In: D. Winnicott, *Playing and Reality*, Chapter 3, pp. 44–61. Harmondsworth, Pelican Books.

Chapter 5

Thraldom to narcissistic objects
The psychotherapy site in a three times weekly therapy

Because the order in which elements of the psychotherapy site are encountered varies from patient to patient, it can be helpful to see the process illustrated several times. The general aim of this chapter is therefore to further illustrate the eventually transformative encounter with elements of the psychoanalytic psychotherapy site. This time the treatment was one that began twice weekly and later changed to three times weekly with use of the couch. The three times weekly structure and the couch were eventually therefore elements of the site, and a second aim of the chapter is to demonstrate that the increased resources represented by these elements functioned to facilitate, eventually, some structural change in the patient's mind. A third aim is to illustrate, explicitly, the subjectivising aspect of the introjection of the site through which the patient develops a greater sense of agency.

Velia: finding a way to begin

Velia was a 20-year-old undergraduate science student from a distant Latin country. She was referred to me by a colleague in a private hospital in Velia's home city where she had undergone inpatient treatment for anorexia prior to returning to resume her interrupted studies at a British university.

Velia declined my recommendation of three times weekly treatment, feeling that attendance once a week was all that her studies would allow. I did not feel however that I could be of use to this very troubled patient in less than twice weekly sessions. Velia had wept and had gone away to ask her doctor for a different referral before, at length, she reluctantly agreed to a twice weekly structure. In view of Velia being a young student from abroad I did not then stipulate that all sessions for which I was available would have to be paid for, but simply suggested that we review the position in a year's time.

Images of the psychotherapy site in the first three months: from school to oriental herbalism

At the outset, Velia recalled hating the feeling of being made to go to school. The time stretched drearily ahead like a long tunnel with no end in sight. The little that she told me became a few stories that settled into repetitive stereotypes, reiterated as though being told to me for the first time.

Velia told me that she had as a child a toy pig with a soft, terry-towelling body but a hard head with ridges at the end of his snout and at the edges of his nostrils: Velia often held the snout clutched in her hand for long periods so that the ridges dug hard into her hand. She told me that she kept this pig by her for a sense of security well into adolescence. It struck me that the pig seemed not to be a true transitional object representing the child's link with his mother's presence, such as Winnicott has described of the small child's security blanket or teddy bear (Winnicott, 1974). Nor did it seem to have been a true autistic object actively substituting for the mother such as Tustin has described in her accounts of autistic children's use of a hard object that is clutched (Tustin, 1980). It seemed to have been something in-between the two. At the age of 14 Velia had decided to relinquish the use of her pig and started to go out with friends for the first time; but quite soon difficulties arose, the going out ended, and Velia started to use her pig again.

The rigidity characteristic of the toy pig's snout seemed to feel necessary to Velia in other ways. After I missed a session through illness, Velia told me that she does not like any break with routine. She continued that a fellow student who had just changed her haircut had an upsetting interview with her director of studies, and Velia explained that in her own mind the two things were related: the girl's reprimand from her director of studies on the day she had a new hairstyle confirmed that if there is a break with sameness, something bad might happen. Velia began to tell me about the year in which she had first developed anorexia and several obsessive-compulsive routines, which began in order to protect her from the dreaded 'something bad', but themselves became tyrannical. Later, she remarked, 'I enjoy these sessions. It's interesting to see what comes out.'

The following week, Velia indicated some interest in the incipient beginnings of a free associative process by telling me that she has more patience with knitting than her mother, because she has the patience to untangle the wool. In the next session, however, reaction set in. Velia said that she was running out of things to say. When I reminded her that she had only to put into words whatever she was thinking or feeling, she replied that she did not really feel able to do it. Later she told me that the supermarket had a two-for-one offer on packs of apples, but that her parents were not there to advise her. When I asked why she needed their advice on whether to buy the apples, she replied that she has little confidence in her own judgement. Evidently the enjoyment of the freedom to follow her thoughts had given way to an experience of the responsibilities of that freedom as problematic and persecutory.

A number of images appeared to be representations of Velia's experience of the psychotherapy site, some three months into her treatment. She spoke of being upset one Christmas when her cousins arrived. 'I'd just got a new toy, and they took it away from me.' (Only later would I learn that Velia's parents were making difficulties about continuing to pay for her treatment.) She spoke too about a girl older than herself whom she likes. 'Her mother and my mother quarrelled, so I won't see her – yet I like her.' We registered that what made her happy was felt to be only precariously available.

Finding how free association works

When a silence fell, Velia said that she was not sure how to think up things to say. I pointed out her anxiety at the thought that we might just wait and possibly be surprised by what might emerge. Velia acknowledged a random thought: she once went to an oriental herbalist about a symptom which the herbalist told her might be related to her kidneys. Later she had read that the tablets that have been prescribed for her can cause kidney damage. I responded that it is problematic for her to know how to think about the treatment that she is having here. Is it something like oriental herbalism that sounds wacky and suspect but turns out in her view to have quite a bit of sense in it after all, or is it a treatment that, despite having been 'prescribed' by her referrer, could actually damage her?

In the following session, Velia told me animatedly of her search for an unfamiliar lecture theatre: the signs to it all pointed in different directions, and she thought she would *never* arrive. But to her great satisfaction she found it, whereas some fellow students had had to text for help.

I inferred that Velia was discovering with surprise, *for herself*, that the act of following her free associations, which seem to point her in different directions, could actually lead her to a desired destination.

Discovery of some other elements of the psychotherapy site

Freedom to make the site one's own

Velia looked at the couch one day and wondered aloud why there was a bed in the room. This was the first time she had remarked on anything she found in the consulting room. She went on to say that she would paint the flat she is getting. I commented that, as with her flat, she now felt able to set about appropriating this place for herself.

Velia told me soon afterwards that she had visited her new flat, which she would re-decorate. 'I want it to express something of me . . .' A fortnight later, she spoke about the social media site 'Myspace'. I inferred that Velia was in the process of introjecting an element of the psychotherapy site comprising its availability for the patient's appropriation, and that this was a step on the road to a more secure sense of subjective agency.

A place where evacuated contents are contained

In a session that took place on the eve of her journey home at Easter (of which she told me only on the day that she was travelling), Velia's mood was irritable.

She remarked that people used to ask: 'Are you *sure*? Are you *sure*?' – for example, asking if she wanted the toilet – and added that she has ended up indecisive, so she always asks people's advice. Velia had, by now, discovered in the psychotherapy site a place where she could obtain relief by evacuating her thoughts and feelings. In the transference, her irritable indecision referred to her uncertainty, at that point, over whether she would find that she needed the therapy. When the session ended, she expressed the uncertainty again: 'I might be back on about the 11th . . . or the 12th . . . ' (In fact she stayed away for much longer, keeping me in uncertainty about when she would return.)

Therapist neutrality

In the sixth month of her treatment Velia relinquished an absolute dependence – up until that point – on her brother's chauffeuring her to her sessions and began to bring herself by bus. She mentioned other external changes – she enjoyed a greater variety and quantity of food, could relinquish a rigid routine of going very early to bed, and was recently making frequent trips to the cinema, often in the company of other students with whom she was beginning to make friends.

Velia wondered aloud in one session whether she was a disappointment to her mother. As a teenager her mother was always being dated, whereas Velia was not very interested in boys. She went on to describe shopping for clothes with her mother. When Velia selected some clothes to try, her mother would try them on herself. She then got tired of waiting while Velia tried everything on.

Later, Velia described a cousin's birthday party during her teenage years when her mother excitedly talked and laughed with the teenagers and was excitedly hoping that a boy there would ask Velia out. I said she was conveying that because her mother seemed not to recognise herself as of a different generation, she seemed more a rival than available in the role of a mother supporting her teenage daughter's trying out clothes or negotiating her own relations with her peer group. Velia remarked that if she had a boyfriend she could not imagine introducing him to her mother. I observed that we were once more hearing how problematic it feels to let her negotiation of her own wishes and her own relationships to be seen by her mother, or by me, because issues of takeover and rivalry are felt to emerge.

A gradually stabilised timeframe

Velia was very elusive about her planned attendance over the summer, was absent in fact for a three month period, was absent for another fortnight just after her return, and then asked whether I could change her time to accommodate a new course.

I replied noncommittally that we could discuss it and asked when she was wanting to change to. Velia said that she was not sure what I had available. I observed that this already told us something that she is wondering about. Taken aback and tearful, Velia said, 'Well – ten minutes earlier?' A long, defensive and circular monologue about boredom followed, but moved to images of roadblocks manned by armed guards who searched the car and even its boot, and an image of a camouflaged soldier aiming a gun. I said that Velia's thoughts about boredom had moved to what underlies the boredom.

Velia told me then that an angry ex-employee of her father's had once set a fire of burning tyres in their garden, and her mother had insisted on telling her about it while she was trying to read her book. I underlined Velia's wish to remain an innocent child and not to have disturbing things drawn to her attention, by her mother then and by me right now. When she spoke of the shock of once seeing the camouflaged soldier, it was possible to reflect with her that the armed guards who searched were felt to be me looking so searchingly at her that it felt persecutory, but there was a question of whether the camouflaged soldier might represent Velia herself. Velia asked why she would point a gun. I reminded her that last session she had expressed great resentment that her uncle at home knows what she is doing but she is not told what he is doing, and linked this first to Velia's not knowing what I was doing while on leave during the summer, and then to her statement on several occasions that she would be absenting herself for a shorter time than she actually did. Perhaps this camouflaged a resentment at not knowing what I have been doing and a consequent wish to train a gun on the treatment.

At the end of that session Velia did not seek clarification of whether I intended to change her session time. On the relevant day I took her in at her usual time. Late in that session, she said: '*The episode of King John and the Magna Carta was not the first time that restrictions were placed on an absolute monarch.*' I heard this as a symbolic representation of a *sufficiently* adequate encounter with a now stabilising treatment frame, and as an implicit acknowledgement that its function of highlighting action on the frame as potentially analysable had been experienced as a restriction on her narcissistic omnipotence. (It was interesting to learn that, after this session, she arrived at her new class in time.)

Approaching the point of watershed

The 'tipping point' of the introjection of a critical mass of such elements of the psychotherapy site, amounting to introjection of the site as a whole, would occur after Velia's encounter with two more elements of the site, which came about in the following way.

The fee: a session having an encounter with a more stabilised frame

Velia spoke scornfully, at the start of one session, about magazines that are all about fashion, make-up and life stories – so annoyingly predictable. She then spoke of staking out the ground for various pre-planned activities. I pointed out the conflict between her wish to have everything pre-planned, which she prefers in here as well, yet her scorn of predictability. Velia retorted that she does not like other people's predictability but does like her own.

She then said that one of her friends had suggested that they meet up. She walked around for a while with 'him'. They were going to have dinner out, but Velia did not want the expense, and had already decided what to have for dinner, so she went home.

I acknowledged her preoccupation with expense but pointed out that it also serves to hold at bay the possibility of negotiating, with the boy, something less pre-planned and more spontaneous. Velia complained of hearing the clock ticking. She then recalled that 'they' had wanted her to take a cycling proficiency test, but she had not seen the point, and added that she does not like being forced. I agreed that yesterday, too, she had expressed her resentment of her parents, right from the age of four, for telling her that she was a big girl – so for most of her life there seems to have been an issue of obstinate refusal.

Velia said in suddenly triumphant tones, 'Yes! You can't force me to do what I don't want!'

I observed that there seemed to be a scenario where one person forces another to do what they do not want. Her preoccupation with the clock ticking acts as a reminder that there are reality dimensions to this therapy in terms of time and money, and a reminder we had arranged to review the position at the end of a year. I then told Velia that until the end of that agreed year I would continue to charge her only for the sessions that she attended, but beyond that time, if she wished and could arrange with her parents to continue, it would be open to her on the basis that she contract for all of the available sessions, including those available during her university summer vacation.

Velia was very taken aback and tearful. She had no friends here over the summer – well, not that she saw friends at home, really, she sees her parents . . . She thought she would ask her parents about this . . .

I acknowledged that since her parents pay for her treatment she would certainly need to discuss it with them, but what about first weighing it up for herself?

Near the end of the session Velia began to speak of her childhood and soon settled into a stereotyped re-telling of familiar tales. I interrupted to ask her to notice how quickly she settled into thinking of herself as a little girl of five, and clung to that – whereas actually she was 21 and a boy, only yesterday, invited her out to dinner.

Velia said, 'I *did* start to wonder if he was interested in me. Maybe a bit *too* interested . . . '

Discovering the representation of bodily states and ownership of them

After a visit to London Velia described, in a very peaceful mood, her liking for the London underground. At some length, she described its tunnels, and described the stations and structure of the Circle line. The trains just go around in a circle. She liked the way the tunnel lights up, so you could tell when something is coming. 'I don't know why I like it so much . . . '

I observed that the body is like a place with tunnels in. In relation to last session where she was describing problems of dealing with intrusion, perhaps it was relevant that the first time in your life that you become aware of having a domain of your very own is at a very, very early age, when you become aware of a tunnel in your body that you can become familiar with, and you can get to know the signs that something is coming.

Velia, a little embarrassed but interested, replied that her parents were very interested in bowel motions, and elaborated this.

Later, she said, 'I feel this session is just going around in circles.' I said, 'Like the trains . . .' Velia replied that other underground lines were built so that trains could move forward, but that there were dangers of striking electric cables, and in some places there was a danger of running into a disused mineshaft, and the whole structure could collapse.

Later she was speaking uninterestedly of potentially having a boyfriend. I said that there was no boyfriend in prospect, yet she seemed to feel that she ought to put on a show of interest, as though she felt that her universe of anality in which things go round and round was disapproved of; she seemed to feel under pressure to take up her disused genital functioning, and moreover with all the dangers she felt of that then bringing about a collapse.

Inferring from a new level of depth that the site as a whole has been introjected

Here are two consecutive sessions from a few weeks later, suggesting a whole new level of depth.

First session of the week: a vivid description of a nuclear catastrophe

Velia told me that she was reading a book about the nuclear explosion at Chernobyl. She told me about it, vividly. The explosion caused deaths and devastation. The site is still radioactive even now, and can cause radiation sickness. It is sad: the Soviet authorities would not admit what had happened, would not admit any responsibility. When people were evacuated they were told they were only going for a few days, so all their things, their photos and so on, are left behind. Velia would like to visit it one day. It is like Pompeii – but Pompeii has become a tourist attraction. Apparently, Chernobyl is very silent. The workers who went in to clean up were killed – by radiation sickness.

Velia had been speaking uninterruptedly for a long time. Finally, she fell silent. I acknowledged that she would like to visit Chernobyl, and then waited to see whether any interpretation was needed.

Velia told me that she went to a play yesterday. Douglas (a boy she had told me she had been attracted to and had fantasies about) was there. She added, 'I felt nothing.'

No, I said. There has been a Chernobyl inside Velia, and the life in her has been devastated.

Velia said she does not know why people ask her things; she tells them what she thinks is the right answer, but she doesn't really have a clue. I interpreted that when I did not speak for a long time, Velia was afraid that I did not have a clue how to help her to find a way to visit the scene where her inner Chernobyl once happened – she did not quite realise, or quite believe, that all that she had said did give us a lot of clues.

Velia's next thought was that in people who have been ill, there can be a temporary appearance of recovery – they *look* recovered – before they fall ill again and die. It's like suicide – they seem recovered, just before the suicide. She added, 'Sorry to sound melodramatic.' I said I did not think she was being melodramatic, and spelled out a link to her previous session.

Velia responded that if Douglas were to ask her out, she would not accept. He wouldn't know – she could not give him . . . She stopped, and said, 'I *have* died inside.'

She said that the real irony about Chernobyl was that it happened when they were testing safety.

Second session of the same week: exploring back in time

Velia began by saying that this room smells like the attic bedroom at home. That's where her uncle slept. But that's not relevant.

(Velia had once casually revealed that her maternal uncle, who lived with the family, bathed her until she was 11, and that as part of the bath ritual she always presented her bottom to be washed by getting up on her hands and knees.)

I asked if she was sure it was not relevant.

Velia proceeded to tell me that they are building a nuclear reactor in France – to explore *just* after the Big Bang. There is a theory that light can be heard as well as seen. It is horn-shaped – you train it on the skies, and as the light from the sun takes eight minutes to reach us, the theory is that the further you go in distance, the further back in time you go. There was an interference, a noise – they cleaned the horn and tried again – and finally found that what they thought was an interference was actually being given back to them from the universe, it was part of their data.

There is some risk (she went on) that in doing this they may create a black hole that will suck in the whole world . . . They used to think the atom was the smallest particle. There is supposed to be a way all the bits fit together.

At Chernobyl – no-one was supposed to be allowed back. But some people *have* gone back and are living there. There are faint signs of life . . . You know, in tower blocks, it looks like no-one is in there, because they are not placed near shopping centres and look deserted – but *sometimes*, occasionally, you can see someone there, if you look very carefully.

I repeated, 'If you look carefully, there are some signs of life.'

Velia agreed, and then said, 'About what you said yesterday – about *my* Chernobyl – I don't know how to move on with an enquiry into it.' I suggested that perhaps she had made a beginning; but it seemed that she was like the astrophysicists, who thought that something was irrelevant. Only they found that it wasn't.

Velia, understanding that I was referring to her opening thought about the consulting room smelling like her uncle's bedroom, said that she thought there was no passion in her family's marriages, not between her uncle and aunt, and not between her parents. But her uncle just slept there because her aunt's tossing and turning kept him awake. At least that's what he said.

Velia began playing with the clasp on her belt and told me how she likes to have something to fiddle with, or to distract herself with. She used to spend long periods telling herself stories, shredding paper while she did so.

'To distract you,' I repeated. I added that there seemed to be something about the stories she made up that required a distraction.

Velia said that if you don't use something, it crumbles away. Then she said she was thinking about the Titanic lying at the bottom of the ocean. It's now crumbling away. Like in Chernobyl – the buildings . . .

I said, 'You do convey a terrible sense of inner devastation.' Velia, in tears, smiled through them and said, 'Maybe there needs to be a solo violin, playing a song of sorrow, just for me.' Then she added, 'Derrida said that the only things worth forgiving are the unforgivable.'

Velia spoke then about demands for total surrender made by the Allies of Germany, that Germany (unlike Russia) was *made* to face what she had done. Velia's next theme was that when atomic bombs are dropped on people directly underneath, there is nothing left, just a shadow. But the only alternative may be a long and costly land war, with battles of resistance every inch of the way.

I reminded Velia that she had mentioned being unsure how the enquiry into her own inner devastation could proceed. She seemed able to imagine only two alternatives – either I drop an atomic bombshell on her, or I invade her by land – but in any case, some form of invasion. Velia pointed out that she might do the invading. Then she said, 'But what could have happened?' I echoed her earlier thought, 'Something unforgivable?' Velia reflected that Chernobyl happened two decades ago.

I observed that that gives us another reference point: time. Velia asked what I meant. I said that two decades ago is very early in her personal history. Velia said, 'I was only one. But – I don't remember!' I suggested that her mind is remembering in its own way. Velia objected, 'But – nothing I've been told from my family history . . . ' I said, 'We are talking about inner reality here.'

Comment

From the sense in these two sessions of full engagement following an associative flow of ideas, and at a greater level of depth with respect to the unconscious,

I infer that Velia had by now introjected the psychotherapy site as a whole, and had discovered herself to be in a working psychotherapeutic situation, analogous to the 'analysing situation' of psychoanalysis to which Donnet (2009) refers. She continued to find new resources in that psychotherapeutic situation – as in the two sessions just described, when she was finding it possible to give symbolic representation to what she could not consciously remember and to an emerging sense of profound libidinal damage.

The move from two sessions per week to three, and to use of the couch

When Velia confirmed having discussed with her parents her wish to continue beyond the second year, I offered her the option of a third session. Eventually, with a re-negotiated fee, Velia secured her parents' agreement, and confirmed her own agreement to three times weekly sessions on the couch.

Her conflicts could now be more elaborated, by being given representative form in a sustained series of images. In September she recalled a performance of *Antigone*, which had impressed her: there is a conflict, Velia explained, between the law of the land and the law of the gods. (I thought silently of what Velia's family's 'law of the land' was felt to have permitted to her uncle and herself, and of the sense of an opposing law of the gods.) In October, finding a worm in an apple disturbed her – 'Finding something alive,' Velia explained, 'where you didn't expect to find it.' Frightening images appeared: at Chernobyl, the concrete tomb in which they buried the reactor was cracking. She told me again that cancer patients, who appear to have recovered, rally and then die. Velia also recalled her childhood sexual researches in secretly read pornographic magazines, at first alone and later with one of her brothers.

A session, after the change, with opposing images of the site

In a session one month into the more intensive treatment structure, Velia recounted a film about scientists whose manipulative efforts to make humanoid creatures better were actually making them worse.

She also described getting glasses. Some photographs she had had developed came out so sharp that she had thought the camera wonderful. Then she realised that because she now had glasses she was seeing properly when taking the photographs, whereas previously she had been unable to see clearly what she was photographing.

I interpreted Velia's two different attitudes to the work in here – a profound distrust of her therapy as manipulating her ('Those scientists played God', Velia put in), yet also an idea that her therapy could amount to glasses that help her to see the world clearly and in focus.

Velia told me then about a machine that opticians have that can show up an otherwise invisible tumour. Some other opticians are in legal trouble for missing a tumour.

I said that the conflict seemed to have intensified. There was a fear of being on the receiving end of my playing God, but also an anxiety that there could be something radically or even fatally wrong with her capacity to see, and that I might fail to diagnose it.

Velia said, 'I don't think I was abused.' With many pauses, and with a disclaimer that the baths with her uncle had any importance, Velia told me that a female member of her family had said she was sexually abused as a child, although she had not understood it at the time.

Velia went on to tell me that after long procrastination about a large hoard of magazines, she had at last got rid of them, and felt better afterwards. She then spoke of feeling tormented by her behaviour during her anorexic breakdown and said something about change.

I said that Velia had been showing us both her recognition that, if she is to change, it may involve being able to relinquish her investment in some of the memories and daydreams she has been holding on to.

The site as firm ladder

A month further on in her now three times weekly treatment, Velia had to climb a ladder. She told me that she had previously felt unsafe on a wobbly ladder, but *this* ladder felt firm and sound.

The final months

During the last months, Velia told me of her mother's excited description of having been spanked by her father. Silently thinking about Velia being bathed by her uncle, I observed to Velia that her mother had an excited preoccupation about a man's hand on a little girl's bottom. From her further associations, it was possible to interpret Velia's being in thrall to the narcissistic exploitation of her by the people important to her, her settling for this, and her secret pleasure in it. Her penultimate session allowed me to interpret that she was afraid of my being hostile to what is important to her.

By now there were various external signs of development in Velia, including the return of her menstruation, a capacity to operate autonomously in the outside world in various ways including independent foreign travel, the forging of some friendships, and the gaining of her degree and of a research post. Her final session suggested the possibility that some structural change in her mind had correspondingly been accomplished. She told me that new flooring is being put into the bathroom at home – the scene of the baths with her uncle – and told me also of a memory there of her father, looking after her constructively by drying her hair. It was father who had at last decreed that she was old enough to bath herself unaided.

A subjectivising process

One vivid image from the final months was that of a man who had seen, but had not realised that he was seeing, a new planet.

Velia also described discovering this city by *walking* it. She at last found a restaurant that she had several times nearly found, not previously going far enough through not believing that there could be anything there. I thought she was describing a subjectivising process . . .

Conclusion

This chapter is the third to demonstrate by means of clinical illustration the piecemeal encounter and introjection of various elements of the psychotherapy site, this time with a patient to whom three times weekly treatment had been recommended. The point at which the site as a whole could be said to have been introjected, and the site discovered by the patient to have been transformed into a working psychotherapeutic situation, was signalled by two images, the buried Chernobyl nuclear reactor and the sunken Titanic, representing the arrival of the psychotherapy at a level of depth in the unconscious. At that point of full engagement in the process of her treatment the patient was able to accept, and to ask her parents to pay for, a third weekly session. This chapter therefore adds to the case examples of the introjected psychotherapy site an illustration of the greater possibilities thereafter, in a three times weekly structure, of the elaboration of the patient's conflicts, and an illustration of the representation, at the end of the therapy, of some structural change accomplished in the patient's psyche (represented by the image of new flooring put into the bathroom). Like Chapter 3, this chapter also illustrates the patient's gradual acquisition, through the introjection of elements of the psychotherapy site, of a more secure sense of being an autonomous subject – in this case in a patient whose sense of individual autonomy and subjectivity had been severely compromised.

Chapter 6 will consider the situation where the clinical activity remains that of psychotherapy, but where external reality explodes upon the scene and appears to take it over entirely.

References

Donnet, J.-L. (2009) *The Analyzing Situation*. A. Weller (trans.). London, Karnac. Originally published in French as *La Situation Analysante*. Paris, Presses Universitaires de France, 2005.

Tustin, F. (1980) Autistic objects. *International Review of Psycho-Analysis* 15, pp. 93–106.

Winnicott, D. (1974) Transitional objects and transitional phenomena. In: Winnicott, D. *Playing and Reality*, Chapter 1, pp. 1–30. Harmondsworth, Pelican Books.

Satish's weekend

Drama on the stage of external reality

Psychotherapy and external reality

This chapter is the final one in Part II of this book that is concerned with psychotherapy: Part III that follows concerns a very different activity, that of social work, which deals very directly with matters of external reality.

In certain circumstances the psychotherapist must be as alert as the social worker to issues of external reality, while dealing with the issue within the confines of his own discipline. Otto Kernberg (2016) draws attention to such a situation in his discussion of transference-focused psychotherapy with severely ill borderline patients who have been caught up in destructive cycles of suicidality and drug abuse. Kernberg points out that such patients characteristically contribute unwittingly to a pattern of life crises external to the psychotherapy, and that the therapist needs to be alert to signs of such a danger in order to intervene in time to alert the patient to the danger of yet another external life disaster. Kernberg's example is that of a patient whose high-handedly arrogant behaviour in the workplace is putting him under threat, without the patient noticing the danger signs, of dismissal from his job.

This chapter focuses on a different way in which external reality can become a particularly live issue within the context of psychotherapy. It sometimes happens that during psychotherapy, external reality bursts upon the scene in such an immediate way that it seems to hijack the space for thinking about internal reality. This chapter discusses this kind of situation in the context of a psychotherapy treatment.

André Green's discussion of projective actualisation of the primal scene

André Green drew attention to what he called the 'dead mother' complex amongst certain borderline patients, by which he meant the difficulties of certain patients who had been confronted during very early childhood with the sudden depression of their mother, 'brutally transforming a living object, which was a source of vitality for the child, into a distant figure, toneless, [and] practically inanimate'

(Green, 1986, p. 142). In the course of delineating that complex, Green referred to a dramatic process which he called the projective actualisation (or the actualised projection) of the unconscious fantasy of the primal scene (that is, an unconscious fantasy of parental sexual intercourse). Green considered a resurgence of the fantasy of the primal scene to be a crucial phase in the treatment of these adult patients because – involving as it does *two* objects – it allows an emotional re-investment of the few remaining vestiges of the memory traces of the mother dating from the very early period relative to the dead mother complex. He observed that for these patients, who use reality as a defence, every resurgence of the primal scene fantasy happens by way of projective actualisation, which ignites the memory traces:

> By 'actualised projection' I designate a process through which the projection not only rids the subject of his inner tensions by projecting them on to the object, but constitutes a *revivifying* and not a *reminiscence*, an *actual* traumatic and dramatic repetition.
>
> (Green, 1986, p. 159)

An illustration taken from a patient in psychotherapy

This chapter illustrates the above situation described by Green.

In the clinical illustration, taken from a three times weekly psychoanalytic psychotherapy, we will hear the patient's account of a happening that was taking place in the course of her treatment, and that I understood as a projective actualisation. The patient's subsequent sessions invite the inference that this projective actualisation implicitly referred back to an *earlier* one that had occurred during the patient's adolescence and that had culminated in a tragedy, although certain details of it appear to have succumbed to repression.

Case illustration: Satish

Satish, at age 23, sought treatment after a breakdown precipitated by the loss of her long-term boyfriend and by bitter acrimony between them. Except for a kindly aunt who lived in Britain, she was geographically and emotionally isolated from her family. The first year of her life appeared to have been relatively stable, but her chaotic upbringing thereafter, with both mother and father coming and going in and out of the household and herself being moved between her Asian homeland and Britain, struck me as that of a poor little rich girl. At the age of about six there had been several episodes of sexual abuse at the hands of a household servant. She had had some counselling from her doctor at the age of 13 when her *de facto* stepfather, who had represented a new-found stability and security and had acted as a buffer between Satish and her mother, had suddenly died an accidental death.

Satish's early sessions were filled with inconsequential chatter, mostly about a succession of male friends.

One year on: a hinge-point

One year on, Satish became anxious that that she was slipping back into a depression – a chemical phenomenon, she told me firmly, for which she became preoccupied with obtaining antidepressants and sleeping tablets.

Soon afterwards she brought a dream and its associations: a prominent figure was that of a tricky, treacherous man who managed to insert himself right inside a couple and to break the couple up. Unusually, it seemed possible for Satish to tolerate – just – my suggesting that this figure might represent a part of herself.

Then the following session took place.

A session at 14 months

Satish, looking very strained, and saying that half her family were not talking to her, described a sequence of events, from the previous weekend, surrounding a cousin's wedding. It had the quality of a dream, or a slowly developing nightmare.

Satish was to drive her brother Avi and his girlfriend Mana, after work on Friday, to the accommodation near where the wedding was to be held. She had waited impatiently for Mana, who had however been expecting to be collected and was frostily silent when, after her eventual arrival, the car journey finally began.

Satish went on, 'Because my brother hadn't explained the arrangements – we'd arranged to stay with Mana's aunt. She lives near the wedding venue. She'd phoned to say that the beds were all made up and ready – there was no way we couldn't stay – but Avi hadn't said that my aunt and uncle had booked a whole suite for us at the hotel.' (This aunt and uncle, I gathered, were the parents of the bridegroom. I did not yet know that Satish's brother Avi had duties as part of the wedding party. It eventually became clear to me that Satish had initiated the accommodation arrangements without thinking to consult her brother as to whether this was necessary.)

I asked, 'For us?' Satish said that there was a double room for her brother and Mana, and a folding bed in an adjoining room for herself. She added, 'It cost £1,000, that's why we couldn't have afforded to stay at the hotel . . .'

It was very late by the time they arrived at Mana's aunt's house, and midnight before they got to bed, when Satish found she had left her sleeping pills at home. Consequently, she had only three hours sleep before getting up to go to the wedding.

After the wedding ceremony and lengthy outdoor photographs, the young people went up to the hotel suite during the brief interlude before the formal wedding dinner. Satish, now exhausted, told her brother she could not manage any further without a nap, and although there was only an hour before the dinner was due to start, she asked him to wake her when it was time to go down for it. She went to sleep – and on waking found to her bewilderment that the time was two hours after the scheduled time for the formal dinner. Why did no-one wake her – what was going on?

She went downstairs and into the reception room, where the guests were at the dessert stage. On seeing her, many of them emanated cold disapproval. Satish, enquiring after her meal, learned that a dinner had been served for her earlier, but had eventually been eaten, and the surrounding relatives generally treated her so coldly that she felt she could not stand it, and got up and left.

Satish sought out the manager and applied unsuccessfully to be served another dinner, and then, crying bitterly, went back up to the hotel room and poured out her woes on the telephone to her mother, about her suffering from depression and her lost pills and how everyone was angry with her and no-one would give her anything to eat. She then could not understand why Mana stormed in, threw something on to the bed, and stormed out again. Later her brother arrived and berated her furiously for her rudeness to the wedding party (apparently, he had woken her before the dinner and she had said she was coming, but she had no memory of this). Avi demanded that she come at once to apologise to her aunt and uncle, and departed furiously when she told him she had been crying too much to appear in public at that point.

Finally, Satish's mother, still on the telephone and evidently recognising the degree to which Satish really was disturbed and distraught, advised her that she could plead illness tomorrow, and meanwhile should sleep, which Satish did. 'But I found out next day that Mana was furious, they came in halfway through the dancing to have a romp in the sheets, well, how was I to know?' Only at this point did I, as listening therapist, grasp that the bed that Satish had been using throughout had been the double bed intended for the young couple, her brother and his girlfriend, *not* the single folding bed provided for Satish in the adjoining room. I asked her about this. She said, 'Oh, I didn't know how to unfold it.'

One feature of the following day was an incident at the hotel breakfast. An order was taken for Satish and two of her cousins, and she was helping herself to toast – the system being that there was one large rack between four people – when an aunt told her coldly, 'That's not yours.' Although another relative, hearing this, intervened to affirm that the toast was indeed Satish's portion, she found it hard to manage without crying.

Satish did finally make her apologies to her longsuffering aunt – after first seeking out the bridal couple in their suite and crying so much, as she said she was sorry, that the bridegroom gave her an enormous hug and told her not to be silly – 'and I cried all over his shirt'.

She repeated with a bewildered air, as her session ended, 'I thought someone would wake me! I can't believe that no-one woke me!'

Discussion

This session, which had a mesmerised and mesmerising quality, struck me as describing the unconscious enactment of a fantasy of intrusion into the primal scene.

Viewed from this perspective, a family wedding had been disrupted as the attention of the whole assembled company was repeatedly displaced from the bride and bridegroom on to the patient as the centre of attention. Moreover, when an amorous young couple had sought to engage in lovemaking in their bed, they found the patient physically blocking their access to it; and, on the morning after the wedding, in the bridal suite, the patient had literally been enfolded, sobbing, in the bridegroom's arms, while his new wife had looked on.

Particular offence had meanwhile been given to two previously friendly female figures, the first being the brother's girlfriend (to whom it must already have become clear, before the travel arrangements debacle, that her own aunt was quite needlessly put to the trouble of accommodating them on the Friday night while their luxury hotel suite lay unused), and the second being Satish's aunt, who had in the past been a nurturant maternal figure to Satish, and whose very generous and costly provision for the Friday night was effectively spurned and wasted.

All this – by a process, I would suggest, of projective identification that externalised the patient's superego – induced in the surrounding relatives an implacably cold, accusing disapproval from which Satish shrank, and against which she found it necessary to mobilise a protective response from her mother and from the offended parties themselves.

Consciously, Satish was quite unable to account for the severity of the general disapproval. *Why* was everyone so angry and so nasty? Yet the voice that said of the breakfast piece of toast, '*That's not yours!*' was vividly in her mind. Now, the bed that she occupied, and the bridegroom in whose arms she was enfolded, were indeed not hers; but the toast that she took at breakfast actually *was* hers. I shall now show that 'That's not yours!' thereby dramatised, very vividly, a central element in Satish's central trauma – namely, her bewildered and terrified confusion about what she *was*, and was *not*, responsible for.

Gradual elaboration

At this time in the therapy, I could be caught off guard by an oscillation between a new and urgent impatience in Satish to understand herself, and an extreme panic terror into which glimpses of insight could throw her.

That happened at this point. During the week prior to the 'wedding' session that has been described, Satish had been expressing a new and determined wish to understand herself better, and in the session immediately prior to the 'wedding' session, she had seemed just able to tolerate my suggestion that a figure in her dream who gets between couples and breaks them up represented an aspect of herself – as also, I pointed out, did other, more constructive figures in her dream. Satish's response had been to tell me that a friend of hers who had gone for a personality test had been initially startled and disbelieving at the picture of himself that came back, but she described why she thought it was accurate and added that she thought that, fortunately, he had taken it on board. I understood her to be telling me that, albeit with great difficulty, she had managed to tolerate and to accept my interpretation that not only did some constructive figures in her dream represent aspects of herself, but so also did the tricky figure who breaks couples up.

It was in this context that it occurred to me that the words with which Satish concluded the 'wedding' session – 'I thought someone would wake me! I still can't believe no-one woke me!' – should perhaps be understood as a plea (in the transference to me as her therapist) that to leave her in a state of unconsciousness would be to abandon and neglect her. Therefore, in the following session, after she announced a plan to move away to a distant city – and in the interim to be unavailable, every week, for one of her three sessions – I tried in good faith to make a link to the events of the weekend (i.e. to the wedding, which seemed to have disappeared overnight from her mind). Satish replied sharply that she did not understand: depression is due to chemical imbalance in the brain, which antidepressants address – is there something else? I was taken aback and perplexed. Eventually, I suggested that we could look at what leads to some of the distressing situations she can find herself in, and whether with hindsight some of the recent ones might have been prevented by taking adequate measures to prevent confusion. It proved possible to do some sorting out at this practical level; but my attempt to link the events of the wedding with past traumas was evidently experienced as a terrifyingly dangerous and intrusive assault, and for a time it was touch and go as to whether Satish would abruptly break off her treatment.

Partial recovery of a partially repressed memory: trauma at age 13

Satish had from time to time spoken of the sudden death of her stepfather – to whom she had been much attached – when she was 13. Her account of how his death had come about had never quite added up. The family – 'we' – had got food poisoning, she had explained, but Manek (the stepfather) had driven off in his car to a friend. He was drunk and driving so crazily that when he was about to depart again the friend (alarmed for his safety on the roads) locked him in to give him time to calm down but should have kept checking on him; while locked in Manek had choked on his own vomit and died. From the truncated, rather garbled nature of the account, I had understood that Satish retained an incomplete memory of something that appeared to be partially repressed.

In a session soon after her account of the family wedding, Satish re-visited, very agitated, the subject of her stepfather's death. 'My mother has just told me that he committed suicide!' Her mother, she told me desperately, wanted to engage her on the telephone in talk about Manek's death – 'but I don't trust my mother, I don't want her talking to me! She twists things and turns them into what she wants, and I won't end up knowing what I remember and what she's told me!' I acknowledged that Satish feels very vulnerable to having her own thoughts and perceptions and memories interfered with and manipulated by her mother and equally so by me.

This interpretation did something to heal what had been a breach in our rapport, and Satish proceeded to add details to the narrative of Manek's death that she had never before supplied.

'At dinner that night there was just me, my mother and Manek. I wouldn't have been there – I was supposed to be staying with a friend, but we'd had an argument, so I stayed in.'

'We got food poisoning. Though it's funny that my mother didn't get it. We all ate the same food. They gave me a glass of wine.'

'Some bits I don't remember. My mum has told me that Manek was dragging me down the stairs with their duvet wrapped around me, she had to haul me away from him. And a neighbour said she saw me lying face down in the street outside the house, just lying there. What I remember is waking up in the car with my mum, I was covered with vomit. We had had to get in the car to get away from Manek. He trashed the house. The next day, I had to go back to get some things, I saw it. Everything was smashed.'

'Manek's friend, he should have checked on him earlier. When he checked on him he could see he wasn't okay, he got an ambulance and we got called to go to the hospital, I hadn't had time to shower or change, but it was too late.'

'My mum didn't talk to me after that. This friend of hers, she said she was shocked at the way my mum treated me. I was ill, and I was only 13, but my mum didn't do anything to look after me. She thought my mum blamed me for Manek's death. But I was missing Manek too.'

Repair of the breach in the stimulus shield

Satish had a partial memory of the events that culminated so tragically in the loss of her loved stepfather, including that she had been given alcohol to drink – it was not clear how much. The recent family wedding scenario, which included the scene of her lying across the bed intended for her brother and his girlfriend, seemed at first to invite a reconstruction of the earlier events, based on an inference of a fantasy of intrusion into, and successful disruption of, the union of the parents: and indeed, I mistakenly started off down that road. The more relevant part of her communication, however, was her pointing out that an ill 13-year-old needed looking after. I came to understand that it was her fragile defences that were most in need of repair.

Green reminds us that it is essential to remain constantly awake to what the patient is saying without falling into intrusive interpretation. He advises: 'To establish links which are proffered by the preconscious, which supports the tertiary processes, without short-circuiting it by going directly to the unconscious fantasy, is never intrusive' (Green, 1986, p. 163). Repeated themes of wanting her possessions back (which I had heard as wanting her projected contents back) had misled me into trying to link the tricky figure who breaks couples up with the events of the wedding, but when it became clear that this was experienced as an intolerable superego attack – Satish spoke grimly of her mother's claim that she did not beat her but that Satish had the scars to prove it – I silently accepted the implied rebuke, and learned to listen in a different way. During the second year of Satish's two year treatment, a series of images of containing structures suggested that the task that was eventually accomplished in therapy was to repair and rebuild her necessary defences – that is, in terms of Freud's conceptualisation of psychic trauma as the piercing of the individual's protective shield against excessive stimuli, to repair the breach that had been torn in her stimulus shield (Freud, 1920).

Conclusion

The purpose of this chapter is to create a double juxtaposition. It has presented a brief passage within a psychotherapy, and belongs unambiguously with the chapters on psychotherapy, in which a primary responsibility of the therapist is to pay attention to the patient's inner psychic reality. Yet it contrasts with the other chapters on psychotherapy in that, during the brief period described, to all outward appearances, and certainly from the point of view of the patient, dramatic events in external reality dominated the scene. In a second juxtaposition, the chapter is positioned at the end of Part II on psychotherapy, just before the book turns to social work practice which has a direct concern with external reality

The case example has illustrated the way that, in the phenomenon of projective actualisation of the primal scene in borderline pathology as conceptualised by Andre Green, to all outward appearances it is external reality that appears to hijack the treatment space, since a real dramatic staging in external reality occurs. The task of the psychotherapist is to remain awake to the unconsciously fantasied dimension of what the patient is saying about external reality, but without intruding those reflections on the patient, whose predominant need may be for ego support.

With its introduction of the issue of external reality, the chapter offers a bridge to the next part of the book. That part deals with the very different domain of social work practice, in which the relation to external reality is a different one. As we will see, the social worker may sometimes be concerned with the interface between inner psychic reality and external reality but, unlike the psychotherapist, the social worker has a direct responsibility to assist with external material and social reality.

References

Freud, S. (1920) Beyond the pleasure principle. In: J. Strachey (ed. and trans.), *The Standard Edition of the Complete Psychological Works of Sigmund Freud* (Vol. 18), pp. 1–64. London, Hogarth Press.

Green, A. (1986) The dead mother. K. Aubertin (trans.). In: A. Green, *On Private Madness*, pp. 142–173. London, Hogarth Press.

Kernberg, O. (2016) New developments in transference focused psychotherapy. *International Journal of Psychoanalysis* 97 (2), pp. 385–407.

Part III

The site in social work

At this point in the book, attention turns from psychoanalytic psychotherapy to the very different realm of social work practice, whose practitioners are charged by society to be directly responsible for dealing with social breakdown. Continuing the theme of therapeutic engagement, the specific thesis in Part III is that it is possible for the social work client to encounter, sense and cumulatively take in various elements of the social work setting (or site), until a point of transformation when he finds himself to be in a 'social work situation' that functions in a meaningful way in relation to his own pressing concerns, and ushers in a spontaneously creative social work process. Although this theory is derived from Donnet's theory of the analytic site as set out in Chapter 2, the ensemble of elements available for introjection in the social work site, far from being the same as those available in psychoanalysis or psychotherapy, is unique to social work practice. A major aim of the chapters in Part III is therefore to specify some of the elements in the social work setting that make it possible for the client to get a sense of the social work situation as something that 'works' for him in relation to what he is concerned about.

Chapter 7 opens this part, bringing to life the abstract theory of the social work site by plunging the reader immediately into a detailed case illustration of what is meant by introjection of the social work site in everyday social work practice. The case example concerns a woman with a learning disability and an urgent financial and housing problem: she eventually became productively engaged on the social work task, which included work on a previously arrested mourning process. The chapter therefore explodes the myth that relationship-based psychodynamic social work practice is helpful only to a minority of relatively middle class, relatively articulate clients not preoccupied with practical problems. It demonstrates that the capacity to become fully engaged in the social work task is *not* a function of pre-existing psychological-mindedness, but is, rather, a function of having taken in (introjected) the features of the social work situation itself.

Chapters 8–12 take time to identify and discuss more fully some crucial elements of the social work site. Chapter 8 looks at recent successful engagement of marginalised families, and concludes that the clients sensed, and took in, their social worker's principled awareness of the inter-relations within a fivefold focus, called here the social work frame of reference. That frame of reference comprises the inter-relations between presenting problem, underlying problem, agency function, unfolding interview material and external crises. Included under attention to the presenting problem is the traditional principle of starting where the client is, which may need to entail a close, imaginative and thorough-going adaptation to the client's starting-point in concrete, practical ways.

Chapter 9 shows that if a part of the social work frame of reference is distorted or missing, such as when the social worker ignores the implications for his work of the function of his employing agency, then the client cannot encounter the missing element and it impedes or prevents the process of introjection and, consequently, of client engagement. By contrast, Chapters 10 and 11 are linked chapters discussing a single case example that illustrates an intact social work frame of reference. Chapter 10 emphasises the dialogue with the clients in which the social worker bridges the gap between the immediate preoccupations of the clients (starting where the client is) and what the social worker herself judges to be relevant. The focus in Chapter 11 is on the social worker's attention to the client-worker relationship as a lens through which sense may be made of a series of escalating crises in the light of the social work frame of reference, and as the vehicle through which the work could be furthered and the crises resolved.

Chapter 12 is devoted to a further detailed case illustration, this time in the sphere of child protection, of the gradual, piecemeal encounter and introjection of elements of the social work site, to a point of metamorphosis where the client became fully engaged in the social work process. It clarifies the relation that may exist between external practical problems and private inner conflict, and it takes time to spell out how the social work frame of reference, discussed in the preceding chapters, represents in large measure the inner logic of the social work situation that the client can sense and take in, or introject, and fully involve himself in. It shows – like Chapters 7 and 11, but this time in relation to the issue of risk to a child – that a crucial resource within the social work situation is the client-worker relationship, not only as a source of support but as the vehicle in which the central problem can be worked on, paving the way to an adequate resolution of the situation of risk to the child.

Chapter 13 sketches the historical context and joins the theoretical and practice discourse of contemporary social work, including the cogent case made by the *Munro Review of Child Protection* for a return to the exercise of principled professional social work judgement that has, since the 1970s, become increasingly constrained under managerialism (Munro, 2011). The chapter's particular thesis is that the basis for successful social work engagement of marginalised families, both in the 1970s and in recent times, has not previously been fully theorised, and it demonstrates how the theory of the introjected site supplies the missing theory. The chapter also suggests that some recent impressive practice initiatives, particularly in Israel, and some recent contributions to social work theory from a critical theory and postmodern perspective, hold out the promise of genuine dialogue with the kind of theory that is set out in this book.

Reference

Munro, E. (2011) *The Munro Review of Child Protection. Final Report: A Child-Centred System. London,* Department for Education. Available from: www.gov.uk/government/uploads/system/uploads/attachment_data/file/175391/Munro-Review.pdf.

Chapter 7

Miss M

The site in social work with a vulnerable adult

This chapter will show how a working class woman with a learning disability and problems with managing household bills became cooperatively involved in a social work process. The chapter firmly challenges a longstanding myth still perpetuated in a modern textbook (Payne, 2014), that casework is only useful for the articulate client who is interested and able to reflect on her feelings and is not for working class clients beset with practical problems. I will argue that what enabled the client in the case example to become so fully engaged was a process analogous to that described in earlier chapters for the patient in psychoanalysis and in psychotherapy. That is, I will argue that she gradually sensed elements of the social work setting (or site) and gradually introjected them (took them in unconsciously) until she discovered the social work situation to be one that was working in an active way for her. She could then make active use of that working, functioning social work situation, to help her to mourn the loss of the mother on whom she had always been dependent, and to help her to find a capacity to take charge of her own life and to look after herself.

A detailed account of the case illustration takes up two-thirds of the chapter. It is followed by a discussion of the social work site that corresponds to the analytic site of psychoanalysis. The discussion specifies the uniqueness of the social work site, specifies some of the elements of the site that were discovered by the client in the case illustration, and points to the evidence for her gradually achieved discovery of being in a functioning social work situation in which she became an active collaborator. The chapter ends with a brief conclusion.

An eviction crisis in outer and inner reality: the case of Miss M

Miss M has remained vividly alive in my mind over the course of several decades. I met her in the course of my former social work practice and worked with her over a period of nearly three years. A presenting crisis comprised a preliminary phase of the work, which had three subsequent phases.

The preliminary phase: an eviction crisis

Referral

An advice-centre worker referred Miss M to our non-statutory family welfare agency for urgent financial help and support. An imminent court case threatened Miss M with eviction from her home for failure to pay rent in the six months since her mother had died; apparently, she had not understood her liability to pay.

The initial meeting

Miss M was hugely obese and exuded personal neglect, with grimy hands, shabby, soiled and greasy clothes, and a fetid body odour. She wore thick-lensed glasses to correct a heavy squint and seemed to have a mild congenital learning disability. She looked heavily depressed, yet caused some commotion by plunging into broken-sentenced remarks and questions, in an indistinct but blaring voice, and drowning out any answers with loud statements of acquiescence and thumps and crashes as she tried to manoeuvre her shopping buggy. She came unwillingly to my room, evidently expecting that the money she had been sent to ask for would have been summarily produced. From what felt, at first, to be the almost unintelligible jumble of her statements, the following emerged.

Miss M told me that she was away from a new job at present with a mouth infection. Once she used to be the tea-lady for a small local firm. Slowly, a picture emerged of a lifetime spent in her mother's ambience, an only child in a bleakly narrow, impoverished home, with her father on the periphery, and little schooling. She had been evacuated during a war-time period, away from her home in a large city vulnerable to bombing, to a family in a provincial town; afterwards, she remained home with her mother, who managed everything. At some unspecified time – in Miss M's late 20s or 30s? – she was given a job. 'I was the tea-lady,' she explained, 'and I ran errands.' She referred to the chatting of the women in the alcove where the cups were kept and washed up; impoverished though it might have appeared, she seemed to be conveying that it represented a social circle, a life of her own at last, outside the home. Then, she told me heavily, her mother's legs were bad. (Her father had died; he hardly figured in the tale.) The mother sent for the doctor, who saw her and then summoned Miss M to tell her that, unfortunately, her mother now needed someone with her all the time, and that she would have to give up work to be there to help. 'You had to give up your job that meant so much to you?' I asked. 'Unfortunate, he said,' Miss M said loudly, blankly and heavily, 'just the way it was, he said, nothing to be done.'

I mused, here, on a fantasy of a grimly controlling woman intent on retracting the daughter and bending the doctor to her purpose. Suddenly I awoke from my reverie to find Miss M, her glasses misty, dwelling on her mother's last illness, death, laying out and funeral. A memory surfaced of university lectures I had attended on grief and the stages of mourning. It struck me that detailed preoccupation with the deathbed and funeral is normally characteristic when bereavement is *very* recent. It occurred to me that no ongoing mourning was in process; somehow, Miss M was stuck fast at the day of the funeral.

When I tried to ascertain whether Miss M imagined that she could continue not to pay the rent and could be rescued again, I was brushed aside and drowned out with brusque statements of outward compliance. Baffled, I nevertheless promised, eventually, to apply on her behalf to a committee for the money that would be necessary if the eviction were to be averted. Subsequently I did so, successfully, with an undertaking (without which I knew that the money could not have been obtained) to try to help Miss M to function independently.

The second interview: weekly casework proposed

Miss M opened the second interview by asking me, in confidential tones, for money for food. Taken aback, I explained that the sum I had just obtained for her was unusually large (for which, irritably, she interjected perfunctory thanks), and that it was impossible to get any more. Miss M greeted this with a dark look; there was no-one to help. She had an aunt, Miss M added grimly, but it was no use looking to *her* for help: the aunt was as hard as nails. Feeling hopelessly that I had been asked for bread and was offering a stone, I said that I could see that it was terribly hard having to cope now on her own, and that, although I could not provide any more money, I wondered whether she might find it helpful to come and see me every week for a while, to talk about her mother and how she was managing without her. Looking askance, Miss M muttered compliance – perhaps to see whether she might eventually get some more money, access to which she seemed to believe I was wilfully obstructing.

Formulation: an outer and inner eviction

The eviction from her flat which Miss M's accumulation of rent arrears was precipitating, and from which she sought rescue, appeared also to express a profound sense of psychic eviction (represented by her mother's death) from her position of lifelong close dependence on her mother. In plain social work language, the problem underlying the eviction crisis seemed to be arrested mourning for the mother who had always managed everything, and this now left Miss M very helpless. I had a dubious mandate for intervening, but decided, despite misgivings over this, to try to help.

Phase I: ten months in the negative transference

Daily realities: job, rent, officials

An early event that assailed Miss M was the unexpected loss of her new job. She had been absent since her first day because she had been unwell. She obfuscated when I tried to approach her probable anxieties about resuming work. She had just been unwell.

In the face of Miss M's insistence that she was unable to manage dealings with the estate agent, we had taken charge of her rent book, inviting her to bring a weekly amount directly to us for sending off. However, the rent arrears mounted steadily once more and, when I warned Miss M firmly of the danger she was courting, she thought it very unreasonable, what with the loss of her job. The next week she arrived, very indignant. Benefit payment to her had resumed; she had just thought things were straightforward – and a gas bill arrived! With her, bills were monsters that arrived out of nowhere to swallow the week's income. I tried to teach her to budget, but soon despaired of it.

She talked mostly about officials at the Job Centre and the Social Security office, who were unsympathetic, difficult and persecuting.

The element of the comical: the intrusion into the toilet

At her weekly arrival, Miss M caused merriment amongst the clerical staff as, in full view of the front window, she halted on the path, hitched up her stockings, brushed down her greasy coat and finally marched forward with squared shoulders to brave the front door (and, evidently, myself!) There was merriment, too, amongst my social work colleagues, as I mounted the stairs with Miss M each week, past their open doors, responding with rapid guesswork to a perfect fusillade of unidentified 'hes', 'shes' and 'theys'.

One day, without preamble, Miss M was describing herself expostulating indignantly with a man who had walked in on her in the toilet. (I gathered, finally, that it was the meter reader for the gas company.) 'I told 'im 'e 'adn't give me a chance to get me knickers up! "Very sorry, I'm sure!" 'e said,' boomed Miss M vigorously, continuing her outraged account. The description at the time was so completely, unexpectedly and irresistibly funny that I was nearly purple-faced with suppressed laughter. It became a turning point, because a struggle went on. I was conscious of thinking that it would hardly matter, really, if I at least smiled, because it was only Miss M, who would hardly notice. Very slowly, as though from an immense distance and battling against a silencer, my professional ego reasserted itself, along with my common humanity. Perturbed, I asked myself how I could toy with an attitude of 'only' Miss M; looking, I saw that she *was* flushed and humiliated. I did not then notice that my enquiries into her job dismissal and rent payment had probably left Miss M with a feeling of being walked in on when one's pants were down; but I did understand in a new way (from the struggle over whether it mattered to smile) that Miss M was apt to have her dignity outraged, by various people including myself, and that she deserved better. I noticed that, when the desire to laugh had passed, and I spoke to Miss M with a new and genuine respect, there was an overwhelming sense of sadness.

That was the last time I felt impelled to explode with laughter.

Negotiating the obstacle to the mourning process

Miss M sometimes spoke about her mother's illness, death and funeral. After the funeral, she had noticed some phenomenon of light in a room in her flat: a comforting neighbour had told her it meant Mum's spirit had stayed there, to keep her company. She conveyed a grey bleakness about life without her mother, whom she doggedly idealised.

I knew (from remembered lectures) that probably the next phase of mourning to be negotiated would be that of resentment or hostility. Miss M began, increasingly, to refer to various figures (nearly all female) towards whom she was very hostile indeed: this or that official, and above all the local aunt. 'She's as hard as Mum was soft,' Miss M would say grimly. I felt I should be interpreting that much of her hatred of these figures was a displacement of her feeling about her mother, but I desisted, feeling that this would be to do violence to the desperately idealised image of her mother that she clung to. Since I was obliged to keep the rent issue to the fore and she had, bleakly, to do some paying, the remorseless intensity of the negative transference to me as representative of the hated, limitlessly depriving aspect of the mother became manifest as a further increase in the references to the aunt who was as hard as nails. Once I said lightly that perhaps she found me more like her aunt than like her mother. Miss M appeared to find this unexpected, sinister and menacing; she grew hot and uncomfortable, and looked terrified.

Interpretation seemed intolerable, both directly about the mother and in the transference to myself. The only solution I could find was to communicate tacitly. I listened attentively to her angry denunciations of this person or that, trying to demonstrate by my interest that the issue of her hatred was important. But I was at pains to resist the pressure to collude with the displacement (which would have abandoned what psychoanalysts refer to as the third position[1]) by actually joining in her indignant denunciations. I hoped to convey, silently, that I did not share Miss M's desperate anxiety that the rage be removed as far as possible from the mother.

Crisis: terrors of the baleful maternal ghost

Miss M became uneasy that her mother's ghost was haunting her flat. Her rent arrears mounted again, threatening to precipitate an eviction; meanwhile, she became increasingly afraid of the ghost and talked of wanting to move. In addition to reality issues, I was concerned that the flat was so bound up with her feelings for the incompletely mourned mother that its irreversible loss *before* resolving her mourning would precipitate further grief for the loss of the flat and further ego depletion. Helped by what the neighbour had once said about Mum's spirit keeping her company, I did now interpret the split in the maternal imago, by remarking that, although it would be nice to get away from the ghost, she would miss her mother's spirit.

A day came when, to my dismay, Miss M conveyed to me that she could not keep going any longer. The ghost was too much; the struggle was too much. Although I showed her as clearly as I could that, in understandably fleeing the ghost that was terrifying her, she would be abandoning much that she might then unavailingly regret, she was adamant and desperate. She begged me to find an institutional home for her. I had a despairing sense that she would become an institutionalised vegetable with an anaesthetised mind, but she would not depart until I promised to look into what could be done, and made an extra appointment to see her.

The crisis, however, had passed its height, and Miss M resumed her erratic payment of rent. The hatred of her mother was, I believe, pushing close to conscious awareness, but had been experienced in projected form as menacing her. She had needed to know that the depth of her terror of the baleful maternal imago was understood.

Phase II: a year in the positive transference

Emergence of the positive transference: a sheltered workshop review

The decisive working through of the hatred of the mother really occurred in the transference relationship to myself. I had arranged for Miss M to attend a sheltered workshop and accompanied her there to introduce her. I saw with misgivings that Miss M and the supervisor (herself a user of the service) took an instant dislike to each other. During her three weeks' probationary period, Miss M missed two appointments with me, and I then learned from the workshop that she had been absent since the first day. She came to see me, at my firm written request, the day before her review was due. She was at her most intractable and talked continuously over anything I tried to say. She had developed a swelling in her legs, she explained loudly, and the doctor said she ought to rest. She did *not* want to hear me ask whether she could have let the workshop know.

This became the turning point of our work. Somatic outcomes following early trauma, in the view of the psychoanalyst Marilia Aisenstein, are last-ditch attempts to mobilise a reparative aim (a kindly response) in 'another' whose availability as a person to be related to, at the relevant time, is imperceptible and uncertain (Aisenstein, 1993). Finding myself otherwise silenced, I confined myself to expressing sympathy for the pain in Miss M's swollen legs. Very, very gradually Miss M then let me move to the misery and terror in the workshop that had preceded the somatic attack. After over an hour of mutinous, terrified deadlock about facing the workshop review (which I considered necessary, having put the workshop's director to considerable trouble on Miss M's behalf), I offered to call at her home and walk there with her, and she finally agreed. When I called next morning, she was ready and waiting, and confided with an ineffably touching air of trusting happiness: 'It's a funny thing, love – me legs have gone right down today!'

Mourning, essential depression and the depressive position

A long period of positive transference ensued, in which – through the medium of apparently monotonous, prosaic trivia – Miss M was more and more able effectively to mourn her mother.

A presentation of the prosaic and the banal was characteristic with Miss M. I do not know whether this can be accounted for solely by borderline intelligence and educational/cultural deprivation, or whether it may also have constituted the semiological 'banalisation', the affective frigidity, which Claude Smadja (2005, citing Marty, 1968) depicts as the distinguishing feature of essential depression. Smadja describes, in essential depression, a *lack* of expression of grief and sorrow, and of psychic representation: pain is not mentalised. He indicates that, as a transference attachment to the clinician gradually, almost imperceptibly forms, it is likely to be in the *counter*transference that the affective dimension of sorrow and grief is first felt. For months, whatever its basis, Miss M gave me just such an impression of a pain which was not mentalised. Then, when she told me so confidingly on our way to the previously dreaded meeting that her swollen legs were better, I looked at her trustingly happy face and could have wept for her.

At about this time, I think that a sign appeared of an incipient capacity to mentalise – by which I mean here, to engage in psychic representation. Miss M told me that the wife of the local undertaker (' 'im what did for Mum', she explained) was in hospital for cancer treatment and was unlikely in Miss M's view ever to come out alive. 'That's where it comes 'ard,' she added seriously, 'if 'e 'as to do for 'is own wife.' For a moment, the hapless figure of the undertaker, thus abruptly conjured, struck me as comically funny. I now think that this imagined image of the newly widowed undertaker, further imagined as obliged to dig his own wife's grave, was an incipient psychic representation of Miss M's own problem of how to look after her need to bury her mother psychically if (as at that time she still feared) there was to be no good object (no kindly person) available to help her: for she was not yet sure of the helpfulness of the social work process and, psychically, a paternal object capable of functioning in the third position was at that time unavailable to her. I see this incipient mentalisation in Miss M as the first sign of a casework analogue of the transference situation in psychoanalysis as described by Christopher Bollas (1987, p. 278), whereby the analysand can live through for the first time elements of psychic life that have not previously been thought, if a certain dosage of time, space and attention allows them to emerge.

In psychoanalytic object relations theory, Melanie Klein, Hanna Segal and others have written of the essential tragedy entailed in the discovery that the hostility and destructiveness directed towards the hated bad object is actually directed towards the dearly loved good object, once the primary object is discovered to be single and whole (Klein, 1975a, 19475b; Segal, 1950). Over the next several months, Miss M, now much more able to be in mourning for her mother, was confronted with this tragedy. When I spoke of the pain of it, inarticulately, to my supervisor, her reply indicated the understanding that was an invincible support to me throughout the work. 'Yes,' she said simply, 'I think she is the saddest of all your clients.'

Reparative wishes surfaced in the transference. Evidently concerned, Miss M began to ask whether I lived alone and felt lonely. Sometimes Miss M would bring some extra money off the rent arrears as though it were a loving present to me. She paid a warm and satisfactory visit to the family to whom she had been evacuated in wartime.

The treatment contract and the 'therapeutic alliance'

One day Miss M told me, puzzled, about someone she had gone to see, who *always* had time to pass the time of day. I suddenly realised, enchanted, that she could not understand what I did in my job, since she never found me busy! Evidently, her mind continued to work at it. Weeks later, she told me about her orthoptist. 'Only a young girl she is,' said Miss M happily, 'but oh! She knows her job!' Since there was warm rapport between us and I was then in my twenties, I took this to refer also to *my* knowledge of my job. I think that Miss M's manifestly warm feeling about this was not only a transference reaction but can be compared also to the attachment of the patient in psychoanalysis *to the analytic situation* (in contradistinction to the attachment of the patient to the person of the analyst) of which André Green (1986) and Donnet (2001) write. Evidently, Miss M had worked out, by then, that we were engaged on legitimate and significant business together, even though she could not have defined it. This could be said to amount to an established therapeutic alliance (although I prefer not to use the term therapeutic alliance because the history of its usage gives insufficient weight to the unconscious aspects of the process of collaborative engagement).

Phase III: integration

During the last year of the work, a continued theme about repairs being made to Miss M's flat seemed to represent a sense of her psyche and her psychosocial environment under repair. Her previous rigid tendency to somatisation diminished.

Accounting: a checking up

One day Miss M asked me casually if I could tell her how the rent arrears stood. Since the rent book was at the estate agent's and the amounts she brought wildly erratic, I obliged by consulting the file and then sitting down to a minute or two of arithmetic. Miss M chattily remarked that she did not understand such things and mentioned a figure she thought it might be. I finished my sum and told her that she happened to be right; whereupon, with another cheerful disclaimer, she electrified me by telling me that she had been writing down, each week, the amount that she brought! This amounted to efficient, accurate accounting!

Bread-and-butter pudding: resolution of grief and mourning

One day, Miss M intrigued me by describing, vividly, how she had made a bread-and-butter pudding. She evoked in my mind an image of her preparing the pudding at her kitchen table. It reminded me of watching my mother cooking such a pudding when I was a child.

The conceptualisation of grief and mourning by Freud, Karl Abraham and Melanie Klein indicates that when the mourner can finally relinquish or let go of his investment in the person who has been lost, a healthy internalisation and identification with the lost person becomes possible, by which an image of the person is installed in the ego so that ego functioning is enhanced (Freud, 1917, 1921, 1923; Abraham, 1924; Klein, 1975a, 1975b). I thought that in her description of cooking the pudding, Miss M was indicating that she had successfully mourned the loss of her mother and was now free to function in identification with her mother, no longer as the watching child but as the woman who cooks. Her enhanced ego functioning could be seen in other ways – in a capacity to organise her life at a level adequate for survival, to scan reality in a new way (such as what was happening to her rent payments), and in an awakened interest in developing new relationships.

The man on the building site

There were still developmental conflicts that Miss M needed to renegotiate in the maternal transference. A workman she passed daily at a building site had been 'chatting her up'; he began to take her out for coffee, and the accounts of himself that he gave her sounded wildly improbable. I felt like an anxious mother whose baby has suddenly shot into adolescence! The affair went on, with Miss M talking more and more animatedly about her beau, and I became alarmed (I think groundlessly) that she might become pregnant. Some weeks later the crash came: 'I found 'im out!' Miss M rapped out grimly and described how she found she had been deceived. Just as there had been pressure to restrict her, now there was pressure to join in a harpies' duet: '*Men!*' (Miss M's mother, it transpired, used to refer contemptuously to her husband as '*Him!*') I did not comply with this pressure, and the upshot of the episode was, I felt, that a paternal figure became available within Miss M's mind, no longer having to remain inaccessible for fear of baleful maternal envy.

A transitional object: the TV-licence money

I once obtained for Miss M a sum of money for the payment of her television licence. On several occasions, not yet having bought the licence, Miss M 'borrowed' from this sum, always seeking my permission in advance, and always 'repaying' herself afterwards. It was an interesting manifestation of Miss M's projection of her ego (and superego) function into me, despite my clarification that the money was now hers to dispose of as she wished. The money seemed to function somewhat like a transitional object, rather like the teddy bear or blanket does for the small child in the way that Donald Winnicott suggested. Finally, she decided to dispense with a television and to use the money for a new purpose of her own.

Termination and after . . .

The many indications of Miss M's development led me to suggest that she could now herself undertake rent payments directly. Her resistance to this was immense, but it was finally achieved, as also, somewhat later, was the conclusion of our work together.

A year later, Miss M called to see me. She looked much healthier and happier, had lost four stone, was cleanly and decently dressed, and told me that she was about to get married. Neighbourhood friends approved and were warmly involved. Although the couple sounded in certain ways bizarrely assorted, I could see a realistic basis for the marriage project and thought it could work, probably with occasional crises requiring limited social work intervention.

The social work site

Parts I and II of this book have looked at therapeutic engagement in psychoanalysis and psychotherapy as a function of the patient's gradual encounter with, and subsequent introjection of, various elements of the treatment site (which means, in a broad sense, the treatment setting). With the description of the work with Miss M on hand to refer to, I will now propose the analogy of the social work site. We can then see the issue of the client's engagement as a product of her encounter with, and her introjection (or taking in) of, elements in that social work site.

A unique ensemble of elements

The social work site is very different from the sites of psychoanalysis and psychotherapy. One difference is that, since social work is charged by society to deal with social breakdown (potential, incipient or actual), it necessarily takes place in an institutional or agency setting. A related difference is that the social worker may intervene directly in the client's life, whereas the psychoanalyst and psychotherapist follow much more stringently the principles of abstinence and neutrality. Some examples of this second difference are that I emphasised to Miss M that it was necessary to pay her rent, and made a temporary supportive arrangement to facilitate this; twice I obtained a financial grant for her; and I insisted that she attend her workshop review and also varied the usual frame to the extent of calling for her and accompanying her there, communicating by concrete enactment (*not* by interpretation) both my support of Miss M as she confronted reality, and also my refusal to allow the joint efforts of the workshop director and myself (embodying a triangulation) to be dismissed.

The nature of the social worker's listening is a third element in the social work site that has important differences from psychoanalytic listening but also an important resemblance to it. A social work frame of reference necessarily imposes particular constraints on the social worker's attention, which cannot therefore be as free from distraction and as free-floating as the listening of the psychoanalyst or psychotherapist. The original presenting problem and the underlying problem are parts of that constraining frame of reference. Thus, not only initially but throughout, it was essential to remember Miss M's original presenting problem – the issue of the maintenance of her home through rent payment – and to be prepared to act on this. The underlying issue, progress with the arrested mourning process, had equally to be kept sight of.

Yet social work listening bears a distant resemblance to psychoanalytic listening. Work in the psychodynamic social work tradition has learned from psychoanalysis not to foreclose too hastily in judging which of the client's communications are relevant to the task in hand. This allows the registering of thoughts and memories that might have been dismissed as inconsequential. For example, consider in Miss M's case her mention of the gas meter-reader's intrusion into the toilet, which helped me to realise how easily Miss M's dignity could be outraged and how easily I could be oblivious of this. Consider too Miss M's remarks about the soon-to-be-widowed undertaker, which communicated to me her uncertainty about whether she might be left to confront alone, without help, the task of (figuratively speaking) laying her mother to rest. These 'apparent irrelevancies' are analogous to the free association of psychoanalysis and may at times prove unexpectedly relevant to the task in hand. Recently, although her elaboration of it differs from mine, Joan Berzoff has likewise singled out Freud's 'evenly hovering attention' as an attitude of listening that is invaluable in psychodynamic social work practice (Berzoff, 2012).

Specifying some elements of the social work site in the case example

It is possible to specify at least four of the numerous elements of the social work site in the work with Miss M. These were: a regular weekly appointment with an almost unvarying time and place; knowledge and an assumption of ethical obligations contributed by professional training; listening in a manner as described above, this being facilitated by the psychodynamically informed supervisor; and the social work frame of reference comprising the fivefold interrelations between (i) presenting problem (threat of eviction); (ii) underlying problem (arrested mourning); (iii) agency function (a non-statutory family welfare agency); (iv) unfolding interview material every week, and (v) external crises (such as my learning from a displeased telephone call from the sheltered workshop that

Miss M had not been attending). This inter-related frame of reference has an inner logic that is always highly specific to the individual case, and can be dimly sensed, in time, by the client.

We can now look at the evidence that Miss M not only sensed some of these elements, but that her doing so had a transforming effect that changed her relation to the social work site and signalled her discovery of it as a social work situation that really worked for her. (The analogy here is to the patient in psychoanalysis for whom the analytic site becomes transformed into the analysing situation that he can utilise, as conceptualised by Donnet (2001) and set out above in Chapter 2.)

Transformation of the relation to the social work site

Three stages are identifiable in the gradual transformation of Miss M's relation to the social work site. Miss M's initial assumptions about the social work site – that is, the place where she found herself in her encounters with me – were evidently that the site dispensed or withheld money: she saw herself as a beneficiary of financial help or a thwarted applicant for it.

Months later, her encounter over many weeks with the relatively invariable space-time frame and other elements of the site gave rise to her puzzled remark about a person she had visited who *always* had time to pass the time of day. This suggests a second stage modification to an idea that what was available in the psychodynamic social work site was someone willing to pass the time of day with her, chatting, if she happened to drop by, and her puzzled air suggests a potential for further modification.

Still later, the specificity, ethics and logic of the functioning of the psycho-dynamic social work method seem to have been borne in upon her. This is evident in her warmly approving remark about the orthoptist knowing her job – 'Only a young girl she is – but, oh! She knows her job!' By this time, it was clear that Miss M felt sure that I (then a social worker in my mid-20s) had a job to do with her in the social work situation that we were in, and that I knew my job. Her remark about the orthoptist marked the transition to an equivalent of Donnet's 'analysing situation' – the *product* of a sufficiently adequate encounter between the patient and the site.

Donnet reasons that the analysing situation 'implies the subjectivised use, through the experience of "found-created", of the resources of the [analytic] site and their singular configuration by the patient', and that this contributes to the development of 'thirdness' (Donnet, 2001, p. 137). By analogy, the 'job' that the orthoptist (standing for myself) 'knew' was, for Miss M, a third term. What Miss M internalised during the second main phase of treatment was a relationship: the orthoptist/worker in relation to her job. This offered Miss M the opportunity to relate not only to me but also to the 'job' – corresponding, in Donnet's discussion of psychoanalysis, to the *method* that is situated, like a third term, between analyst and analysand. From that time onwards, Miss M and I were working on the job together, and she took on an increasingly active role.

So, then, the worker's focus on the fivefold interrelations between presenting problem, underlying problem and currently unfolding interview and extra-interview material, all in the context of institutional or agency function, can be inferred gradually and at a level *below* that of consciousness, by the social work client. *These interrelations, at the interface of the internal and external world, constitute the logic and specificity of the psychodynamic social work method.* By virtue of the client's introjection of something of the logic of this method, together with other crucial elements of the site, a relatively autonomous social work process gets under way, corresponding to the analytic process of psychoanalysis.

What evidence is there of Miss M's introjection of the elements of the psychodynamic social work site during the first two phases of her treatment, and of her 'subjectivised use' of the site thereafter? As evidence of the process of introjection, I have already pointed to the metamorphosis of her experience of the site, from being a place where money is dispensed or withheld, through being a place where someone is willing to chat to her, to being the place of a work of significance with a method and logic with which she sensed I was conversant. Her 'subjectivised use' of the site from then on, with her own 'singular configuration' of its 'resources' (both terms borrowed from Donnet's discussion of the analytic site) is visible in the idiosyncratic but productive use that she was able, latterly, to make of her treatment.

Late in the second phase, she was learning to rely on the available listening resource. Because she was beginning to trust my way of listening to her, she could use it to make psychic representations, as when the undertaker image, with its question of whether the undertaker might have to dig his own wife's grave, approximated to an early proto-symbolic representation of her question about whether she was to be helped with the process of mourning her dead mother.

In the third phase of the work, she was able to renegotiate an adolescent-level oedipal anxiety (and a newly appropriate adaptation to reality) through the preoccupying episode of the man on the building site, whose appearance in her life at that juncture is a particularly striking example of paradoxical created/found discovery. This added a further dimension – some 'thirdness' – to the new reality adaptation she was achieving as she separated psychically from her mother. (This re-working of adolescent-level anxiety while I was still available as a transference figure was to stand her in good stead after the work with me ended, when she demonstrated a capacity to find a partner in life and to marry him.) Again, she could reveal her survey of her accounting of the money we handled in trust for her, on the understanding that I would not *prematurely* disturb her fiction that she was incapable of conducting any such survey, for the idea that she had such capabilities of her own was still frightening to her. Miss M started to lay this fiction aside a few months later. Then she practised some trials in budgeting with the help of the TV-licence money and attained a further stage of autonomy when she finally appropriated that money, permanently, for a different use determined by herself. Only then did I have to act, by broaching the issue of her taking over the execution of her rent payment. By then, her 'created/found' configuration of the resources of her treatment had carried her a very long way.

Conclusion

The analysis of the case example in this chapter demonstrates on clear theoretical grounds, as well as in practice, why effective client engagement in the social work process is in no way dependent on any prior capacity to reflect on, or to articulate, emotional difficulties. The client's full engagement as an active, subjective agent in the social work process comes about not because of any prior capacity for psychological-mindedness, but as a result of his gradual discovery and (unconscious) introjection of the social work site or setting, which he discovers to be a social work situation with an inner logic that he can make use of. This corresponds to the analysing situation of psychoanalysis as conceptualised by Donnet (2001), which I have set out in Chapter 2. The ensemble of elements in the social work site differs markedly from the elements of the analytic site or the psychotherapy site. Some of the elements that uniquely characterise it have been specified, particularly the social work frame of reference that must constrain the social worker's listening.

The next chapter will explore the social work frame of reference in contemporary social work practice.

Note

1 The third position and 'thirdness' were discussed in Chapter 2. Here, the issue implies that Miss M could see only two possible positions (points of view), that of the person she was denouncing or her own. I hoped to convey the possibility of a third viewpoint, which here would imply less need for vehement denunciation of the person onto whom rage with the mother was displaced.

References

Abraham, K. (1924) A short study of the libido, viewed in the light of mental disorders. In: D. Bryan & A. Strachey (trans.), *Selected Papers of Karl Abraham*, pp. 418–450. London, Maresfield Reprints, 1927, reprinted London, Karnac, 1979.

Aisenstein, M. (1993) Psychosomatic solution or somatic outcome: The man from Burma. Psychotherapy in a case of haemorrhagic rectolitis. *International Journal of Psychoanalysis* 74 (2), pp. 371–381.

Berzoff, J. (2012) Why we need a biopsychosocial perspective with vulnerable, oppressed and at-risk clients. In: J. Berzoff (ed.), *Falling Through the Cracks: Psychodynamic Practice with Vulnerable and Oppressed Populations*, pp. 1–39. New York, Columbia University Press.

Bollas, C. (1987) *The Shadow of the Object. Psychoanalysis of the Unthought Known.* London, Free Association Books

Donnet, J.-L. (2001) From the fundamental rule to the analysing situation. *International Journal of Psychoanalysis* 82 (1), pp. 129–140. Available from: DOI: 10.1516/3FUH-9WTT-E68B-WF70.

Freud, S. (1917) Mourning and melancholia. In: J. Strachey (ed. and trans.), *The Standard Edition of the Complete Psychological Works of Sigmund Freud* (Vol. 14), pp. 237–260. London, Hogarth Press.

Freud, S. (1921) *Group Psychology and the Analysis of the Ego*. In: J. Strachey (ed. and trans.), *The Standard Edition of the Complete Psychological Works of Sigmund Freud* (Vol. 18), pp. 65–143. London, Hogarth Press.

Freud, S. (1923) *The Ego and the Id*. In: J. Strachey (ed. and trans.), *The Standard Edition of the Complete Psychological Works of Sigmund Freud* (Vol. 19), pp. 3–66. London, Hogarth Press.

Green, A. (1986) The dead mother. K. Aubertin (trans.). In: A. Green, *On Private Madness*, pp. 142–173. London, Hogarth Press.

Klein, M. (1975a) A contribution to the psycho-genesis of manic-depressive states. In: *The Works of Melanie Klein Vol. 1: Love, Guilt and Reparation and Other Works 1921–1945*, pp. 262–289. London, Hogarth and the Institute of Psycho-Analysis.

Klein, M. (1975b) Mourning and its relation to manic-depressive states. In: *The Works of Melanie Klein, Vol. 1: Love, Guilt and Reparation and Other Works 1921–1945*, pp. 344–369. London, Hogarth and the Institute of Psycho-Analysis.

Marty, P. (1968) A major process of somatisation: The progressive disorganisation. *International Journal of Psychoanalysis* 49 (1), pp. 246–249.

Smadja, C. (2005) *The Psychosomatic Paradox: Psychoanalytical Studies*. A. Brewer (trans.). London, Free Association Books.

Chapter 8

Engaging families 'mired in deep distress'

The next several chapters will develop the theme of the characteristics of the social work site that the client can discover and take in.

Modern experience continues to bear out Freud's shrewd hunch, with regard to potential therapeutic help for the poor, that 'often, perhaps, we may only be able to achieve anything by combining mental assistance with some material support' (Freud, 1919, p. 167). This chapter will develop the theme of social work engagement by commenting on some contemporary social work projects that have successfully engaged the collaboration of marginalised families, partly by recognising, in the way that Freud had suggested, the importance of combining some material support with attention to emotional and relational difficulties.

The chapter falls into three parts. First, attention will be drawn to the ways in which the cardinal principle of 'start where the client is' has been given new life by imaginative listening and response to clients' perception of their own needs at the level of organisational arrangements and of concrete material provision, as well as at other levels. The chapter then focuses in more detail on a particular example of an intensive family support project for families whose children were on the edge of being taken into care. Finally, in an analysis of that same example, I will point to evidence that these client families, in feeling supported and attended to, at the same time sensed the relation of the social work process to the issue of the care of their children. In other words, they were encountering elements of what they were gradually discovering (through a process of introjection) to be an effectively functioning social work situation, and were themselves becoming involved in the social work process.

Goodness of fit

Certain social workers, in different parts of the world, have been making strenuous efforts to help people who are in deep economic distress and who are additionally distressed in multiple other ways. A research study of these efforts in Israel is informed by the clear conclusion that the 'satisfied client' is one who has received a response both to his/her concrete *and* emotional needs (Knei-Paz, 2009). Other research findings from the past two decades concur

(Rosenfeld & Sykes, 1998; Berry et al., 2003; Hall et al., 2012; Mason, 2012; Charles et al., 2014; Ingram et al., 2015). This chapter considers some recent effective social work attempts, in different countries, to work collaboratively with populations who are, in Knei-Paz's apt phrase, 'mired in deep distress'. The two most characteristically salient features of this multiply burdened distress are chronic poverty, and the fact that social work agencies have previously been inclined to give up on the families concerned.

In connection with the second of those features, very important collaborative work has come out of Israel during the past 25 years. It has followed a seminar organised to study some successful projects working with families with young children whom others had considered beyond help (Rosenfeld et al., 1995). We can notice that the literature on these projects often parallels, but is not coterminous with, the literature on child protection.

Where social services do give up on certain families, a self-perpetuating cycle gets established, in which the cause of the giving up is perceived as located in the character of the families – who are described in such terms as 'dysfunctional', 'resistant', 'long-term multi-problem', 'uncooperative' and 'hostile'. In a helpful shift of this frame of reference, Rosenfeld and Sykes (1998) have characterised these families as *inaptly served* by the available service provision. They have observed three particular characteristics which predispose groups of families to be inaptly served by their society's service organisations and providers: namely, they tend to be excluded from mainstream societal participation; they face multiple, ongoing and oppressive life burdens; and their extended families and communities cannot or do not provide the supplementary resources required. Their burdened state is lucidly portrayed by the authors, who point out that any given one of the burdens would severely tax anyone's capacity to cope, yet for these families the burdens are multiple as well as unrelenting:

> When these burdens are combined and become 'chronic', the families and their coping resources are overwhelmed and exhausted. Having become incapacitated, to struggle on their own also diminishes their ability to acquire the resources required to cope and do more than survive.
>
> (Rosenfeld & Sykes, 1998, p. 287)

Projects in Israel with these families which were not inapt but instead developed relationships of mutual trust and had a positive impact, *over time*, were found to contrast markedly with the work that took place in other social services (Rosenfeld et al., 1995; Rosenfeld & Sykes, 1998). The most noticeable feature was the practitioners' ongoing efforts to develop a high sensitivity and responsiveness to the people they wished to help, in their organisational arrangements as well as in their practices. A dynamic process took place through which a goodness of fit was achieved between family need and provisions given, on the one hand, and the relationships through which they were transmitted on the other. Such a goodness of fit is the antithesis of inapt service and can only take place, these authors emphasise, through a process of ongoing dialogue between providers and recipients which genuinely leaves room for both participants to bring their experience to bear on how goals are to be defined and also the processes by which they are to be attained. In Britain, Dominelli has articulated in many of her writings an approach to the provision of social work services which she describes as anti-oppressive practice, and which is in some ways similar to the approach just described (Dominelli, 1996, 2002).

Such an improved goodness of fit, as a result of the kind of dialogue described by Rosenfeld and Sykes, has also proved to be possible in Queensland, Australia, by means of a two year project at a branch of 'Centrelink', the large statutory agency which deals with social security claims and which has often been criticised as punitive, especially in relation to jobseekers (Hall et al., 2012). Many of the Centrelink clients, with complex difficulties such as long-term unemployment and histories of violence, abuse, homelessness and mental health problems, had dropped out of their mental health treatment, counselling support and relationships with families and friends, but continued to visit Centrelink. Consistently, clients who were consulted at the pre-planning stage of the project said they wanted more time from staff – *not*, as managers preoccupied with efficiency expected, to have such matters as the conditions of benefits explained to them more clearly, but to have their own circumstances listened to (c.f. Towle, 1973). Many of these previously isolated clients, on feeling more listened to in the course of several months in the project, continued to reject what might have seemed the obvious services for their circumstances (such as mental health or domestic violence services), but were able to start to forge support network connections of their own (Hall et al., 2012).

This concerted effort to be highly attuned to the perceived needs of the clients or families themselves is one of the most salient features of projects with multiply burdened families in other countries. This is true both of work from within the social service agencies, and of highly structured, time-limited family support programmes such as the imaginatively ambitious relationship skills intervention programme entitled Strong Couples-Strong Children (SC-SC), an impressively client-friendly venture in North Carolina set up with the aid of federal funding under the Obama administration. This project targeted poverty-stricken young couples having their first baby and mired in multiple problems including poverty, unemployment, drug addiction, chaotic changes of household, involvement with the criminal justice system, and relationship strife (Jones et al., 2013).

A comprehensive review of the American literature on child neglect carried out in 2003 had pointed to the same associated multiple family burdens and, as Rosenfeld and Sykes (1998) had done in Israel, emphasised the need to look beyond the existing rules and targets of the service agency to seek an alliance with the family, looking collaboratively for ways to decrease the family's amount of chronic stress (Berry et al., 2003; c.f. Reding & Wijnberg, 2001). These authors emphasise that services for families in which children are neglected must not only be multi-faceted and comprehensive but must also offer very long-term involvement – much longer than is needed for families in which children have been physically abused (Berry et al., 2003, p. 17). Again, in line with Freud's hypothesis, it is recognised that the provision of concrete services is very important in the eyes of the family, and that quite simple services, if offered effectively at the beginning at the beginning of the work, can greatly facilitate the family's building and maintaining a relationship with the social worker (Berry et al., 2003). Across countries, it is increasingly understood to be vital to enquire into and respond concretely to the family's own identified priorities with the mobilisation of outside resources, because this helps to overcome hopelessness and builds trust (Berry et al., 2003; Ingram et al., 2015).

An intensive family support project

This issue of the function of concrete services has been illustrated, vividly and movingly, by a British research analysis of the components of effective relationship-based social work, utilising a follow-up study of parents' perspectives on an intensive support project with families whose children were on the edge of being taken into care (Mason, 2012). In the setting up of this project, the social workers were given caseloads small enough to allow direct contact with each family for several hours per week, and there was a telephone service that covered nights and weekends. In the follow-up study, one mother said to the researcher:

> I was very tired when [project worker] got involved and he showed me ways to build my energy level up, he showed me how to make a decent omelette. They didn't throw the goals in my face; they went through it all with me.
>
> (Mason, 2012, p. 374)

The mother went on to describe the project worker's driving her to and from the doctor's surgery, arranging for a counsellor, his willingness to help her with shopping if needed, and her overall sense of his reliable availability. How eloquently this speaks, first of all of the worker's capacity to contain his child protection concerns to a degree that allowed him to listen, really to listen, when the mother spoke of being 'very tired'. His listening and interest evidently led him to enquire further – has this mother consulted the doctor about her tiredness? No? It's hard for her to get there? And – is she getting adequate nutrition? Can she cope with the regular shopping? The children's needs are not neglected by the project worker, who knows that he is there exactly because the children are on the borderline edge of being taken into care and who, in time, will talk very fully with the mother about what needed to be achieved in the care of the children ('. . . they went through it all with me'). But he starts where the client is. Because his listening is imaginative, he appreciates the depth of this mother's despairing hopelessness. We may infer from the mother's response that his idiosyncratic offer quite early in the history of their contact to show her how to make an omelette was made in tune with what he sensed might, at that point, be most likely to be experienced as supportive and helpful.

Mason's study bears out the observation that, in this setting and for clients such as this, simple and effective services early in the contact facilitate the establishment of a solid relationship between caseworker and client. One mother recalled how much it meant to her that her project worker, rather than telling her that she should tidy her house, would help her with the tidying. This remark takes on full force in the context of standard child care practice in Britain at this time, which has or had become (the current effectiveness and extent of recent reforms is not yet clear) intrusively dictatorial to an almost unimaginable degree. One of the mother's in Mason's follow-up study volunteered a comparison between the nervousness she felt about visits from the regular child protection social worker, for whom she felt everything had to be spotless, and the cheerful approach of the project worker, who would herself make a pot of tea for them both on her arrival and would then turn to and help out. The worker's making the tea and helping with the housework was part of the establishment of a relationship that was felt by this mother to be supportive. Another mother recalled how frequently her project worker ran errands for her, and how willingly this was done.

Memorably, yet another mother recounted that her worker visited at ten o'clock at night to deliver a bottle of Calpol (Mason, 2012, p. 374). This is a particularly touching example of the social worker's imaginative appreciation of the acute stress that such a burdened family can experience – on top of everything else, one of the children is ill and feverish, the other children are in bed, the doctor's surgery and the local chemist are closed, all help feels out of reach . . . Mason observes that acts of kindness such as this one, where the worker appeared late in the evening with a bottle of medicine for the sick child, were highly significant in building strong relationships (Mason, 2012, p. 374). Similarly, when crisis overtook another family at one o'clock at night, a duty worker was available. Yet another fervent comment was about the difference from other services in terms of availability, that the project workers could be turned to when there was an urgent sense of need, 'like when A got sent down' (Mason, 2012, p. 373).

We saw earlier that Rosenfeld and Sykes (1998), when looking at what characterised interventions that were helping families previously despaired of by others, drew attention to the efforts made by practitioners to develop a high sensitivity and responsiveness to the families *in their organisational arrangements* no less than in their practice: and we can see the immense importance of such organisational arrangements in the project that Mason describes. The workers were given caseloads small enough to allow direct contact with each family for several hours each week. There was a duty telephone service available covering nights and weekends, should a family be in a state of acute crisis outside normal office hours, such as happened when one of the family members was taken away to prison. Instead of being hampered with bureaucratic prescriptiveness, the workers were evidently free (with the support, one infers, of reflective supervision) to work in a principled but very flexible way, which lent them the confidence to initiate, as and when appropriate, spontaneously creative individualised responses.

Re-stating the defining issue: allegiance to the logic, ethics and specificity of the social work method

Mason, whose article (just described, above) is well worth reading for the eloquence with which her research style lets clients speak for themselves, rightly challenges 'non-engagement' as a given, arguing instead that engagement with 'hard-to-reach' families must be seen as a two-way process. She analyses the components of a facilitating, effectively reaching-out caseworker relationship, concluding that they are: respectful communication, negotiation of a shared goal, practical assistance and reliability.

Accurate as far as it goes, this analysis does not do full justice to the data that Mason presents. For a comprehensively accurate analysis of what social workers such as those in the project described are putting on offer in such a way as to facilitate the clients' engagement, an additional descriptive category, of a different order, is required. What springs to mind is Donnet's characterisation of the very different method of psychoanalysis, when he speaks of that method's *logic, ethics* and *specificity*. We cannot do without descriptive categories of this order.

What does this mean? I drew attention earlier to the first project worker's capacity to contain his child protection concerns while he *first* paid attention to the concerns of the parent, not perfunctorily but in a way that took them very seriously. Evidently this was true of all the project workers. The parents in this project knew that their project worker was connected to, and implicitly sent by, the statutory social services agency with its child protection function – as Mason herself underlines, quoting again the mother who remarked, 'I just didn't like social workers . . . As soon as they handed over to [project worker] I felt much better . . .' (Mason, 2012, p. 374). Another parent, a father, observed judiciously that he was very wary at first and did not trust the project workers because he knew that they had been sent by the Social Services Department. He went on to say that while he remains clear-sighted about that connection, he appreciated the project worker's frankness and honesty in always discussing with the family everything that she was writing in her reports, which she showed to the family in advance. His wife added that the three goals that they had established had all been accomplished, and were all things that she herself had wanted too.

This issue has to be central to the definition of what facilitated the families' engagement. These comments certainly indicate the clients' sense that their worker was putting on offer, in the professional relationship, the respect, practical assistance, reliability and negotiation of a shared goal that Mason has identified. Crucially, however, these clients were also registering the worker's capacity to embody, in a contained way, *an ensemble* that included a principled professional awareness of the following inter-related issues:

- the *presenting problem* (here, societal concerns about the welfare of the children in the family), linked to;
- *agency function* (here, a special family support project, linked to the social services statutory child welfare and child protection function), while the worker looked at;
- the *underlying problem(s)* (here, the multi-faceted stresses and strains overwhelming the family's capacity to care for the children); and
- the preoccupations most immediately concerning the family – a starting-point which always bears a logical relation to the stresses and strains referred to above, and to which the worker regards himself as ethically bound to pay respectful, sustained and active attention in the long-held basic social work principle: 'Start where the client is.'

Mason (2012, p. 375) rightly points out that these project social workers operated in a manner that 'facilitated a process' whereby the families in question gave permission for the worker to confront difficult issues, notwithstanding the initial mistrust engendered by the knowledge that the worker was sent by social services. In the worker's lively and imaginatively sympathetic concern for the parent(s), there was therefore a capacity to hold on to an awareness of the children's welfare, and of his/her own agency role, in such a way as to make interventions on the children's behalf that were appropriately timed, individualised and tactful. The social worker's ethics are implicit in all this: Rosenfeld and Sykes have summed up a crucial ethical aspect of 'good enough' services as the practice of unconditional connecting, by which they mean that the social worker does not make his continued concern for the client in any way conditional on mutuality or reciprocity, let alone personal gain or the wielding of power over another (Rosenfeld & Sykes, 1998, p. 286).

To return to the project: what facilitated the clients' engagement was, therefore, gradual appreciation of the worker's capacity to offer a relationship embodying (i) the logic and (ii) the ethics of the above inter-related ensemble, and (iii) tact informed by an understanding of the issues as *specifically* manifest in the particular family. To put it differently: as the clients encountered what Mason has described as a relationship marked by respectful communication, negotiation of shared goals, practical assistance and reliability, they gradually came to sense also the underlying logic, ethics and specificity of the casework method.

Allegiance to the site means allegiance to the social work frame of reference

There is nothing startlingly new in this method. Certain changes in social work theory and method as well as very marked changes in the context of its practice have become manifest over the course of the past 50 years, some of them in the progressive direction of the development of a critically reflective and international perspective on social work that goes beyond what was once the (mostly) agency-based social work of the Anglo-American social work tradition, and these will be discussed in Chapter 13. One of those changes is a revival in some quarters of a preparedness to facilitate corporate action amongst client groups, and another is the revival, in the form of an orientation known as Family Support, of an active facilitation of the utilisation of informal support networks within the community (Devaney, 2015). For the present, however, I want to underline what has all too easily been uncritically discarded and lost from social work's collective professional memory in too wholesale a reaction against traditional casework. Along with the fundamental principle of 'start where the client is', it was once axiomatic that the social worker should ask herself the following questions:

- *What is the presenting problem* – that is, when the client comes voluntarily, what is the problem that the client brings and that is seen by him as the difficulty? If the client does not come voluntarily, what is the presenting problem and who brings it to the agency?
- *What is the underlying problem* – and, if there are multiple problems, how are they related?
- *What is the function of the agency* to which the social worker belongs, what bearing does that have on the social worker's role and scope for action, and how do the presenting problem and the underlying problem relate to it?[1]
- *What is uppermost in the client's preoccupations today, and how can that preoccupation be related to in a way that is meaningful to the client and is also consistent with attention to all of the above?* – That is, the principle of 'start where the client is' remains paramount not just at the point of initial contact but right throughout the work.
- *If some crisis is looming – whether apparently unrelated or not – how can it be taken into account in a way that keeps sight of all of the above?*

These basic elements of social work method, its essential frame of reference, were once fundamental to mainstream social work in the Anglophone world – that is, in Britain, Australia, New Zealand, Canada and the USA. Within a neo-liberal political ethos and widespread introduction of market principles and the New Public Management into social services and health and social care provision, it has become much harder for social workers under tightly constraining prescriptive control to find sufficient autonomy to operate in a principled way, employing that basic frame of reference (Featherstone et al., 2014). But the principles are not altogether lost, nor everywhere lost. As demonstrated above, for example, they are fully and implicitly present in the social work project in Britain described by Mason in 2012, which appears to have been conducted under the auspices of a scheme allowing certain authorities experimental freedom from bureaucratic control, and about which there was a high degree of client satisfaction (Munro, 2011; Mason, 2012).

Conclusion

I have proposed that those basic elements of the social work method came to be sensed by the clients in the project that Mason describes. This silent 'sensing' by the client has a transformative potential: in the project described by Mason, the clients could sense that the respectfully detailed interest and support being offered by the social worker was related to the issue of the care of the children. They could begin to sense that they themselves, together with the social worker, were part of an effectively functioning *social work situation*: as the mother quoted above said of the goals that were set: 'They were all things I wanted too.' It is this gradually acquired sense of the dynamic potential of the social work situation that allows the clients to become engaged in the social work process.

This transformative process as specifically found in social work has been illustrated very fully in Chapter 7 with the case of Miss M from my own former social work practice, while the present chapter has illustrated it from accounts of contemporary social work. The social work frame of reference at work, together with its function of facilitating change for the client, will be illustrated again in Chapters 10, 11 and 12.

First, however, we will look at some difficulties that can arise over maintaining allegiance to the social work frame of reference.

Note

1 I do not see the identifying of a problem as necessarily at odds with the ethos of strengths-based and solution-based social work, provided that it is done in the context of recognising and respecting strengths, such as the sheer capacity to survive under multiple life burdens.

References

Berry, M., Charlson, R. & Dawson, K. (2003) Promising practices in understanding and treating child neglect. *Child and Family Social Work* 8 (1), pp. 13– 24. Available from: DOI: 10.1046/j.1365-2206.2003.00262.x.

Charles, P., Jones, A. & Guo, S. (2014) Treatment effects of a relationship-strengthening intervention for economically disadvantaged new parents. *Research on Social Work Practice* 24 (3), pp. 321–338.

Devaney, C. (2015) Enhancing family support in practice through postgraduate education. *Social Work Education* 34 (2), pp. 213–228.

Dominelli, L. (1996) Deprofessionalizing social work: Anti-oppressive practice, competencies and postmodernism. *British Journal of Social Work* 26 (2), pp. 153– 175.

Dominelli, L. (2002) *Anti-oppressive Social Work Theory and Practice*. Basingstoke, Palgrave Macmillan.

Featherstone, B., White, S. & Morris, K. (2014) *Re-imagining Child Protection: Towards Human Social Work with Families*. Bristol, Policy Press.

Freud, S. (1919) Lines of advance in psycho-analytic therapy. In: J. Strachey (ed. and trans.), *The Standard Edition of the Complete Psychological Works of Sigmund Freud* (Vol. 17), pp. 157– 168. London, Hogarth Press.

Hall, G., Boddy, J., Chenoweth, & Davie, K. (2012) Mutual benefits: Developing relational service approaches within Centrelink. *Australian Social Work* 65 (1), pp. 87–103. Available from: http://dx.doi.org/10.1080/0312407X.2011.594956.

Ingram, S., Cash, S., Oats, R. & Simpson, A. (2015) Development of an evidence-informed in-home family services model for families and children at risk of abuse and neglect. *Child & Family Social Work* 20 (2), pp. 139–148. Available from: DOI: 10.1111/cfs.12061.

Jones, A., Charles, P. & Benson, K. (2013) A model for supporting at-risk couples during the transition to parenthood. *Families in Society* 94 (3), pp. 166–173.

Knei-Paz, C. (2009) The central role of the therapeutic bond in a social agency setting. *Journal of Social Work.* 9 (2), pp. 178–198.

Mason, C. (2012) Social work the 'art of relationship': Parents' perspectives on an intensive family support project. *Child & Family Social Work* 17 (3), pp. 368–377.

Munro, E. (2011) *The Munro Review of Child Protection. Final Report: A Child-Centred System.* London, Department for Education. Available from: www.gov.uk/government/uploads/system/uploads/attachment_data/file/175391/Munro-Review.pdf.

Reding, K. & Wijnberg, M. (2001) Chronic stress: A conceptual perspective. *Families in Society: The Journal of Contemporary Human Services* 82 (2), pp. 345–354.

Rosenfeld, J., Schon, D. & Sykes, I. (1995) *Out from Under: Lessons from Projects for Inaptly Served Children and Families.* Jerusalem, JDC-Brookdale Institute.

Rosenfeld, J. & Sykes, I. (1998) Towards 'good enough' services for inaptly served families and children: Barriers and opportunities. *European Journal of Social Work* 1 (3), pp. 285–300. Available from: DOI: 10.1080/13691459808413790.

Towle, C. (1973) *Common Human Needs.* 3rd edition. London, Allen and Unwin.

Chapter 9

A question of allegiance to the social work frame of reference

This chapter and those that follow will develop the theme of the social work frame of reference. This framework in the social worker's mind was introduced in Chapter 8 as an essential part of the social work situation that the client can potentially sense, and take in.

The chapter is structured as follows. An introduction proposes that an important part of the social work frame of reference is agency function. Two case examples follow, in which agency function was ignored, together with its implications for the social work role and task. There is then a discussion of a common misconception that psychodynamic principles are thought to mean imitating the psychotherapist. Discussion then returns to the two case examples, for the way that they illustrate the logic and specificity of the basic social work frame of reference. The chapter concludes that absence or distortion of the frame of reference prevents or impedes the establishment of a viable social work process.

Agency function as a part of the social work frame of reference

Chapter 8 began by registering some successful 21st century attempts, in different parts of the globe, to work collaboratively with families previously despaired of (Berry et al., 2003; Hall et al., 2012; Jones et al., 2013; Charles et al., 2014; Ingram et al., 2015). Crucial to the success of such attempts is the willingness to orient the service to the point of view of the client families: and in practice this includes the provision of concrete practical assistance with the families' material needs as well as attention to their social and emotional needs (Rosenfeld & Sykes, 1998; Knei-Paz, 2009).

We could see this as an effective implementation of a basic social work principle, which is also a psychodynamic one: 'Start where the client is.'

Chapter 8 later looked at research concerning the satisfied clients of a special family support social work project (Mason, 2012). These satisfied clients had been able to sense, in their project worker's approach to them, the effects of principles such as the one just stated *and* of an implicit social work frame of reference.

The idea that such a frame of reference can be sensed by the client(s) merits closer investigation, and the next four chapters study this question. First of all, it will be helpful to look more closely at the frame of reference itself, starting with an approach from a negative perspective. This chapter illustrates some work in which the social work frame of reference had, at least temporarily, gone missing, and it illustrates the effect of that on the clients.

The missing element in both cases was a sound grasp of agency function and of its implications for the conduct of the work. Agency function simply means the function of the agency or institution in which the social worker is employed, such as a hospital, a service for refugees, a school for the blind, a statutory probation and parole service, a statutory social services department and so on. It can be important not to interpret agency function too narrowly – as Marion Bower has pointed out, for example, workers in a drug addictions service may forget to take full account of the fact that their clients may be parents, while workers in a child and family service, in seeing the same clients as parents, may fail to take cognisance of the depth of the difficulties overwhelming them (Bower, 2005). With the proviso not to interpret it too narrowly, it is a common-sense part of ordinary social work to take cognisance of agency function as part of an implicit frame of reference. Occasionally, social workers who are frustrated or unhappy in their setting, or irked by its constraints, do their best simply to ignore their role as defined by the function of their institutional setting (rather than to subject it to critical scrutiny and challenge). This can limit the effectiveness of their work, as the following examples illustrate.

Case example I: a mother speaks of an unsafe edifice on the stairs

At a case discussion seminar that I led during the 1980s, an educational social worker, Peter, spoke to us about the case of Dennis T, a 12-year-old boy with recently developed school behaviour problems.

Dennis attended one of the several schools that lay within the remit of Peter's job. Peter was employed as a social worker within the educational department of a metropolitan council, and spent part of his time in the council's educational headquarters and part of his time at the schools allocated to him. Peter told us that he liked the freedom that his job gave him to work intensively with selected cases but was irritated with routine duties such as attending school case reviews. He described the referral and his assessment interview with the T family. After the initial meeting with the family he had referred Dennis for appropriate educational help and, on the basis of the careful assessment interview in which he developed considerable rapport with both of the parents, he offered to them, and they accepted, some joint interviews.

Mr T did not then attend, while Mrs T presented herself in an anxious and distressed state and invited Peter's concern and interest in her personal preoccupations. In a long series of individual appointments with Mrs T, Peter listened to her inner states of feeling and memories of childhood, and discussed them with her. Meanwhile Dennis settled into his new school, although in a recent interview, in which she complained also of a sense of hopelessness about her own depression, Mrs T mentioned that Dennis had been spending much time at home using various household items to build large and precarious structures for himself on the stairs, climbing in them in what sounded like a foolhardy and risky way and inviting his younger brother to join him. During the seminar discussion, several social work colleagues said how impressed they were that Peter was conducting a piece of work so like real therapy.

Eventually I intervened, suggesting that Mrs T's reported preoccupation with her son's building a large and precarious edifice on the stairs might be not only a conscious communication about an item of external reality, but also a transference communication about the long series of interviews about childhood memories and feeling states and Peter's comments on them. Perhaps the mother felt that it all amounted to an unsound and precarious edifice, which might even be unsafe.

In the startled silence that followed, I drew attention to Peter's opening remarks about his job satisfaction over intensive casework with selected clients but his irritation, from time to time, at being brought up against the bounds of his particular job in educational social work. The admiring remarks evoked by his presentation, that he was practically doing real psychotherapy, suggested that an idea was around for everyone present that if only a social worker could operate within the same parameters as a psychotherapist, the work could proceed untrammelled. There seemed therefore to be some attempt to eliminate from everyone's mind the social work aspects of Peter's job. Yet the irksome social work setting carried with it a potentially helpful frame of reference with a clear reminder to keep somewhere in central focus the presenting problem of Dennis's difficulties at school. Was it possible that a real loss of this focus could have led his mother to feel that the work with her had become an exercise without point?

As Peter was to volunteer some weeks later, he was divided between a sense of outrage over these remarks and a sense of lively interest in their content, which did in the end, he would later tell us, prove apt and useful. Meanwhile, the discussion proceeded.

Janet Mattinson had written a decade earlier about the reflection process in casework supervision, showing that a dynamic between supervisee and supervisor sometimes reflects, and can potentially shed light on, a dynamic between the social worker and the client or client family (Mattinson, 1975). This social worker's successful struggle to master his chagrin in the seminar was illuminating in itself in this regard, as it was plain enough that the relevant issue for the referred client, a boy who was approaching puberty, and for his father (who had let himself be side-lined) was one of male potency – whether and how it could be allowed or assumed, whether it was to be spurious or genuine. In the relationship between the mother and the social worker, Mrs T's implicit question could be read as asking whether Peter was only a boy, building structures for his own pleasure and for display, or whether he was a man capable of engaging in a purposeful and fruitful professional exchange with her. If she should find that she was encountering the latter – perhaps through Peter's talking to her about this very question, if and when he saw fit – we predicted that the issue would then become whether she could allow male potency variously in her social worker, her husband and her sons, or whether she was driven to undermine it.

Work with her on this issue would aim to assist Dennis by freeing him from some of the parental pressures against which his behavioural and academic difficulties seemed to have been in part (as Peter himself had originally judged) a reaction.

Case example II: a foster child builds a spaceship cocoon: social work, or therapy?

Background

A local authority Social Services Department social worker brought to the same case discussion seminar the case of a seven-year-old boy, Ricky. Ricky was being looked after in a temporary foster care placement pending an application for a full Care Order and, should this be granted, a move to a long-term foster home. Ricky's father was meanwhile appealing against a recent court order which had terminated parental access.

It was after being kicked against a wall by his mother that Ricky had been taken into care two years previously on a Place of Safety Order (this being prior to the Children Act of 1989). Ricky had suffered being hit, pushed downstairs and subjected to bizarre maternal threats, such as that cars in the street would eat him. Ricky bit people, would scream for hours, soiled himself and urinated anywhere and on anything. Gradually, the efforts of the foster parents to help Ricky were rewarded. He calmed down and now attended school.

The visit and its arrangements

The social worker, Angela, had been assigned the case some months previously. Parental access visits had been terminated after it was found that, during them, the parents had not only confused Ricky in gross ways but had once burned him with a cigarette. Angela told us that she then embarked on a piece of therapeutic work. She asked the foster mother to arrange for her to spend an hour alone with Ricky each week during her regular visits to the foster home, and she took with her each time a box of play materials. She took infinite pains to demonstrate a warm, empathic concern for the child, and listened to all that he said and did with respectful attention, doing her best to respond aptly. She also told us that as there was little supervisory support in her department, she was paying for private supervision from a child psychotherapist.

Angela described a visit in which Ricky spent the time taking some of the play materials that she had provided, and enlisted her help in building a cocoon-like structure around himself which he explained was nice and safe and comfortable, and was a spaceship. His mood was quiet and contented, and she found the way that he enlisted her help very appealing and touching. Angela offered an interpretation. She told Ricky that she thought he was showing her how much he wanted to be able to go far away to somewhere safe and comfortable with just himself and herself there. Ricky's response indicated that he felt warmly understood.

Discussion: the potential helpfulness of a sound grasp of agency function

As far as it went, Angela's interpretation of Ricky's wish to be in safe, comfortable place in her presence was both sensitive and correct. I asked the case discussion members to think about whether it was also incomplete, since it left out any reference to the anxieties about Ricky's real life situation from which he was wishing to build himself a refuge as far away as possible – including, we might infer, the fundamental question of what was to happen to him now that he had been in the temporary foster home for two years. Angela had shown her understanding of the content of the child's defence but had omitted to interpret its character as a defence *against anxiety*. A more complete interpretation might have added something along the lines of: '. . . and you are showing me, too, that you wish you didn't have to be here where you really are, with things that worry and upset you so much that you try hard not to think about them.'

Did the incompleteness matter? We were soon to find out, when Angela presented the case again. At this point we could reflect that, had Ricky felt that the pervasive anxiety underlying his wish to feel safe in Angela's presence was understood, he might have felt in a position to voice the nature of his worries and so receive some help with them, at least to the extent of feeling that they had been shared. The trouble with the incompleteness was that as soon as Angela was gone, Ricky was left a prey to all his uncertainty about what might soon become of him, without it having been shared with or understood by Angela while she had been available to help him with it.

Ricky's case highlights the need for psychodynamically informed social work to take place within an ordinarily appropriate frame of reference that includes the function of the agency from which the social worker is operating. Angela was largely using child psychotherapy as a model for her work with this traumatised child. Up to a point, it served: but what would most have assisted her to be alert to Ricky's pervasive underlying anxiety would have been a simple grasp of her role as a local authority social worker, and hence her central task with this child, which was to mediate for him matters to do with his placement. This placement was currently in a state of uncertainty, pending the imminent court hearing of the application for a full Care Order and the contested access hearing. A child and family social worker would therefore expect to be alert for signs of how this uncertainty was weighing on the child, and for clues as to how it might be helpful to him to express his experience of that uncertainty.

Ricky asks, 'Will it be like Ivy House?'

Angela reports her colleagues' view of the issues for discussion

Soon afterwards, Angela brought the case again for seminar discussion. She said that her local authority colleagues had reminded her to tackle two issues: should she do some life history work with Ricky, and how should she work with him on the issue of his mixed race identity? Angela then told us that her time with Ricky in the foster home had seen so many interruptions that she had arranged to see him instead at the local Child Guidance Centre. Meanwhile, Ricky had been regressing again. He was aggressive to other children, and the foster mother said he was being cocky, rude and aggressive to her. Angela thought Ricky was probably reacting to the departure of one of the children from the temporary foster home, and to the fact that the other children had told Ricky, 'You'll be next.' The foster mother, however, thought that Ricky was reacting to Angela's way of working with him.

The visit to the room in the Child Guidance Centre

This was Ricky's first visit to the Child Guidance Centre, and Angela collected him from school by car. Immediately before this she had had to endure a half hour harangue from the foster mother, who complained that Ricky was being rude and aggressive to her while being angelic with Angela, and that she thought Angela's way of working with him in sessions was responsible for the deterioration in his behaviour. Angela mentioned that she was feeling beleaguered on all sides about her attempts to work psychotherapeutically.

In the car on the way to the Centre, Ricky asked if it would be like Ivy House. This was the venue at which parental access visits had taken place until they were stopped some months previously. On arrival, Ricky asked to carry the toy box up to the room. He explored the room, said he would build a spaceship, and then played with increasing aimlessness. He cut sheets of paper and shredded them, picked up toys and dropped them, scribbled aimlessly and at the end, when the floor was littered with bits of paper, wanted Angela to clear up the mess. She had been unable to make sense of any of this and felt her few ventures to make contact with him did not succeed.

The clue to what was on the child's mind

One misleading consequence of Angela's attempt to model her social work on child psychotherapy was to exalt in her mind the idea of a psychotherapy *session*, with the same kind of place boundary and time boundary as in psychotherapy. Because of this, what happened in the car on the way to the session seemed not to count. Yet the all-important clue to Ricky's worries surely lay in his question during the car journey: 'Will it [the Centre] be like Ivy House?' Ivy House was where he used to meet his abusive parents, and it suggests that he was wondering whether he was shortly to have contact again with his parents. His subsequent restless behaviour, unable to settle to anything, suggests that he was very anxiously preoccupied. Bearing in mind that the first five of his seven years of life experience led him to expect adults to inflict sudden, unheralded shocks on him, it is not impossible that he thought he might meet his parents in the Centre quite soon, perhaps that very day, especially as he may have picked up in the foster home some inkling of the uncertainty pending the court cases. He does seem to have felt that he was being left in a mess which he was neither equipped nor responsible to handle, as witness his expressed desire that Angela should clear up the littered mess.

Ricky's question 'Will it be like Ivy House?' reveals something further. The question asks Angela what kind of a place she is taking him to. It was a significant question for Ricky not only in relation to the venue of his sessions with his social worker, but far more importantly and fundamentally in relation to his home. Angela herself had observed that he was currently very preoccupied with the looming up of his eventual departure from his (temporary) foster home, as shown by his regressed and aggressive behaviour and the remarks of the other children, 'You'll be next.' We can infer that one component of his urgent question was whether on leaving the foster home he might be discharged back to his natural parents – and if not to them, to whom and where?

It was understandable that Angela did not notice this. Supervision to help her to integrate psychodynamic principles with appropriate contextual reference points seems to have been unavailable. The torrid half hour with the foster mother left Angela annoyed, depressed and inclined to batten down all hatches until she and Ricky reached the quiet of the room at the Centre, where she felt she could begin to concentrate on her 'real' work. A cheerful and supportive supervisor might have helped her to see that the foster mother's information and view, despite being caustic, were extremely valuable in situating Ricky, and the help that he needed, at that point in time. Far from being a bit of unimportant administrative business tacked on to one end of the visit and so disposed of, the conversation with the foster mother conveyed information vital to the conduct of the casework. Ricky was highly exercised about his fate on leaving the foster home; and a supervisor could remind Angela that it was helpful to know this, given that an essential social work task in this child and family work was to protect Ricky from meaningless details of the court procedure affecting him, yet to keep him properly informed about what was so closely concerning him. A supportive supervisor, able to appreciate all that was valuable in Angela's work, might also be in a position to help her to ask herself whether the foster mother had a point: whether Ricky's distressed and aggressive outbursts after and between Angela's visits might indicate that something could be better handled. Supervision might then help to establish what had been missing in the spaceship session, and might have reflected too that Ricky's question about Ivy House suggested a fear of being confronted with his parents.

A real obstacle standing in the way of Angela's learning from her Social Services Department colleagues had been that while they tried to alert her to the fact that her role with Ricky was that of a child and family social worker, their recommendation that she should do 'life history' work, and work with him on his mixed race identity, meant that their advice came in a form that was instrumental/ procedural. She could not hear in this anything that she felt was really relevant to his needs. It was necessary to recognise and acknowledge the value of her capacity to be sensitive to Ricky's feelings: only then could she be helped in her work with him by linking up the way that he felt with the information that she had thought to be extraneous but that actually was crucial for its focus.

Prevalent misconceptions or equivocations over psychodynamic principles

Of course, it is not only in social work that acquired psychodynamic knowledge needs to be appropriately integrated. Sue Kegerreis has articulated this point very lucidly in relation to teachers and residential care workers working in schools for children with special needs (Kegerreis, 2013). Notwithstanding her own position as a teacher on courses about psychodynamic principles for such practising front-line professionals, Kegerreis points out that there can be unintended consequences for professionals who are attending such courses and who are reading texts based on clinical work. Therapy can become over-valued, and the teacher or care worker can either lose sight of the value of their own work or be misled into trying to copy the therapist in settings that do not have the necessary parameters. Work is required to integrate the new-found psychodynamic understanding into the particular role, task and setting of the professional concerned, usually being appropriate to more ordinary front-line interactions with children by staff in these residential settings, as Clare Winnicott's republished work has demonstrated (Winnicott, 2004).

Neil Altman's *The Analyst in the Inner City. Race, Class and Culture through a Psychoanalytic Lens* is a passionate book that documents its author's enthusiasm and dedication, as a young newly trained psychoanalyst, to bring his psychoanalytic know-how out of the leafy suburbs of privileged America and into the shabby milieu of an inner-city public health child psychiatry clinic (Altman, 2010). He writes eloquently on behalf of his patients and their families. His ardour and the perceptiveness and sense of much of what he writes are impressive. However, there are also points on which one cannot but register a certain naivety. One of them is that many of the issues that arose during his years in the child psychiatry clinic are longstanding issues in social work theory and practice, such as the question (which arose in connection with providing snacks to the clinic's child patients) of when, and when not, to offer concrete goods and services. The most perplexing point is that Altman couches his discussion of several case examples in terms of his offering 'analytic therapy'. At no point, however, does he actually tell the reader in what capacity he was employed at the child psychiatry clinic.

The question of his actual role, in relation to agency function, is never clarified; we are never told in what capacity he was employed there. The reader has the impression that it did not occur to Altman that it mattered.

The persistent equation of psychodynamic principles with copying the therapist, and even the psychoanalyst (doing something vaguely thought of as 'analytic therapy'), sometimes still continues. The veteran American social worker Schamess writes as though still uncertain on this matter. He describes, but in an apologetic tone, his appropriate environmentally supportive work as a psychiatric social worker during the 1960s in the Bronx Child Guidance Clinic in New York, which included advocating on behalf of his poverty-stricken clients with schools, housing agencies, child welfare and other agencies, and sometimes arranging financial support. He writes apologetically of this environmentally supportive aspect of his work, 'Although providing environmental support violated any number of traditional analytic principles' (Schamess, 2013, p. 219). His text makes it clear that by 'analytic' in this context he means 'psychoanalytic': but since those principles apply to the conduct of psychoanalysis, the reader is left puzzled as to why Schamess thinks it relevant to speak of their 'violation' when the activity is that of Child Guidance Clinic social work. He writes further: '. . . did (do) my failures result from ignorantly or wilfully deviating from the proper analytic frame, or did (do) they stem from my reluctance to abandon a rigid, unhelpful therapeutic posture?' 'The proper analytic frame' – again, the reader is left wondering, proper to what? Schamess is discussing the advice on neutrality given by the American Psychoanalytic Association to 'dynamic therapists'. Something has prevented him from being clear that advice specifically intended for the practice of formal psychoanalysis, and/or formal psychotherapy, is not designed for application to the entirely different activity of Child Guidance Clinic social work practice.

Psychodynamic principles seem to me to be often at their most helpful when they further illuminate matters which have been arrived at in the course of acquiring practice wisdom. Practice wisdom is a concept whose theoretical development has been fuelled in recent years by a reaction against the imposition of the scientific paradigm as the only appropriate one. Chu and Tsui articulate it as based on the assumption of another kind of understanding (other than that of the scientific paradigm) in the course of practice in a human realm (Chu & Tsui, 2008). I mention practice wisdom here because, in the development of my argument about an adequate frame of reference that the social work client can sense, I have been referring to the work of a number of the social work practitioners described in the literature who are not avowedly applying psychodynamic principles at all but whose relationship-based work is consonant with many of those principles. The most obvious example of this is the way that some social workers become aware of a transference dimension in the way that their clients relate to them without conceptualising it as such but with a capacity to respect it, tolerate it and recognise how to work within its vagaries. A second example is that some such social workers recognise instinctively that many apparently inapposite remarks that the client may make can have a place in the scheme of things in the course of the work, and that receptive listening is not only respectful but may also be functional for the work itself.

Specificity and logic of psychodynamic principles integrated with a social work frame of reference

Let us return to Peter's case of Dennis and his parents Mr and Mrs T, and to Angela's case of Ricky.

It needs to be made clear that both Peter and Angela were competent professional social workers. They and their colleagues had sought out a case discussion seminar conducted by the staff at a British psychotherapy clinic specifically for social work practitioners, at a time in the 1980s when a series of child deaths, and then the Cleveland 'dawn swoop' crisis, had already led to a sharp increase in bureaucratic prescriptiveness and instrumental control of social workers, as well as hostile portrayal of social workers in the media (Cleveland, 1988). There was a significant tension between regulation and the exercise of professional judgement that led many other social workers to retreat into defensive practice since, as Howe would point out only a few years later, there would otherwise always be *some* detail of procedure or guideline which the practitioner could be shown not to have observed (Howe, 1992). The social workers who had come to the case discussion seminar were amongst a minority who were trying hard *not* to retreat into defensive compliance with bureaucratic requirements. They were trying to hold on to the value of relationship-based social work and to the associated exercise of judgement in a climate increasingly inimical to this. Given the immense strain that they were under, is understandable that they seem to have hoped that in the case discussion seminar, held in a psychotherapy clinic, they could take refuge in a psychotherapy world which would leave reminders of their social work world behind – a defensive move in a direction opposite to that of the majority. However, they wanted to learn, and they did so.

Angela's capacity to have a warm and sustained interest in Ricky as a person, and to relate to him at a level appropriate to a young child, were vitally important. Perhaps in the first seminar discussion (about the 'spaceship session') she was disappointed in her hope that this would be explicitly recognised, and tried to blot out our discussion in the way that she tried to blot out the Social Services Department setting of her work. However, her concern over not having understood Ricky's restlessness at the Child Guidance Centre led her to realise, once it was pointed out, that his question did indicate an association in his mind between the place where he used to have frightening meetings with his parents and the place she took him to, and revealed also that she needed to attend to his preoccupation with all that had and was going to happen to him. At last the issue of agency function and her social work role made coherent sense as a relevant point of reference in relation to her relationship-based work with Ricky.

We can notice the issue of specificity here. Previously, agency function and the task of mediating a child's placement had not made sense as applying in any meaningful way to the work with Ricky. Ricky's question – 'Will it be like Ivy House?' – allowed the jigsaw pieces to fall into place.

Peter had conducted a competent and collaborative assessment with the T family, made appropriate arrangements for Dennis, and offered appropriately to think further with the parents about some tensions between them which appeared to be impacting on their son. Marital and family therapists will know that that the next thing to happen was a common one: despite an agreement to meet with the couple, only one spouse attends. Different practitioners handle this variously. The problem for a while in Peter's work with Mrs T does not necessarily have to be construed as a failure to insist on meeting only with both parents as agreed, although some practitioners would do so. Rather, Peter seems temporarily to have lost from his mind the whole social work frame of reference implicit in agency function. That is to say, he forgot that his role with Mrs T was not that of a clinic psychotherapist with an individual patient. Instead, it was that of a social worker employed by an education authority to which Dennis's school belonged: and Peter was forgetting to keep somewhere not too far from the forefront of his mind the relation of the underlying problem, the marital tensions, to the presenting problem of Dennis's school behaviour problems.

Once again, we see the logic and specificity of the integration of a psychodynamic perspective with the social work method. The unfolding interview material with Mrs T had lost its focus until (and unless) it could be brought back into focus as the task of working on the marital tensions, identified as the problem underlying the presenting problem of Dennis's difficulties. At the same time, that unfolding interview material, listened to with a psychodynamic ear, allows us to infer that at a certain level Mrs T herself registered that, at that point, Peter had lost his appropriate professional focus. She could not sense the presence in his thinking of the social work frame of reference because right then it was not operative.

Conclusion

The 'sensing' to which reference has just been made has implications for the theory of the introjected social work site and the discovery of the social work situation as a 'working' situation. On this occasion the sensing was negative, an occasion when there was no adequate encounter with a crucial element of the social work site. Such a state of affairs, unless rectified (and there were good grounds for hoping that rectification would take place in the cases that have been described) prevents or impedes the establishment of a viable social work process.

Recognition of this problem allows us to draw a contrast with occasions when an adequate encounter with such an element does take place. The next chapters will illustrate this.

References

Altman, N. (2010) *The Analyst in the Inner City. Race, Class and Culture Through a Psychoanalytic Lens.* New York, Routledge.

Berry, M., Charlson, R. & Dawson, K. (2003) Promising practices in understanding and treating child neglect. *Child and Family Social Work* 8 (1), pp. 13–24. Available from: DOI: 10.1046/j.1365-2206.2003.00262.x.

Bower, M. (2005) How to use this book. In: M. Bower (ed.) *Psychoanalytic Theory for Social Work Practice: Thinking Under Fire*. London, Routledge.

Charles, P., Jones, A. & Guo, S. (2014) Treatment effects of a relationship-strengthening intervention for economically disadvantaged new parents. *Research on Social Work Practice* 24 (3), pp. 321–338.

Chu, W. & Tsui, M. (2008) The nature of practice wisdom in social work revisited. *International Social Work* 51 (1), pp. 47–54.

Cleveland 1987 (1988) *Report of the Inquiry into Child Abuse in Cleveland 1987*. London, Her Majesty's Stationery Office.

Hall, G., Boddy, J., Chenoweth, L. & Davie, K. (2012) Mutual benefits: Developing relational service approaches within Centrelink. *Australian Social Work* 65 (1), pp. 87–103. Available from: http://dx.doi.org/10.1080/0312407X.2011.594956.

Howe, D. (1992) Child abuse and the bureaucratisation of social work. *The Sociological Review* 40 (3), pp. 491–508. Available from: DOI: 10.1111/j:1467-954X.1992tb00399.x.

Ingram S., Cash S., Oats R. & Simpson A. (2015) Development of an evidence-informed in-home family services model for families and children at risk of abuse and neglect. *Child & Family Social Work* 20 (2), pp. 139–148. Available from: DOI: 10.1111/cfs.12061.

Jones, A., Charles, P. & Benson, K. (2013) A model for supporting at-risk couples during the transition to parenthood. *Families in Society* 94 (3), pp. 166–173.

Kegerreis, S. (2013) 'Knowing all this just makes it harder': Psychodynamic ideas on the frontline (2011 Ellen Noonan Annual Counselling Lecture, Birkbeck College, University of London). *Psychodynamic Practice: Individuals, Groups and Organisations* 19 (1), pp. 4–21. Available from: http://dx.doi.org/10.1080/14753634.2013.750091.

Knei-Paz, C. (2009) The central role of the therapeutic bond in a social agency setting. *Journal of Social Work* 9 (2), pp. 178–198. Available from: http://journals.sagepub.com/doi/abs/10.1177/1468017308101821.

Mason, C. (2012) Social work the 'art of relationship': Parents' perspectives on an intensive family support project. *Child & Family Social Work* 17 (3), pp. 368–377.

Mattinson, J. (1975) *The Reflection Process in Casework Supervision*. London, Institute of Marital Studies, The Tavistock Institute of Human Relations.

Rosenfeld, J. & Sykes, I. (1998) Towards 'good enough' services for inaptly served families and children: Barriers and opportunities. *European Journal of Social Work* 1 (3), pp. 285–300. Available from: DOI: 10.1080/13691459808413790.

Schamess, G. (2013) On knowing and not knowing: Theoretical and relational transformations during 50 years of practice. *Journal of Social Work Practice* 27 (3), pp. 217–233.

Winnicott, C. (2004) Casework techniques in the child care services. In: J. Kanter (ed.), *Face to Face with Children*, Chapter 6. London, Karnac. Original work published 1955.

Chapter 10

After starting where the client is, what next?

This chapter illustrates a process inherent in the social work task: the encompassing and the bringing together of a polarity. It is essential to recruit the point of view of the user of the service, and to register the nature of his immediate and latent preoccupations. This is articulated in the traditional social work principle: 'Start where the client is.' Yet the social worker must also consult her own knowledge, thought and judgement, and *must bring these into relation to the point of view and immediate preoccupations of the client(s) in the course of a dialogue with him (or them).* The aim of this chapter is to elucidate that process. It may entail, as it eventually did in this case, paying attention to evidence of an unconscious dimension of the point of view of the client.

The case described here was presented on three occasions to a case discussion seminar by an educational social worker based in a school.

The problem of how to help

The social worker visited the home of an 11-year-old pupil, Michael Mills, after his mother had telephoned the school to say that she suspected him of truanting. Distressed, the mother explained that Michael had always found it difficult to settle and concentrate at school, and was still poor at reading and writing, though he liked music, drama and sport. He was always losing things. He seemed especially anxious about attending school on Mondays and Fridays. The social worker suggested a period for Michael in the school Sanctuary and some individual help with reading and writing.

At a second home visit, the mother spoke in passing of a man with whom she was having a relationship. Before Michael's birth, in her late teens, she had moved to a city in which she was a stranger, and quickly became pregnant. Having had no idea how to cope with a baby, she had had to go for help to Social Services. The mother cancelled the next home visit. The social worker happened to see mother and son at the school. They both said that there were no problems now.

Two terms later, the mother telephoned. During those terms, the social worker had heard that Michael had briefly attended the Sanctuary but then disappeared from school for a while, apparently on a visit with his mother to her distant parental home. Then it was heard that Michael had been cautioned by the police for stealing a motor-cycle. Finally, Mrs Mills telephoned to say that Michael was refusing to go to school.

First home visit since re-referral: Children's Home requested

When the social worker responded with a visit to assess the situation, Michael spoke very negatively about school. He had been put on report but failed to comply. When then given detention, he did not attend. He was therefore excluded from class. He then refused to go to school and had an asthma attack.

The social worker asked Michael directly what he wanted. Michael said that he wanted to go to a Children's Home, as this would get him off the streets. His mother seconded this, saying that Michael was so persistently defiant that she was unable to cope with him, that he had got drunk, and she thought he had been smoking dope.

The social worker digested this joint request. Reflecting that here was a boy and his mother both asking that he be controlled, it occurred to her to ask about a feature of the household which had not been mentioned: how did matters stand with the man with whom, as she had mentioned a year ago, Mrs Mills had been having a relationship? Mrs Mills replied that this relationship had broken up two months previously, and Michael suddenly interrupted to announce that he would go back to school on Monday.

The social worker replied that she did not think that he should simply do so without their giving the matter some careful thought. She suggested a contract: two conditions specified Michael's time for coming in, and his pocket money. Michael complained of having to climb five flights of stairs regularly to have his report signed and the social worker agreed to raise this with his Head of Year. Subsequently she learned that Michael's tutor was very angry about this, which he saw as undermining his authority.

Second home visit: the problem of how to help

The social worker was dissatisfied with this second visit, telling the seminar: 'Just as you arrive at the problem it disappears, and there is nothing to work on after all.'

On her arrival at the second visit, Michael appeared in his pyjamas, yawning – school was closed due to strike action. His mother told the social worker that the contract had gone well, as Michael had kept to everything. Michael added that sometimes he had been in earlier than five o'clock because he had been playing football every night at school.

The social worker asked, 'Is this new?' Michael explained that school football had resumed: '. . . and we won 4:2 last night. The teachers played and made real idiots of themselves. You should have seen Mr Pleasance!' (This was the mild, benign teacher based in the Sanctuary.) The social worker responded, 'Oh,

I didn't know he played football.' Michael answered, laughing, 'Well, he doesn't really.' The teacher then asked specifically about coming in at night, and about school. Michael replied that he had gone to school every day, that it was okay, and that he had done his first piece of work for Mr Gritt yesterday. (This was his class teacher, with a reputation for strictness about which Michael had previously expressed hostility.)

Mrs Mills now produced a letter from the school saying that Michael had not done his homework. The social worker asked Michael directly about this. He replied, 'Well, I don't get it every night, and I didn't get any last week as I was away.' The social worker clarified, 'You mean you were away the week before?' Michael said, 'Yes, and I've lost my folder.' His mother added, 'He loses everything. He can't always play PE as he has lost his kit, too. I just bought him new pencils, pens, ruler and now he's lost it.' Michael supplemented, 'And the Tippex. I left my bag in the changing room and when I went back it was gone. It must have been stolen.' When the social worker asked if he had enquired for it in school, he said he would do so tomorrow.

The social worker then said, 'So, you find it difficult to organise yourself in school. Do you work on this with Mr Pleasance?' (Michael was to meet on Mondays and Fridays with this teacher for counselling with any problems he was having at school.) Michael now claimed to have been told nothing of this arrangement until Mr Pleasance found him last Friday, by which time it was too late. After pointing out that she had told him herself and receiving his denial, the social worker said, 'Well, that's a shame, as it's the thing you like best in school.' Michael answered, 'Yes, I really like it. I'll go first thing on Monday.' The social worker then raised the issue of Michael's lateness the previous Monday, saying she had telephoned to find out what had happened. His mother replied that Michael had refused to get up and go in as the subject that morning was one he hated. Then she herself had fallen asleep again until mid-morning. 'But the important things have been much better, and we've been getting on really well. Haven't we, Michael?' Michael nodded, but was fidgeting and rubbing his eyes.

The interview became desultory. Mrs Mills had given Michael all the pocket money he said he needed.

Discussion

Losing things

At the first visit, Michael's sudden undertaking to go back to school confirmed, dramatically, the relevance of the social worker's question about Mrs Mills's partner. We could reflect that, in this family, things get lost tangibly (such as folders, pencils and sports kits), but *things get lost also from their minds.*

The arrangement to see Mr Pleasance has been lost from Michael's mind. So, has the sense of there being a problem! A year ago Mrs Mills said there was a problem, but when the social worker began to enquire into it the problem was said to be over. A week ago, the sense of there being a problem was back, but by today it has been lost again. A problem of homework not done retreats almost to disappearing point as soon as there is an attempt to get hold of it ('I don't get it every night', 'I was away last week'). Then, when the social worker asks about last Monday's lateness, the mother hurries it away – the important things are all better. Again, in the previous visit the departure of Mrs Mills's partner comes to light *and evidently coincides with the recent escalation of Michael's uncontrollability*; but no sooner does the social worker learn of it than attention is diverted to Michael's sudden resolve to return to school, and from that point the issue seems to have remained lost from their minds as a matter of recognisable importance.

Michael's ambivalence about authority

The social worker's remark that seeing Mr Pleasance was what Michael liked best in school was made on the basis of comments he had previously made. He had conveyed hostility about the strict class teacher, Mr Gritt, and liking for the benign, accommodating Mr Pleasance. Moreover, his explicit and conscious reason for refusing to get up for school on the Monday on which he was late was that he was due to have a subject he hated. As, although he had forgotten this, he was due to miss the assigned subject in order to see Mr Pleasance, was he unconsciously avoiding Mr Pleasance? His remarks about the after-school football match suggest a certain sneering contempt for Mr Pleasance.

Did the tale of Mr Pleasance and Mr Gritt have transference implications for the different faces of authority represented by the social worker? Michael, we might infer, seemed to agree with the tutor that the teachers (with the social worker considered as one of them?) had made 'real idiots' of themselves by complying with his request that he should not have to walk upstairs to get his report signed. Yet Michael clearly recognised the social worker's firm and sure authoritative handling of him in other respects. His spontaneous remark, 'I did my first piece of work for Mr Gritt yesterday' shows his respectful appreciation (at that moment in time) of firm handling and of his response to it.

Michael's father

The seminar heard later about the two visits that followed.

Third home visit: a surprising revelation

Mrs Mills cancelled the next visit on grounds that it was half term. When the social worker next visited, Michael had truanted from school on the previous two days. This interview had an angry start, with both mother and son shouting. Mrs Mills wanted Michael to be 'put away' as she could not control him. The issue became one of who was going away, and Michael complained that their life was nothing but rows and break-ups. Here the social worker asked whether this was what had happened with Ed (the mother's partner). Michael suddenly began to cry, and ran off.

The social worker asked Mrs Mills how long she had been with this man. Much to her surprise she learned that the man was Michael's father, and that he has always been either a member of the household, or around, since the time of the pregnancy with Michael.

The social worker then asked to be allowed to get Michael. She found him hiding in the bathroom, still crying. She persuaded him to return to the living-room, where they did then talk about Michael's father and how greatly Michael missed him.

Michael declined the social worker's offer of a lift back to school in her car, but at lunch-time as she passed through the school playground she was hailed by a yell of 'Miss! Miss!' from a beaming and wildly waving Michael.

Fourth home visit

Early in the next home visit the social worker asked Michael whether he had been doing his homework. After a lengthy skirmish about his folder not having been found, the social worker brought Michael back to the question, 'So what have you done for your homework?' Mrs Mills showed three screwed up pieces of paper. One was Michael's Report Card, which had been torn in pieces and stuck together with adhesive tape.

The social worker said at once, 'Michael, this is awful. I would think your teachers would be angry to see your report in this state. How did it get like this?' Michael said that it was not his fault, that Mr Horne (the music teacher) had torn it up. Prompted by the social worker he described a noisy 'pretend fight', evidently provocative, in the corridor with another boy; Mr Horne had come out and shouted at them and refused to sign Michael's report, whereupon Michael told him he was stupid, and the teacher replied by tearing up the report. The social worker observed, 'So you really wound him up before he tore your report.' Michael said he supposed so. The social worker added, 'And now I suppose you can't do drumming.' Michael said, 'No, he will let me.' The social worker commented that Michael was probably rather lucky that the teacher was willing to continue.

After a silence, Michael muttered, 'I'm brainy. All the teachers are wallies. They're stupid.' The social worker asked him seriously what made them so. This failing, she asked at a venture, 'Is your dad stupid?' Michael denied this angrily. 'Is he brainy too?' 'Yes.' 'So, you are like your dad?' 'Yes.' The social worker asked what Michael's father thinks of his truanting. Mrs Mills replied that he tells Michael to go, and the social worker asked Michael whether he listens to his father. Michael said yes, and his mother suddenly put in that he really does, he never argues with his father and has always done things with him and likes to be seen with him – unlike herself, with whom Michael is embarrassed to be seen and so makes her walk in front of him in the street. Michael added, 'I used to go sailing, ice skating, scrambling and everything with my dad.' The social worker asked Michael if he still does those things. He answered, 'Yes, all of them, but not now because he's away.'

Here the social worker asked Michael directly what his father would say about his truanting last week if he had been here. Michael said that his father would tell him to go to school. Mrs Mills interposed an explanation that Michael's father had himself been taken to court at the age of 11 and sent away to Approved School from which he kept running away and had to be sent back for increasingly lengthy periods. He wanted Michael to go to school and not end up like he did.

The social worker asked Michael what he thought of that. When she asked specifically whether he thought it was right to have sent his father away, Michael said at once, 'Of course not. I'd run away like he did if I was sent to boarding school.' The social worker said, 'So you think you are like your dad in this way too?' Michael said that he did, and his eyes filled with tears.

Mrs Mills said, 'But everyone tries to help Michael.' She began a complicated account of how she and some friends were clubbing together to have Michael's ice skates mended, and Michael wandered off.

Discussion: an emerging theme of undermining by the mother

The social worker had carried the issue of the lost man/father figure in the forefront of her own mind, and so was quickly sensitive to those points in both interviews when it was palpably relevant. This lay behind the dramatic results of her intervention in the third home visit, when Michael suddenly began to cry and ran off, and she learned that the 'man' was actually Michael's father. It also lay behind the freeing up of Michael's uncommunicativeness in the fourth home visit, when he proved hostile and uncooperative until she engaged him in discussion of his father's handling of him.

A diagnostic issue of central importance was emerging: the mother's ambivalence about allowing Michael to be engaged effectively and authoritatively, whether by Michael's father, or by the social worker, or by the school. Despite her conscious wish and attempts to deal with him appropriately, evidence was mounting that the mother acted to undermine and disrupt Michael's relations with all three.

First, in relation to the social worker, a moment of close rapport between Michael and the social worker, when Michael had tears in his eyes, was disrupted by mother's tale of the ice skates. The mother also disrupted the work by cancelling appointments – for example, at half term – just when the social worker had begun or resumed effective work with herself and Michael. There was also the implicit gesture of contempt towards the social worker by not keeping to the agreed amount of pocket money.

Secondly, in relation to the father, a hypothesis to be born in mind was that some of the ruptures of the family unit were provoked by the mother, possibly because of her difficulty in tolerating Michael's closeness to his father. This will be discussed in more detail in the next chapter.

Thirdly, in relation to the school's authority, there was the mother's remaining in bed until mid-morning on the Monday that Michael refused to get up for school, which must have clearly conveyed to Michael that she was not prepared to be consistent in her support of the school's requirements, especially when the ringing telephone was left unanswered. Then there was the matter of the lost homework folder. Mrs Mills said she had provided Michael with a yellow folder but he would not use it. Eventually Michael clarified that the school had told him that he would have to replace the actual *contents* of his school folder – namely an exercise book for each of the eight subjects. The mother was neither prepared to replace them nor to tackle Michael about paying for them out of his pocket money. This subtly undermined the school's authority since Michael continued to use the lack of proper equipment as justification for not doing his homework.

'Getting engaged' and 'wading upstream'

The social work task, in cases where there are emotional problems to be worked on, can be conceptualised as having three stages: the initial, ongoing and termination phases. The work on the Mills case so far could be described as a successful negotiation of the initial stage.

In this initial 'getting engaged' stage, there is often a gulf to be bridged between the worker's and the family's intentions, often because the family is defining the problem in limited and concrete terms (Mattinson & Sinclair, 1979). Here, a crucial and immediate test on re-referral was Michael's request, and his mother's, for a Children's Home. Would the social worker minimise the problem and dismiss the sense of urgency? Alternatively, would she unthinkingly go along with the family's definition and proposed solution to the problem, and remove Michael from his home without allowing for any ambivalence behind the request? This social worker did neither. Rather, by referring back to Mrs Mills' remark on a previous occasion about a relationship to a man, she bridged the gulf between what the clients were telling her about a boy in escalating trouble whose mother was worried about him, and her own sense that what was missing was a father figure. Confirmation that the gulf had been bridged was immediate: as Mrs Mills replied that the man (still not revealed as Michael's father) had left two months before, Michael interrupted to announce that he would, after all, return to school.

A second main requirement of 'getting engaged' is that the social worker has to show the family that she can *stay with* the emotional problem. Mattinson and Sinclair explain that this means '"bearing with", "staying with", "sticking with" the clients, their problems, and their fear, rage, despair, anxiety *and above all, their ambivalence*' (Mattinson & Sinclair, 1979, p. 183; italics mine). Repeatedly, as soon as the social worker responded to the Mills family's anxious request for help, she was pushed away or evaded because of the extreme ambivalence of their wish to have Michael taken authoritatively in hand, and their ambivalence about having the issue of the father's significance opened up and worked on. The sheer perseverance called for in the monitoring of Michael's homework, and in staying with the issue of the father, was immense.

Also needed, early, is 'some demonstration either in word or action of an ability to recognise and accept some basic aspect of the clients' emotional needs' (Mattinson & Sinclair, 1979, p. 187). Through the steadiness with which Michael's social worker, undaunted by evasions, pursued questions of his homework and conduct, and through the combined tact and relevance with which on repeated occasions she opened up the subject of Michael's father and his authority, she demonstrated understanding and acceptance both of Michael's need for father and father's authority, and yet also of his hostility towards authority and the paternal principle it represented. This bears out the observation that it is, above all, the clients' ambivalence which the social worker must bear with.

A major feature of the ongoing phase of work – called by Mattinson and Sinclair 'wading upstream' – is that the social worker repeatedly finds, after hard won achievements, that she is 'back to square one' (Mattinson & Sinclair, 1979, pp. 200–201). We saw this at the discouraging outset of the fourth home visit, following the rapport so effectively established in the third. Even very experienced social workers need a supervisor, a seminar group or a workplace case discussion group to restore their belief that their own capacity to survive is what will strengthen their clients (Mattinson & Sinclair, 1979; Ruch, 2011; Munro, 2011).

The continued story of the Michael case bears this out. Chapter 11 forms a sequel to this one. It discusses the theory informing the social worker's stance about Michael's father, and continues the narrative of the case.

References

Mattinson, J. & Sinclair, I. (1979) *Mate and Stalemate: Working with Marital Problems in a Social Services Department.* Oxford, Blackwell.

Munro, E. (2011) *The Munro Review of Child Protection. Final Report: A Child-Centred System.* London, Department for Education. Available from: www.gov.uk/government/uploads/system/uploads/attachment_data/file/175391/Munro-Review.pdf.

Ruch, G. (2011) Where have all the feelings gone? Developing reflective and relationship-based management in child-care social work. *British Journal of Social Work* 42, pp. 1315–1332.

Chapter 11

Weathering a crisis

Relationship with the social worker as touchstone

In Chapter 10, a description began of the case of Michael Mills. The social worker's alertness to the question of a man in the household informed her listening, which established an effective working rapport and enabled Michael to convey how much he was missing his father. Michael's behaviour difficulties could be understood as a reaction to protracted uncertainty about the father's departure from the family, culminating in his actual departure. The father had always had an ambiguous, constantly threatened position on the edge of the family.

This chapter begins by considering the significance of the father from the perspective of oedipal theory. The second part continues the narrative of the case through a crisis. In the third part, the social worker's efforts to resolve the crisis are discussed in terms of her relationship with the family, using the concept of the transference. A brief fourth section links this case discussion to some social work literature on reflexivity and on the function of professional structures such as the seminar in which this case was discussed.

Michael's absent father in the light of oedipal theory

Michael behaved ambivalently towards authority figures. One potential way of understanding this is to consider Michael's attitude to authority figures as a displacement onto them of the son's ambivalence towards his father, which in psychodynamic theoretical terms may be ultimately oedipal in origin. This concept may be most easily accessible through a modern exposition (Blass, 2001). It refers to Freud's Oedipus complex theory: namely, the son's rivalry with father for mother and consequent impulse, at an unconscious level, to annihilate the father (or his relationship to mother); while ranged against this impulse is the fear of father's retaliation, fantasied as castration, and also the lurking realisation that, since father is also loved and is really one person, to eliminate the hated father is to lose the loved and needed father (Freud, 1900, 1913, 1920, 1924, 1926).

It follows that a child whose father departs or dies may be prey to the unconscious fantasy that his unconscious wishes have caused the departure or death;

also, a barrier to the fulfilment of unconsciously fantasied incest wishes may seem to have been removed, giving rise to intense anxiety.

In Chapter 10, Michael's repeated loss of his school stationery and sports kit was noted as a possible dramatisation that *something has been lost.* Were there clues as to what that 'something' could be? The social worker discovered that the recent departure of Michael's father from the family was a keenly felt loss. Moreover, Michael lost, specifically, those things that enabled him to function: and he said that they must have been stolen. Constantly losing things might be an expression of his sense of the loss both of his father and also of a sense of his own potency, since without the father he lost his things and so felt robbed of the equipment necessary for him to function, a symbolic castration. At the same time, he was so much in the throes of very determined onslaughts on authority – truancy, a motorcycle theft, and a bout of drunkenness at age 12 – that he seems to have been trying to destroy any semblance of paternal authority. His behaviour difficulties might have signified both an attempt to smash authority, representing his (oedipal) father, and also an angry, despairing outburst expressing the rage and despair he felt at having lost his father, without whom he might feel he could not function effectively.

A child's own conflicts can be exacerbated by parental behaviour that reflects unresolved parental conflict. Michael's mother, notwithstanding her evident love and concern for her son, seemed to be colluding with his flouting of authority. She had virtually acknowledged to the social worker that it was difficult to tolerate Michael's closeness to his father, when she had described Michael as always listening to and never arguing with his father, and as being eager and proud to be seen with him but ashamed to be seen with her. Moreover, she consistently minimised the importance and standing of Michael's father. Joyce McDougall has proposed that such maternal inability to give an adequate place to the father in her own mind – often because of a continued oedipal identification with the child who is excluded from the parental sexual union – creates difficulties for the child (McDougall, 1989). There was a history of repeated separations from Michael's father. Was Michael's insecurity exacerbated by a need on his mother's part to undermine the father's position in the family?

Michael's father did seem to have accepted a tenuous, undermined and now absent position in the family. All three family members seemed to contribute to maintaining this absence or, at best, tenuous presence. The seminar conjectured that this was the state of affairs which underlay Michael's difficulties.

Crisis

Michael's father had been talked about again during the fifth home visit. Mrs Mills cancelled the next appointment. The social worker asked Michael to tell his mother that she would call again the following week as usual, and paid a sixth visit to the house, but found no-one at home.

Seventh home visit: social work contact terminated at mother's request

At the next interview, the last in December, the social worker suggested that they take stock of their work together. Michael said that he was 'not bothered' if the social worker's visits continued. His mother, however, was quite clear and insistent that the visits should stop, 'to reward Michael' for the improvements in his behaviour. Michael made some remark about a fight between his parents, which might suggest that he sensed a hidden conflict between his mother and the social worker. Finally, feeling that no other non-intrusive option was open to her, the social worker agreed to terminate her contact with the family.

A gathering state of crisis

Eventually the social worker heard that Michael was in considerable trouble at school, and on piecing the information together she learned that he had begun truanting the day after her visit. She told the seminar that, at the time, the idea of rewarding Michael by stopping had not felt right, but that under the pressure of the moment she had been unable to think why. (On reflection, Michael's getting into trouble always followed *interruptions* – of his schooling, and of his father's presence, and now of the social worker's visits.) The school holidays intervened and then, the social worker heard from the teachers, Michael began to be in further trouble.

With regard to the social work frame of reference, this learning from the teachers of Michael's being in trouble is an example of what is meant by an 'external crisis': it is a crisis of which the social worker learns from someone other than the client, and/or where a connection to the social work process may be far from obvious, at least to others including the client(s). The social worker, having noticed that Michael's truanting began the day after she had agreed to terminate her work with the family, decided to contact them: but some administrative confusion delayed her and then a sudden death in her own family obliged her to go abroad. On her return, weeks later, Michael was suspended from school for a week, pending review. He had harassed some girls sexually, tweaking their nipples and intruding on them in other ways in front of some teachers, and had also followed some girls into the toilet.

Michael's mother telephoned the social worker as Michael was refusing to attend the meeting at school that week to review his behaviour. The social worker offered to take them, but Michael refused this.

The following day the mother telephoned again, extremely shaken. Michael had hurled a heavy glass ash tray at her, which smashed on the wall just above her head. The social worker visited that day.

An emergency (eighth) home visit

She took up the violence directly with Michael. He asked for a transfer to a boys' school, which she acknowledged as reflecting his sense that issues of sex would not arise there, but spelled out the support he had had from his present school. Michael still refused to attend the meeting about himself at school that week, and the social worker simply responded that she thought he was feeling very embarrassed and ashamed. In the end the meeting took place without Michael and the school re-admitted him.

Resolution of the crisis

The ninth home visit took place a week later. Mrs Mills answered the door after a while, having been woken by the social worker, and called Michael. Mrs Mills told the social worker that, yesterday, Michael had truanted from school at breaktime and that, later, a boy had been beaten up outside the school: Jake, the usual ring-leader, had told a teacher that Michael had arranged it. She did not know what was going on or what to do. Since Christmas Michael was worse again, was rude and insulting, came in late and would have to be sent away: what else could she do?

The social worker, who had throughout all these multifarious crises perceived clearly the strong reaction to her having agreed to stop working with the family, at once took the opportunity to go straight to the heart of the matter. She said, 'Well, we have talked about this, and Michael did seem to want to change things before Christmas. Perhaps we shouldn't have stopped then, and it's a shame we couldn't have met sooner this year when things first started to go wrong.'

Michael came into the room, looking half asleep and rubbing his eyes. (It is probably significant that he appeared immediately after the social worker's acknowledgement that her own absence had been unhelpful.) Mrs Mills went to make tea in the kitchen, from where, however, she could hear the conversation.

The social worker greeted Michael and said it seemed a lot had been happening. Michael said no, school was all right. The social worker pointed out that he had only attended for two days – was that right? He mumbled vaguely. Despite the social worker then asking him directly about what it was that had happened at school yesterday, and prompting him, his eventual story of the previous day did not fit together. His mother, who had returned with the tea and shouted at him, became so frustrated that she hurled herself at him, shouting. Michael got up and swore at his mother. He then left the room saying that he had had enough and was going back to bed. His mother started after him, shouting.

The social worker intervened, suggesting that Michael should be left for a minute. Mrs Mills said flatly that Michael would have to go; it was getting worse. The social worker asked whether he was coming in during the evenings. He was; but the mother was afraid. The social worker engaged Mrs Mills in discussion of what she was afraid of from Michael, and learned of her fears of police trouble, gluesniffing, male prostitution and prisons. She admitted on questioning that she had no actual grounds for these fears, but said she would rather give Michael up now than watch him get worse and end up in prison. The social worker made it plain that she regarded the option of putting Michael away as unrealistic and unhelpful, but said that they could look at ways of supporting her and Michael. Mrs Mills was still very angry, so the social worker then offered to ask Michael if he was willing to return.

She found Michael in bed, facing the wall. He agreed to talk but not to go back upstairs. He said, 'Why can't we just stay here? She gets on my nerves, just going on and on.' The social worker remained firm about her function: 'I know it's hard for you to hear what she is saying, but that's why I'm here: to try to help you and your mother to speak to each other and hear each other.' Michael muttered that he did not want to listen to his mother, that she was crazy. The social worker asked, pertinently, whether he wanted his mother to listen to him. He answered, 'Yes, but I can't. She won't listen.'

Here the social worker went straight to what she thought was *the boy's leading anxiety. She said, 'Michael, I think you were very angry that we stopped meeting before Christmas, and that you have let us know very clearly that you want these meetings to continue. We have only half an hour left, and I know it's important to you not to waste this time.'* In this intervention, and in the one Michael had overheard just before he had entered the living-room, the social worker gathered up the threads of the case *in the relationship to herself* (conceptualised as the transference).

She was rewarded. Michael jumped immediately out of bed and ran upstairs, and the social worker followed. Michael sat next to his mother on the sofa and the social worker repeated the gist of their conversation to Mrs Mills.

Mrs Mills said, 'I do want to understand Michael, but I feel duped.' Michael asked her what she meant. She answered that he had been behaving so well before Christmas and then it had all changed. Michael looked at the floor in silence. His mother said that she could not stand any more, that she did not think he could stay any longer if he was going to be bad like this. Michael defended himself. His mother asked him angrily to tell her why he wanted to stay. Michael shouted, 'Why do you think?' His mother said wearily that she did not know any more, and then said, 'Well, go on, then – why *do* you want to stay?' Michael swore at her savagely. His mother said, 'See, you won't listen. People trying to help you is no use, you don't even know why you want to be here. It doesn't matter to you, does it?'

Michael made a real effort, and said to his mother, 'Well, it's a house . . . and you are my mum.' His mother turned on him. 'It's a house! Is that all you can say!' Michael, crying hard, told his mother that he had known she could not listen. Mrs Mills repeated, angry and sneering, 'It's a house!'

Here the social worker interposed that she thought Michael was saying it was his home where he belonged.

Mrs Mills got up, took a cigarette to the other side of the room, and lit it. Michael continued to cry, and shouted to his mother between his sobs that yes, it was his home, and he did not want to go anywhere else, not even to his dad's, but that she had packed his bags and was always trying to get rid of him. His mother challenged him to say why she had packed his bags. Michael answered,

'You didn't hear what I said.' His mother denied this. Michael challenged her: 'Repeat it, then.' Mrs Mills repeated, more or less word for word, what he had said. Michael began to sneer at his mother. 'See, she didn't hear. She just goes on smoking, smoking, smoking. See, she didn't hear anything.'

The social worker intervened again, saying that his mother had certainly heard all his words, but perhaps what she left out was how painful it was for him to say them.

There was a very long silence.

Mrs Mills came back to the sofa and the mood changed as if the fury had never been. They discussed some arrangements and some school issues, including Michael's worry about being expelled.

The relationship with the social worker as touchstone

The accumulation of incidents and successive crises involving Michael which awaited the social worker on her return from overseas was capable of engaging the attention in a scattered way as a series of separate, unrelated events.

Yet, just when it seemed that this case was about to disintegrate hopelessly, it was the social worker's *reflection on the relationship with herself as the touchstone*, making sense of the chaos and escalating trouble, which guided her intervention and enabled her to contain the situation in so moving a way. In the seminar, we thought in transference terms, conjecturally, about the recent crises in relation to the central problem.

The seminar's transference hypothesis about Michael's earlier loss of the social worker

Because of the firm, consistent and effective manner in which she generally managed to embody the school's authority, as shown in Chapter 10, we thought that the social worker may have been experienced as a father-figure – or, to put it in more precise psychodynamic terms, to have been experienced in the paternal transference. Moreover, her relationship to the school may have been experienced as that of a couple not to be tolerated without attack: in Chapter 10 we saw her unwitting collusion with such attack and her subsequent concern about it, when Michael's tutor felt that his authority had been undermined at Michael's instigation.

What had the termination of the social worker's involvement before Christmas meant to Michael? Our transference hypothesis was that this re-enacted Michael's repeated and deeply troubling experience of losing an important and authoritative figure, who represented both the *father* to whom he was attached and also a (phallic) *potency* – or sense of (masculine) effectiveness – which he felt unable to hold on to securely without a continuity of paternal presence and support. This would mean that when he lost the social worker, Michael could have felt as if he were losing his father all over again – and he may have felt, moreover, that this 'paternal' loss had perhaps come about through the destructive effect of his hostility to the parental couple both directly and symbolically.

The social worker judged that, in order to establish rapport, it was necessary for her to address what had gone wrong in the relationship with herself. In the ninth visit she did this, which then allowed room for her sensitive mediation in the distressing row between mother and son.

The transference hypothesis in the light of other findings

Postmodernist perspectives on social work underline the significance of one's own contribution to a situation as opening up a site for change (Fook, 2016). Earlier practitioner-researchers found that the most transformative moments in their work with vulnerable families were those rare occasions when the social worker's clarification of the clients' interactive strategy had included a recognition and acknowledgement that social worker herself had (albeit unwittingly) joined in the very behaviour that was problematic (Mattinson & Sinclair, 1979, p. 203).

Similarly, we saw in Chapter 10 that Michael's social worker, who could normally be relied on *not* to collude with the familial pattern of disregarding the importance of the father or of anyone representing to Michael the paternal principle, had in the course of the pre-Christmas visit – according to our hypothesis – been drawn into the Mills family's interactive strategy. Through this, a conflict-ridden interaction between two parental figures, this time the social worker and the mother, resulted in the interruption of Michael's secure possession of the 'paternal' figure of the pair (this time the social worker herself, in her capacity as a paternal transference figure). She had belatedly realised this and had begun to talk to the clients about it: she conveyed, during the ninth home visit, her understanding that the escalation to crisis point of Michael's behaviour problems was a violent reaction to the mistake she had made when she agreed to stop seeing them. This restored the working alliance, and gave her the opportunity to mediate in the distressing row that followed.

That row between Michael and his mother expressed distress and rage *about feeling pushed out and rejected.* Michael was furious and hurt that his mother had packed his bags and was always trying to get rid of him, while his mother was furious and hurt that Michael seemed to her to want a house but not her. During the crisis-ridden weeks they also seem to have felt abandoned by the social worker. It is as though, by means of the row, they were saying to her as well as to each other: 'Do you understand how enraged and, above all, how *rejected* I feel?' Sensing this, and having related earlier in the interview to the sense of rage, the social worker responded by relating directly to the feeling of rejection. Their response showed how greatly they felt understood and comforted.

Michael's father and the 'third position'

With the help of the social worker, including her reinstatement of the sense of father's place in the family, Michael and his mother could begin to be more reflective. This is vividly illustrated by the dramatic effect of her two quiet interventions in the angry and distressing row during the ninth visit, when she re-stated from a different viewpoint what Michael was saying. She did not need to 'take sides' with one or the other because she could see from a *third* position what Michael was trying to convey and the way that his mother was hearing him.

In an analogous way, the seminar functioned for the social worker, as do comparable professional structures such as supervision or workplace discussion groups, as the embodiment of a third position in the three-term situation of social worker-clients-seminar (c.f. Mattinson & Sinclair, 1979; Bower, 2005; Munro, 2011). The theoretical concept of the third position has been discussed above, in Chapter 2.

The agency from which the social worker operates has the potential to function positively or destructively in this third position. At the time of the third seminar presentation the work in the Mills case remained ongoing, but was to be destructively interrupted by large-scale administrative re-organisation which abolished the social worker's attachment to the school and, of course, re-enacted the original trauma.

Conclusion

These two chapters about relationship-based social work with Michael have further developed the theme of the social work frame of reference that, if adequately internalised, guides the social worker's interventions and can consequently come to be sensed by the clients.

Chapter 10 looked at the process by which the social worker must encompass and bridge the gulf between societal concerns (in the Michael case, concerns about school misbehaviour) and a genuine interest and respect for the clients' preoccupations. We saw in Chapter 10 that the social worker's carrying the issue of the lost man/lost father figure near the forefront of her mind helped her to intervene in a sensitively relevant way. The present chapter showed how the family's ambivalence about a father figure came to be played out in the relationship to the social worker herself, albeit in a series of crises that had apparently nothing to do with this relationship. The social worker's understanding that the disrupted relation to herself was crucial guided her successful attempt to restore working relations with the family.

The next chapter returns to a closer focus on the process of introjection by which the social work client becomes, eventually, actively involved in the social work process. The chapter will enumerate some of the ensemble of elements that characterise the social work site and are available for potential introjection.

Importantly though not solely, those elements include the social work frame of reference that has been under consideration in the past several chapters. Most of the chapter will be devoted to illustrating this theory in action, in a case of non-accidental injury to a small child.

References

Blass, R. (2001) The teaching of the Oedipus complex: On making Freud meaningful to university students by unveiling his essential ideas on the human condition. *International Journal of Psychoanalysis* 82 (6), pp, 1105–1121.

Bower, M. (2005) *Psychoanalytic Theory for Social Work Practice: Thinking under fire*. London, Routledge.

Fook, J. (2016) Critical reflectivity in education and practice. In: B. Pease & J. Fook (eds.) *Transforming Social Work Practice: Postmodern Critical Perspectives*. 2nd edition. Abingdon, Routledge.

Freud, S. (1900) *The Interpretation of Dreams*. In: Strachey, J (ed. and trans.), *The Standard Edition of the Complete Psychological Works of Sigmund Freud* (Vols 4 & 5). London, Hogarth Press.

Freud, S. (1913) *Totem and Taboo*. In: Strachey, J (ed. and trans.), *The Standard Edition of the Complete Psychological Works of Sigmund Freud* (Vol. 12), pp. 1–162. London, Hogarth Press.

Freud, S. (1920) *Beyond the Pleasure Principle*. In: Strachey, J (ed. and trans.), *The Standard Edition of the Complete Psychological Works of Sigmund Freud* (Vol. 18), pp. 3–64. London, Hogarth Press.

Freud, S. (1924) The dissolution of the Oedipus complex. In: Strachey, J (ed. and trans.), *The Standard Edition of the Complete Psychological Works of Sigmund Freud* (Vol. 19), pp. 173–179. London, Hogarth Press.

Freud, S. (1926) *Inhibitions, Symptoms and Anxiety*. In: Strachey, J (ed. and trans.), *The Standard Edition of the Complete Psychological Works of Sigmund Freud* (Vol. 20), pp. 87–175. London, Hogarth Press.

Mattinson, J. & Sinclair, I. (1979) *Mate and Stalemate: Working with Marital Problems in a Social Services Department*. Oxford, Blackwell.

McDougall, J. (1989) The dead father. *International Journal of Psychoanalysis* 70 (2), pp. 205–219.

Munro, E. (2011) *The Munro Review of Child Protection. Final Report: A Child-Centred System*. London, Department for Education. Available from: www.gov.uk/government/uploads/system/uploads/attachment_data/file/175391/Munro-Review.pdf.

Chapter 12

Ruth and Mrs F

The site in a case of non-accidental injury to a child

This chapter traces the gradual, transformative introjection of the elements of the social work site, by the mother of a little girl who was found to have been non-accidentally injured.

In addition to focusing on that most preoccupying of social work concerns, child protection, this chapter carries forward the book's argument in a number of ways. In particular, the discussion elucidates the frequently complex interrelation, in social work practice, between external practical problems and the client's emotional state.

The chapter proceeds by detailed discussion of a single case example in the sphere of child protection. The aims of the case discussion in this chapter are:

- To show the relevance to child protection of the theory of the social work site.
- To furnish another detailed demonstration that it is the transformative introjection of the social work site that secures the client's full engagement in the social work process.
- To clarify how the inner logic of the social work site can be discovered and introjected, by illustrating the client's encounter with the inter-related social work frame of reference.
- To clarify how external practical problems may relate to the client's inner psychic world.
- To show how the relationship with the social worker can function as a vehicle in which a central difficulty (here, central to the child protection issue) may achieve adequate resolution.

Following discussion of the case, the final section of the chapter draws together some conclusions.

Ruth and her mother Mrs F: the preliminary phase

When Mrs F's student social worker left our family casework agency, Mrs F requested another social worker, and I was asked to assess the situation. Mrs F had been referred by the statutory Social Services Department after her partner's death, depressed and unable to cope with her two-year-old daughter, Ruth. I knew that the student had arranged day nursery care and had worked energetically to help with several chaotic financial tangles; she had also tried to help Mrs F to mourn the death of her partner and the earlier deaths of her father and sister.

A feisty lady, Mrs F announced loftily, in a telephone response to my offer of an appointment, that she did not make personal visits to the office – and was, besides, unwell. Mildly, I agreed on this occasion to visit. Mrs F received me with a pointed demonstration that she was ill, collapsing feebly back into bed with paroxysms of coughing. In came a neighbour, who lavished pointed attentions on Mrs F. I decided to take a rallying tone with Mrs F, who responded by dismissing the neighbour. On exploration, it seemed that despite intense panic before the student's departure, Mrs F's theatrics now masked a resentful sense that we would force her to remain, as she put it, 'like a cripple on a stick'. We parted cordially; she could re-contact us if necessary.

Shockingly, just at the point where the Duty Senior at Social Services was noticing a series of separate approaches from Mrs F about apparently unrelated practical problems, her daughter Ruth, who was now three, was found by the day nursery to have multiple but fading bruises all over her back, buttocks and thighs. A Social Services worker visited at once, and in the bewilderment and guilt on all sides and in a legislative context differing very considerably from that of the present, we all agreed to Mrs F's request to be referred back to me.

The legislative framework then, and the case in relation to it

The most straightforwardly reliable way to secure statutory authority for child protective measures then, early in the 1970s, was to apply summarily, in the event of actual injury, for a Place of Safety Order authorising emergency removal of the child for seven days. This allowed application through the courts for a Care Order, which was more likely in practice to be granted if the child was already in care. Social Services did not request an emergency order for Ruth – deterred, probably, because the bruising was fading when reported. It would have been unusual to apply for a Supervision Order, perhaps because child protection intervention was often rigidly equated with removal into care, and it was not thought of for Ruth at this juncture.

With hindsight, the referral back to me, in a voluntary agency setting and without application for a statutory order, was questionable. It was made in the context of prior mistakes and in the panic-stricken, horrified atmosphere just after publication of the report of the Committee of Inquiry into the death of Maria Colwell, in which it was difficult to think. No-one had passed on to me, or recorded on our file, the information that the original referral to Social Services (prior to the student's involvement) was made because the Health Visitor saw Mrs F strike Ruth violently, knocking her across the room. In ignorance of this, I had made an error of judgement in closing the case. The subsequent injuries were reported late.

The nursery staff, leaderless due to a vacant post, had been so shocked when Mrs F had displayed Ruth's bruised legs, accusing them hysterically of having allowed another child to kick her, that it took a fortnight for them to doubt the story and have the child medically examined, by which time the bruises were fading.

We all failed to see the potential seriousness of my not having the formal authority that a statutory worker with a Supervision Order[1] would have commanded.

Assessment visit following the injuries

Visiting, I walked into what felt like a war zone. Mrs F spoke hysterically of prying and informing neighbours, at one point producing a severed telephone cord with a garbled tale of how a neighbour had come in and cut it. She launched into a dismaying tale of practical disasters. She thrust at me a distress warrant (a notice of legal authorisation for the seizure of her possessions) for an unpaid rates bill. Later I learned that, in respect of an earlier unpaid rates bill, there was actually a warrant out for her arrest. She launched into a hysterical tale about her landlord: annoyed over outstanding repairs, she had withheld payment until he took her to the court, which ruled that she must maintain weekly rent and also pay arrears weekly through the court. I later learned that over this court debt there was another active, although suspended, warrant for her arrest. Electricity bills were pressing and hopelessly in arrears. Mrs F expressed not only fury but desperation about it all, and about Ruth.

So, we talked about Ruth, and what it would mean if I thought Mrs F had 'battered' her. Quieter now, she told me of her visit after her partner's death to his mother overseas. She described the prior obstacles, the endless channels that she had had to go through, in trying, for a long time in vain, to trace and reach this de facto mother-in-law. Something eloquently insistent about this near-despairing search for a mother figure reminded me of the flurry of visits, apparently about practicalities, to the Social Services Duty Team: and I replied how sorry I was that I had not understood all her efforts to get back to myself.

This established at last a rapport that was sorely needed, because it was still not clear what it was that I had originally failed to understand at my first visit and that had led Mrs F, after all the student's hard work on sorting out the financial problems, to allow such catastrophic levels of debt and harassment to mount up again – indeed, it seemed likely that after the student's departure, not a single payment can have been made towards any of the bills and debts. Once I had responded to the tale of her quest for a mother figure, Mrs F revealed her still deep preoccupation with the partner, father and sister of whom she was bereft. I had been wholly mistaken in thinking that her mourning was adequately accomplished. She was still at the early grief pang stage – but even this was mostly blocked off with a manic denial such as had deceived me at our first meeting.

Why was her mourning arrested? She now told me a series of tales, first of her father, then of her sister, then of her partner, and a pattern unfolded – in each of these tales, she had contact with a person, who subsequently died. Moreover, after her visit to her partner's parents overseas, his father died. These recent deaths came traumatically together, probably reviving a pre-existing infantile trauma. I recalled her having told the student that her baby brother died when she was two, and that her parents blamed her in childhood for serious accidents to her younger sister. She seemed in the grip of an unconscious fantasy that, perhaps because of hostile feelings she was deeply afraid to acknowledge, she had caused all these people to whom she was so deeply attached to die.

Early encounters with elements of the site

The visit after Ruth was injured shows that some elements of the psychodynamic social work site had already been introjected from the work of the student and from my single preliminary visit. True, I had severed communications, as Mrs F showed me graphically during the post-injuries visit while I sat opposite her, holding up to me a severed telephone cord that 'the neighbour opposite' had come in and cut. Yet her tone conveyed that I was also felt to be a kind of embodiment of the mother-in-law figure whom she had, in near despair, tried so persistently to reach (an embodiment for which the psychoanalytic term is the transference). This sense of me as a mother figure she had been trying to reach suggests something in the social work site felt to be potentially helpful.

Inner logic of the site laid bare in the post-injuries visit

The specific inner logic of the psychodynamic social work site, with its external/ internal interplay, was discernible in that visit. The social worker's respect for it and response to it helps the client to begin, dimly, to discern and take it in. We can re-examine the details for that inner logic.

Having exploded over prying informants and her persecuted, cut-off state, Mrs F moved at once to the financial disasters – a part of her original presenting problem, which was that of being left unsupported to cope with Ruth's emotional and physical needs, including her domicile. So, the external crises of non-payment of bills, arrears and debts expressed, indirectly, Mrs F's unspoken rage over being left by her partner to cope, debt-ridden and unsupported. As was consistent with my institutional role (consistent, that is, with the function of my agency), I accepted the distress warrant that she proffered, signalling my preparedness in this crisis to support her initially by direct reality intervention. We had then talked of Ruth, whose injuries constituted the even more pressing aspect of the current presenting problem, originally presented by Mrs F, urgently and wordlessly, when she had struck Ruth before the Health Visitor almost a year earlier. Mrs F voiced the question of whether I thought she had 'battered' Ruth. When I asked what it would mean if I did, she referred obliquely to Ruth being taken away from her. After this issue became explicit, Mrs F told me of her long and weary search for her dead partner's mother, her de facto mother-in-law.

Should the interview then have been redirected to relevant, prioritised discussion of Ruth's injuries and whether Ruth might have to be looked after for her own safety? Child protection procedures and guidelines have burgeoned since then, but the pressure to bear them all in mind can crowd out the mental space for diagnostic listening (Howe, 1992; Grimshaw & Sinclair, 1997; Munro, 2011). Far from being irrelevant, as a strictly bureaucratic approach to child protection might suggest, the mention at that precise point of the mother-in-law implied, crucially, *that what had happened to Ruth was a product of some conflictual burden that Mrs F was carrying*, which she felt could only be dealt with if she could reach the requisite figure of help and understanding.

I needed this conflict identified. To proceed further, Mrs F needed confirmation of her tentative sense that she had reached such a figure of understanding now, so I took the unusual step of rendering the transference link explicit, by replying how sorry I was to have misunderstood all her attempts to get back to me. (It was not yet clear why she had felt unable to approach our agency directly but had gone several times to Social Services instead.) This reply enabled her to confide the preoccupations from which I could infer her central conflict. With its implicit respect for the relevance of Mrs F's unconscious processes to the child protection task in hand, it will have constituted a new and important element in the social work site that she encountered and introjected.

We can then see Mrs F relating to the task as much at the level of unconscious as of conscious cooperation. She revealed at last her unabated grief and told connectedly and vividly the events allowing me to infer that each, traumatically, seemed to her to confirm the truth of an unconscious fantasy that she was guilty of that person's death – father, sister, partner, partner's father. (The warrants for her arrest appeared to dramatise her appalling inner psychic situation, as well as her external one, of being under threat of imprisonment as a guilty person deserving punishment.) That such things can be told is itself a discovery to be internalised.

Ongoing work and its bearing on child safety

Ruth's name was placed on the recently established at-risk register, and I was designated as her key worker. I averted the looming practical disasters and liaised with the newly appointed leader of the day nursery, who undertook to monitor Ruth's wellbeing directly and to keep me informed. I liaised also with a named Team Leader at Social Services, who remained available as the representative of statutory authority.

During my weekly visits, the pent-up agony of Mrs F's losses could sometimes find release before something would freeze over, like a shell of ice around her heart. This work on her bereavement was integral to the child protection work, because Mrs F's desperation about the series of deaths was the context in which Ruth had been attacked. Diagnostically, I hypothesised that Mrs F had an unconscious fantasy that her hostility been instrumental in the deaths of her father, partner and sister, and that this probably revived an unconscious infantile fantasy that her jealous rage had brought about the death of the baby brother who had once supplanted her. I came to believe that Mrs F had secondarily projected on to Ruth, and attacked in her, the imago of her own guilty-little-girl self – an archaic imago dating, I conjectured, from the death of the baby brother, reinforced in childhood when she was blamed for accidents to her little sister, and revived by the trauma of the recent cluster of deaths.

She always had a pot of tea freshly made for my arrival. Thereby she not only expressed a strong attachment to me, but also investigated another element in the site: how reliably would I arrive at the appointed time, a minute after the tea had been made? There came a period of countertransference resistance when I came late, which she marked by politely asking if I would like her to make a fresh pot of tea? Struggling during that month with my resistance to setting off punctually, I longed quite frantically for my colleagues to push me out of the door in time, Ruth's safety being at stake.[2]

A therapeutic and management problem: rage denied, split off and acted out as debt

Mrs F refused absolutely to wait for free Health Department repairs to her blocked toilet – and paid the plumber with the money intended for the court debt on which there was a suspended warrant for her arrest! After moving to a new house weeks later she incurred, despite my further warnings, a massive hire purchase debt on a new carpet and washing machine. My heart sank, originally with her casual remark that she would have to hire a plumber, as I feared that to remind her of unwelcome realities would jeopardise my usefulness to her as someone with whom she could grieve. Despite my dread of having to address such issues, I knew that if Ruth was not ultimately to be placed in the same perilous situation as before, I must warn Mrs F against provoking a crisis from which I could not promise any further rescue. As we saw in Chapter 7 in the work with Miss M on the dangers of eviction, direct work on external reality often entails taking up with the client her difficulty in managing that reality, thereby occasioning anger and frustration. At first Mrs F's anger with me for opposing her over the plumber was expressed indirectly – by incurring the hire purchase debt! When I remonstrated that she already had overwhelming debts, she argued furiously that her partner's debts should be cancelled, and the rent arrears could be left as she would move.

Such provocations expressed, indirectly, her cataclysmic rage – with her partner for having abandoned her to the debts and the lonely care of Ruth, and with her family and me for failing to shelter and provide for her as she so deeply longed.

Flight

Soon my firmness about money made it much harder for Mrs F to maintain her precarious defence against conscious awareness of her hatred of people who mattered to her – of the loved ones she had lost, of myself whose help she needed, and of Ruth. It would not have mattered that she was furious with me – except that I had previously been experienced as a good, understanding figure, and it was frightening for her to start to realise that she could harbour hatred towards persons whom she felt positively towards or loved, including the lost partner and family members and her little daughter. This incipient shift in her defences threatened in turn to bring closer to consciousness her unbearable sense of guilt – her unconscious fantasy that, because she had harboured feelings of hostility towards her family members, she was responsible for the damage to them that resulted in their deaths. This sense of being under terrifying accusation was now felt to be threatening her from 'out there' in the form of creditors, courts and bailiffs, whose real existence acquired an augmented sense of sinister menace. A veteran house mover over vast distances, Mrs F was soon planning and arranging to flee abroad. (Miss M, as we recall from Chapter 7, had likewise felt so threatened by her mother's ghost in her home that she had all but put herself on the streets to escape.)

I listened. I said only that it was indeed terrible to be living in such desperate circumstances, and that of course she had a right to move abroad if she chose: but that it worried me greatly that Ruth would be uprooted from the nursery where she was so settled, and that Mrs F would be lonely and far from my help.

She heard me, and accepted instead a Housing Association offer of a local move.

Dangerous stalemate

Soon after her house move, Mrs F ceased to open the door to me – furious, probably, over my questioning the hire purchase debts. I knew she was in a vulnerable mental state. She had taken to lying in bed and stroking the pillow until she had conjured up a sense that her partner and father were there for her to talk to. Bursting into terrified tears, she had confessed to me a nearly hallucinated sense of their really being there.

The door remained shut – except once, when Mrs F demanded money and I pointed out various expenditures that I knew of, such as a daily taxi to the nursery. My letters, and tactful encouragement from the nursery, did not induce her to relent. Eventually I became seriously alarmed that Mrs F was relying on me to get back to her despite her opposition, and that her disappointment and desperation at my failure could be vented on Ruth. This fear was confirmed when the nursery reported their concern that Ruth was being delivered early and collected late – by her 18-year-old half-brother, who was treating her roughly.

Resolution

In a situation grown dangerous for Ruth, I took a calculated risk. First alerting Social Services, I wrote to Mrs F, telling her that I now accepted her evident wish to work with me no longer. Therefore, any further contact would have to be initiated by her.

This broke the deadlock. Mrs F telephoned, panicking about an electricity bill mix-up, and I visited. She said desperately that through a misunderstanding they were threatening to *disconnect the supply*. I said that I would handle the electricity bill situation, but that perhaps Mrs F felt that I, too, had been 'threatening to disconnect the supply' of help that came to her from our agency through me. Then, for the first time, we could discuss Mrs F's mixed feelings, not yet about others such as Ruth (that would come later) but about me – how officious she sometimes found me, and yet how she realised that she wanted and needed to go on working with me.

The achievement of transformational introjection and the functional client/worker relationship

Did the visit after the electricity bill mix-up mark the transformation of Mrs F's capacity to sense, and fully utilise, the social work situation?

The next period would be difficult, fraught and dangerous. Mrs F developed hallucinations of the dead and dangerously fixed suicidal intentions. With her agreement, Ruth was temporarily looked after in local authority foster care. For this I introduced a Social Services colleague to Mrs F at a joint visit and cooperated closely with her while still visiting weekly. Notwithstanding all our labours, exhaustive and exhausting, there was a time when Ruth was snatched angrily home and then flung back, two days later, into local authority care.

Nevertheless, when Mrs F recovered from her pathological state of grief, Ruth achieved a planned return home, achieved entry (as I later heard) into school, and was eventually removed from the at-risk register. Mrs F's more thoughtful use of the social work was visible in an ordinary way after Ruth's return home, when we worked on issues of mourning that were further brought into focus by Ruth's approach to school entry age, a milestone about which Mrs F, who still spoke of her as 'the baby', was almost hysterically anxious. Finally, I told her that I would be leaving the agency. Real transformation in Mrs F was evident as we worked on parallel themes of mourning and relinquishing, respectively, the dead partner, father and sister in whom so much was still invested, the mother/baby tie to Ruth and the transference object located in myself.

Mrs F's transforming introjection of the psychodynamic social work site was therefore demonstrable after Ruth's return home. Yet I think that it was already accomplished at the visit after her distraught phone call about the electricity bill, which ended our estrangement. Thereafter, however testing, difficult and apparently uncooperative she was still to be, she was fully engaged with our enterprise. The prior issue between us of her flouting the demands of reality in the financial domain had been crucial here, when I had stood for the reality principle, survived her rage, and allowed her to discover in the relationship to me a whole person who was *both* the officious meddler she had wanted to be rid of *and also* the helper she valued, trusted and needed. She found herself in a social work situation that gave her vital further opportunities to work out, in relation to this whole object (person) that she found in me, her capacity for raging opposition. Without this opportunity to test me out in this way, and the discovery that I could survive it, she could not begin to approach the terrors of what she feared she had done to the loved ones she had lost, nor could she approach her frightening ambivalence about Ruth.

Klein (1975a, 1975b) describes the depressive anxiety that is aroused, originally in infancy, on beginning to perceive the object as a whole, when the fantasised attacks on the hated bad object are understood to have been attacks on the loved good object. The baby becomes anxious that he has damaged the mother he loves and is anxious that he may have lost her and her love. As Mrs F's move towards whole object perception brought her depressive anxieties closer to consciousness – her anxieties, that is, about the damaging effect of her rage on the people who mattered to her – the domain in which the struggle and opposition was worked out was less that of finances than that of making realistic rather than unrealistic plans for Ruth. The episode of Mrs F snatching Ruth and flinging her back was just the outwardly visible evidence of how tremendously testing was this new struggle over reality constraints. Only with better assurance of my survival of all this testing could she embark, with my help, on some disentanglement of the strands of a rational and an irrational sense of responsibility, in psychic and external reality, with respect to the loved ones who had died – and later in relation to Ruth, from whom the projection of the guilty little girl could eventually be withdrawn.

The idiosyncrasies of created/found

Some of Mrs F's uses of the social work site had the characteristically idiosyncratic stamp of created/found (a concept discussed theoretically in Chapters 2 and 14, and already illustrated elsewhere). One of these allowed me to mitigate my earlier censoriousness. Her deceased partner's mother paid for a Christmas visit, and the flight was delayed by 12 hours. The airline gave overnight accommodation, but instead of being mollified Mrs F embarrassed them with a shrill, hysterical torrent of complaint that she and the 'baby' had no change of clothes accessible – and was given £100 to buy some! I said with twinkling eyes, 'Mrs F, I think you quite enjoyed yourself!' There was a gleam of satisfaction in her own eyes . . . In telling me this, I think she discovered a way of assisting me, without giving way to her, to take up a less confrontational stance in the financial domain – thereby creating/finding another helpful element in the psychodynamic social work site, as the splits in her inner world became better integrated.

Conclusion

The present chapter has furnished another example, this time in the field of child protection, of the piecemeal encounter and introjection of various elements of the social work site, to a culminating point of transformation. The transformation signalling the client's full engagement was visible in a visit that took place, at the client's request, after a period of estrangement.

One such element encountered by the client was the kind of social work listening (adapted from the 'evenly suspended attention' of psychoanalysis – Freud, 1912) which is not in a hurry to dismiss apparent irrelevancies, is informed by the social work frame of reference, and is sometimes called psychodynamic listening. This was exemplified by the client's description of her search for her mother-in-law, a description which appeared also to communicate an attempt fraught with difficulty to reach the social worker, the reasons for those difficulties only subsequently becoming apparent.

The chapter has developed the theme of that crucial element in the social work site, the social work frame of reference, by discussing very fully the details of its inner logic as revealed in a home visit paid after non-accidental injuries to the child came to light.

Another function of the chapter has been to illustrate the often complex relations between external practical problems and inner psychic states. In the case example described, the piling up of debts and of arrest warrants in connection with them expressed in action an otherwise unexpressed misery and rage over being abandoned by the partner who had died, and also a burden of guilt so terrible, even though largely unconscious, that it may seem to the client herself to have merited prison.

Finally, the chapter has clarified how one of the most crucial of the resources in the social work situation, the relationship with the social worker, can be the vehicle through which the conflict central to the risk to the child may be adequately modified. In the case described, the risk to the child arose through the traumatised mother's unconscious fantasy that her own destructiveness had brought about the deaths of her loved ones. This made it frightening to acknowledge and face feelings of rage towards anyone important to her, but rage which is denied is more prone to erupt suddenly and uncontrollably, including towards a small child. It was only after the mother in this case had been able to tolerate experiencing trust in the social worker and also raging opposition to her, and after finding that the relationship survived, that she could then acknowledge and work through her ambivalence towards, and mourning for, the loved ones she had lost, and finally could acknowledge and receive help with her frightening swings of feeling towards her child.

Notes

1 A Supervision Order would give the social worker formal authority to visit, in order to oversee the care of the child. If access were repeatedly refused, application could once again be made to the court, one logical possibility being that a Care Order might then be made, and the child removed from home.
2 Social workers come face to face with very powerful feelings in their clients and can in turn have powerful feelings stirred in themselves, without quite recognising what they are in the grip of; this phenomenon is known as countertransference. Reflective discussion with colleagues with an understanding of unconscious processes can be a particularly valuable aid in the struggle with such feelings (c.f. Agass, 2005).

References

Agass, D. (2005) The containing function of supervision in working with abuse. In: M. Bower (ed.), *Psychoanalytic Theory for Social Work Practice: Thinking Under Fire*, pp. 185–196. Abingdon, Routledge.

Freud, S. (1912) Recommendations to physicians practising psycho-analysis. In J. Strachey (ed. and trans.), *The Standard Edition of the Complete Psychological Works of Sigmund Freud* (Vol. 12), pp.109–120. London, Hogarth Press.

Grimshaw, R. & Sinclair, R. (1997) *Planning to Care: Regulation, Procedure and Practice Under the Children Act 1989*, pp. 12, 44, 47–48. London, National Children's Bureau.

Howe, D. (1992) Child abuse and the bureaucratisation of social work. *The Sociological Review* 40 (3), 491–508.

Klein, M. (1975a) A contribution to the psycho-genesis of manic-depressive states. In: *The Works of Melanie Klein Vol 1: Love, Guilt and Reparation and other Works 1921–1945*, pp. 262–289. London, Hogarth and the Institute of Psycho-Analysis.

Klein, M. (1975b) Mourning and its relation to manic-depressive states. In: *The Works of Melanie Klein, Vol. 1: Love, Guilt and Reparation and other Works 1921–1945*, pp. 344–369. London, Hogarth and the Institute of Psycho-Analysis.

Munro, E. (2011b) *The Munro Review of Child Protection. Final Report: A Child-Centred System*. London, Department for Education. Available from: www.gov.uk/government/uploads/system/uploads/attachment_data/file/175391/Munro-Review.pdf.

Chapter 13

Joining the discourse of contemporary social work

Purpose and structure of this chapter

The present part of this book has been depicting the process by which the social work client can discover that he is in a quasi-autonomous 'social work situation' that is effectively addressing the issues that most closely concern him, and in which he is actively engaged.

During the past 50 years the landscape in which social work is practised has undergone radical change. The specific purpose of this chapter is to discuss the relevance to contemporary social work, especially in Britain, of the theory and practice described in this book. Contexts that pose new challenges call for adaptation and change: but if we cannot draw on existing knowledge and traditions we are in danger of spending a long time re-inventing the wheel rather than devising advanced adaptations of it to meet the new conditions. In the upheaval and dislocation of the changes to the administrative context of social work, a great deal of inherited knowledge and skill was lost (O'Neill, 1999; Munro, 2011a). It is in order to bring this point home that this chapter follows a trajectory from social work's past to its present.

The chapter is structured in three main parts. First it outlines the history and changing context of professional social work in the Anglo-American tradition. Secondly it focuses on the ferment in British social work during the 1970s and identifies, in a Social Services Department casework project from that time, evidence of a process of introjection (a process not yet conceptualised) on the part of the client families that allowed them to discover a 'social work situation' that was, they could feel, working for them (Mattinson & Sinclair, 1979). Finally, the chapter discusses the contribution of the theory of 'site' and 'social work situation' to comparable social work possibilities in the administrative and theoretical contexts of the post-Munro present.

The Anglo-American social work tradition

The central importance of relationship as the most influential component of the helping process (Goldstein, 1990; Samson, 2015) has been understood right from the beginnings of modern professional social work in the 1860s. As Octavia Hill set about improving the dreadful housing conditions of the London poor she talked to her tenants over tea as she collected the weekly rent, and was in no doubt about 'the sweet subtle power of human sympathy' and about the potential empowerment inherent in noticing aspirations which circumstance has discouraged and crushed (Maurice, 1913, p. 258). The Settlement Movement that was begun by Canon Barnett at Toynbee Hall in London, and by Jane Addams at Hull House in Chicago, was based on respect for the local residents as neighbours and fellow citizens. Community consultation was practised and was followed by effective social action: William Beveridge and Clement Atlee, who were to play such significant parts in establishing the post-World War II British welfare state, had both spent time as young men living in Toynbee Hall (Cohen, n.d.). Jane Addams, who campaigned successfully in Chicago for the abolition of child labour, the first Children's Court, the first Probation Officers, improved midwifery, improved public sanitation and garbage disposal and a host of other improvements in the living conditions of the poor, had a particularly fine gift for facilitating the identification or new emergence of networks of support and of lobbies from within the community (Segal, n.d.). As cited by Murdach, Addams described her work as an attempt to lead social life by giving it focus and form, and compared her activity to the work of the director of a musical chorus who 'receives in exchange for the music of isolated voices the volume and strength of the chorus' (Addams, 1965 [1902], p. 83, cited by Murdach, 2007, p. 212).

Implicit in all of this was an appreciation of the importance of the person and of the environment. This was given explicit theoretical form when Mary Richmond proposed that the focus unique to social work, irrespective of social work's different specialist fields, is on the person-in-his-situation – the element of situation mattering as much as that of person (Richmond, 1917). Social work treatment, she stated, should aim to intervene to support existing networks within the family and kinship structure and should take account of the importance of mutual aid and of neighbourhood and community resources (Richmond, 1917; also Richmond, 1899, cited by Murdach, 2007). Richmond maintained, too, that caseworkers should also engage with social reform programmes, and that any observed 'recurrences' – such as noticing that in a number of cases, a man with tuberculosis had been working in a hat factory – should actively be made known to colleagues with an expertise in social action (Richmond, 1917, pp. 32, 351–355).

The ensuing years have been referred to as the 'psychiatric deluge', as psychoanalytic ideas brought back from Europe were eagerly espoused by American social workers struggling to understand troubled children in the new probation systems and then, as psychoanalysts and psychiatrists arrived during the 1930s as refugees from Nazi Germany, social workers joined psychiatric colleagues in Child Guidance Clinics and were influenced by them. Over three decades, the authors of several textbooks worked at integrating with caseworkers' fieldwork experience the ideas derived from psychoanalysis (Robinson, 1930; Taft, 1933; Hamilton, 1940; Perlman, 1957; Hollis, 1964).

The energies devoted to the intensive cultivation of social work's professional casework tradition had not, however, been matched by energy devoted to the Jane Addams tradition of community work and social action, which had lapsed. A veritable trumpet call for change was sounded by Evelyn Burns in her 1958 Presidential address to the National Conference on Social Welfare, as she called on fellow social workers, in a speech as cogently argued as it was passionate, to emerge from the cocoon of the private agencies in leafy suburbs and to study and campaign for the needs of the poor (Burns, 1958).

In Britain, amongst the relatively few social workers who were professionally trained, the optimistic 'golden age of casework' was the 1950s (Yelloly, 1980). Several prestigious trainings were based on psychodynamic principles – the psychiatric social work training, the child care training at the London School of Economics (LSE), and the Tavistock Clinic's Advanced Casework Course. Meanwhile in 1954 Eileen Younghusband established at the LSE the first generic social work training, modelled on the American casework tradition.

During the 1960s, to correct a deficit of training in local authority social work, two year certificated social work training courses burgeoned (Davis, 2008). Many of these new courses were staffed by sociologists, some of them Marxist, others imbued with the critical theory tradition of the Frankfurt School which had taken time to penetrate British academia. In some quarters, there was disillusion with casework; in others, casework was seen as immoral, an active collusion with an inequitable system that was oppressing the poor, savagely lampooned in the satirical magazine *Case Con*: in one cartoon the earnest social worker asks the weary young mother in the slum dwelling how she *feels* about being poor (Ferguson & Woodward, 2009). (The casework thus satirised was inaccurately portrayed, as this chapter will soon illustrate from a 1970s project and as Chapters 7 & 12 have already made plain.) Besides, the recommendations of the *Seebohm Report* for an amalgamation of Children's Departments and Welfare Departments into generic Social Services Departments was implemented in 1971, and there were widespread hopes that community work could be practised instead of the casework now regarded by some with disillusion if not with outright condemnation. Radical social work was born (Bailey & Brake, 1975; Corrigan & Leonard, 1978).

Although some viewed with dismay the dismantling of specialisms such as psychiatric social work, others had a sense of a brave new world. Then, suddenly and shockingly, came the news in 1973 of the death of seven-year-old Maria Colwell – starved, beaten and finally kicked to death in the family to which social workers had returned her. In the attempt to ensure that such a thing could never happen again, the beginnings of the bureaucratisation of British social work were now set in train with the Children Act 1975. In the wake of a continuing series of child abuse scandals, the Children Act 1989 brought social workers under yet further heavily prescriptive managerial control.

The introduction of marketplace principles into the organisation of welfare in 1993 in England and Wales saw an even more fundamental change in the conditions of practice. A split was introduced between purchaser and provider, the local authority no longer taking direct responsibility for the services it now purchased through Trusts, quangos and other intermediate bodies (Cooper & Lousada, 2005). Adult and children's services were separated. The role of the social worker was re-designated as that of case manager, effectively establishing a call centre culture in which tasks were split up and the routine parts of them performed by untrained staff (Stepney, 2012). Social work training was meanwhile re-designed as a series of discrete competencies. Lena Dominelli subjected this system to a trenchant critique at the time, concluding that it lent itself to even greater bureaucratic control and was inimical to the development of the professional capacity to make principled judgements within the context of establishing a relationship (Dominelli, 1996).

The immensely important *Munro Review of Child Protection*, commissioned in 2009 by the Secretary of State, demonstrated conclusively that the unintended consequence of bringing social workers under ever tighter bureaucratic control, ever since Maria Colwell's death in 1973, has been the disastrous erosion over several decades of social work's scope and capacity for relationship-based professional practice entailing the exercise of principled judgement (Munro, 2010, 2011a, 2011b). *The Munro Review* specified a series of major reforms of the profession which were to be seen through by the newly formed College of Social Work. But the pressure to revert yet again to the solution of bureaucratic control has been relentless. By 2014 the *Narey Report* on social work education was recommending that for those students who were intending to specialise in children's services, the second year of social work training should be stripped of much of the history and theoretical principles of social work in order to concentrate instead on routine form-filling tasks that would be encountered in the field (Narey, 2014). In 2015, shock waves went through the profession when the recently formed College of Social Work was abolished; the whole situation has been referred to as 'The struggle for the soul of social work in England' in an article of that name (Higgins, 2016; Golightly & Hollway, 2015). It may still be too early to tell how effective the Munro reforms can be in the absence of the body that was to have been the independent voice of the social work profession in Britain. The unresolved questions of Brexit render the future even more uncertain.

The watershed of the 1970s

Let us now look at the problem that psychoanalytically derived theory had become pushed away from social work largely before there had been time for an emerging profession to use it appropriately (Stevenson, 2005).There were those, including some outside the psychiatric social work tradition, who understood its appropriate use in settings such as child care practice (Winnicott, 2004; Stevenson, 2005). But a sound grasp of how to make appropriate use of psychoanalytic ideas in social work was not everywhere to be found, nor were structures allowing for reflection in supervision and between colleagues. There was a persistent and quite widely prevalent idea at the time that the goal of intensive casework was to promote something called 'insight'. Evidence of interest in aspiring to this 'insight' and of its accomplishment came to be looked for in the discourse of the social worker's client, and it was not long before an idea grew up that the social worker interested in doing casework needed to find the client who was 'well-motivated' and had 'verbal skills' – and who was not beset by preoccupying practical problems. Disillusion set in for many as this mythical client proved hard to find, especially amongst the clientele of the big Social Services Departments that were established with the implementation of the *Seebohm Report* in 1971, and in which frequent structural changes absorbed most of any energy that might have been available to integrate theory with practice.

Yet as disillusion was setting in for some, others were robustly demonstrating that effective psychodynamic casework could indeed be negotiated with families in a statutory Social Services Department.

'Site' and 'social work situation' in a 1970s casework project in a Social Services Department

In 1975, the Institute of Marital Studies (IMS) embarked on a project in a London Social Services Department with families about whom previous social workers had despaired. A full length book, often very moving and sometimes very funny, describes the nature of the work vividly, lucidly and humanely (Mattinson & Sinclair, 1979). The research demonstrated that sustained psychodynamic marital casework could be conducted effectively and helpfully in a Social Services Department with families about whom there were grave child protection concerns, an important criterion of a good outcome being whether the care of the children had improved. This past research has been cited in a trenchant critique of the *Laming Report* on the death of Victoria Climbié as evidence of the sophisticated psychological understanding that is urgently needed now in child protection work, and needs to be recovered (Ferguson, 2005).

The data published in the IMS study reveals something more which was not yet conceptualised. It is a vital issue because it demonstrates on clear theoretical grounds why the persistent myth of the irrelevance of psychodynamic theory and practice for marginalised populations is fundamentally misconceived. There is evidence that the clients in the IMS study gradually encountered elements of a 'casework site' or 'social work site' that at a certain point they discovered (I infer, through its introjection) to be a functioning 'social work situation'.

Clients have their own unique ways, which may not be fully conscious, of investigating what is being put on offer to them as well as of conveying the nature of their concerns. In one initial home visit, the couple complained heatedly about each other when the IMS worker spoke of possibly visiting regularly to see if thinking about their concerns might be helpful. Every time he tried to offer a comment, the noise of the heated argument increased. Finally, he *bellowed* over the din that perhaps what they wanted to know was whether he could *stand* coming to see them every week. Complete silence fell. Mildly, the husband replied that, yes, in a manner of speaking, he supposed that you *could* say that. Rapport being thus achieved, they agreed to work together! Such work requires faithful persistence in the face of repeated discouragement (Mattinson & Sinclair, 1979).

The case of 'Mr and Mrs Whiteside' documents the progressive process by which the sense of a social work site was acquired. The initial four months of work had included a period of mutual rejection (that is, the clients had rejected their IMS project social worker, but she, too, had inadvertently rejected them, and had had to recognise this). This was resolved. At the four month point, the worker asked:

'Why do you still want me to come every week?'

'I can't explain', said Mrs Whiteside. After much thought, she added, *'You sits.'*

Three months later, when asked again, she got a little further.

'I still can't explain, but you sits and you listens; that's all I can say.'

Five months later she herself reopened the subject.

'I've got it now why you have to keep on coming. You sits, you listens, and when you do that, then I don't think I'm as silly as I used to.'
                                        (Mattinson & Sinclair, 1979, pp. 190–191)

How are we to understand this? At the four month point, Mrs Whiteside has discovered one of the elements in the social work site: a *reliable presence* ('You sits.') At the seven month point, she has discovered another crucial element of the social work site: the *listening* that is on offer ('You sits *and you listens.*') At the 12 month point, she conveys her own sense of an important discovery, which she volunteers of her own accord – 'I've got it now!' She has discovered the *effect* of the listening. She expresses it as 'when you do that, then I don't think I'm as silly as I used to.' To explain what we see here as a version of maternal containment, as conceptualised by the psychoanalyst Wilfred Bion, would be a correct but only a partial explanation (Bion, 1977).[1] It is because of the whole of *the logic, ethics and specificity implicit in the social worker's listening* that the client feels less 'silly'. To put it differently, she feels less vulnerable to being dismissed as 'silly' by herself or others, because things are now felt to make sense. She finds that there is an inherent logic implicit in the social worker's listening, and that her own individual concerns and difficulties (and those of her husband) are being taken account of and are understood – *and* that their being taken account of bears a relation to the vital issue of the care of the children. The sense of being engaged in an enterprise, a process that in some dimly conceived way works effectively according to its own logic and rules is as much implied here as is containment in the maternal transference. This enterprise in which the client finds himself engaged is what is called in this book the *social work situation*.

There are other graphic descriptions in the IMS study of the gradual arrival at this sense of a social work situation. The couple called 'Mr and Mrs Gilcrux' had at one stage told their social worker, idealised at that point, that she was their family, but she had had, gently, to demur. Later, during a depressed phase, the husband had announced: 'I know what we're doing. Sweeping out from under the carpet!' – but his wife was doubtful. Later still, having been talking together before her arrival, they told her confidently of their arrival at a conclusion: 'We've decided you're helping us to grasp the thistle. We say that in Scotland. You can't hold it like that; you have to hold it like this.' Here was their discovery of the social work situation, their engagement on a project with their social worker's aid.

Subjectivised, idiosyncratic use of the social work situation, from which one may infer a secure process of introjection (c.f. above, Chapters 2, 7 & 12), was usually achieved late in the work with these Social Services Department clients. In one very deprived family, during a late stage in the work, the social worker was asked to read the family a story. One parent asked it of the social worker, the other parent fetched the child's book, and the child chose the story and sat on the worker's knee as she read it: and there was a sense that the whole family derived comfort and nurture from the experience. As this example reminds us, the indications of a development of a sense of personal agency in the use of the resources of the social work situation are always highly individual (the interested reader can find evidence for subjectivised uses of the social work situation, during a late phase of the work, in Mattinson & Sinclair, 1979, pp. 186, 205–214, 219–220, 235–239).

Bridging the gap from the 1970s to the changed landscape of context and theory now

Implicit assumptions within the same legislative context: prescription versus process

Social work as an activity has become an increasingly contested domain and so has the theory considered appropriate to it (Gray & Fook, 2004). Many have agreed, historically and now, that social work is concerned with person-in-situation (Richmond, 1917; Hamilton, 1940; Fook, 2002; Cornell, 2006). Perhaps the only point on which there is unanimity is the central importance of relationship within the helping process, whether the intervention takes place at the level of individual or family, of group or of community (Goldstein, 1990; Samson, 2015). Professor Eileen Munro chose to place on the facing page of her interim report the following simple observation on the part of a parent whose child, one infers, was considered to be at risk of harm:

It's all about relationships. We are talking about people with problems, with painful stuff. You have to know someone, trust them. They must be reliable and be there for you if you are going to be able to talk about the things you don't want to. The things that scare you.

(Munro, 2011a. Quoted from 'Family perspectives on safeguarding and relationships with children's services' – The Children's Commissioner for England, June 2010)

For today's social workers, as the *Munro Report* has argued in detail, the atmosphere of being under managerial surveillance with heavily prescriptive guidelines does add immeasurably to the difficulties of practising relationship-based social work in a principled way (Munro, 2011a, 2011b). It is helpful that the editors of a modern British social work textbook encourage prospective social workers to realise that institutional guidelines do not remove the practitioner's scope for reflecting on *how* those guidelines might apply in any given instance, in a context that includes the wishes, preferences and situation of the client(s) concerned (Adams et al., 2009, p. 4). Nevertheless, a problem about establishing effective, relationship-based collaboration with families, particularly where the children in them may be at risk, is that language such as that of 'partnership' or 'contract' may conceal fundamentally opposite approaches.

In this connection, research by Silvia Fargion in Italy has established that even within the same legislative and administrative framework, a concept such as establishing and working with a contract can be understood and approached in mutually contradictory ways (Fargion, 2003). All of the social workers in Fargion's study, when asked to describe what they meant by 'contract', volunteered the same basic features *at a general level*: they referred to the contract as an *agreement*, and they referred also to goals and tasks – in short, to the *structure* of the intervention. Despite broad agreement at this level, these social workers had ideas of 'contract' that differed as significantly from one another as do the perceptual organisations of ambiguous figure-ground images, such as the well-known black and white image which appears to be a vase on a black background when the white part is seen as the figure, but appears to be two faces on a white background when the black part is seen as the figure (Fargion, 2003).

The analogy is a telling one: where *structure* was perceived as the 'figure' or important feature of the contract work, the issue of agreement became a background issue. One such social worker explained that the contract allows the practitioner to divide complex problems into manageable parts and to devise a practical working plan with measurable outcomes in relation to defined tasks – for which both parties but especially the client can then be held accountable (Fargion 2003, p. 522). For example, when requiring parents to be in contact with their child's school, frequency of meetings and a timetable should be specified. Any verbal 'yes' on the client's part was equated with agreement. The substance of contract work was seen as persuading the client to accept the social worker's plan.

In Britain, Jordan denounced such annexation of the language of contract and of 'partnership' (enshrined in the Children Act 1989) to an ethos of unilateral imposition and intimidation (Jordan, 1990, p. 95). Munro has similarly pointed out that the Children Act 1989 employed a rhetoric of collaboration that was actually highly manipulative, while others have pointed out that new Labour's 'respect' agenda also used a rhetoric that disguised a controlling and coercive approach (Stepney, 2010; Munro, 2011a).

For a second group of social workers in Fargion's study, what was perceived as the 'figure' was not the structure of the intervention, but rather the *process of arriving at agreement*. One social worker explained that it is problematic if an acceptance at surface level covers a misunderstanding or the client's need to please the practitioner. This calls for full, careful and respectful negotiation that includes a clear definition of what each of the two parties thinks is important. Explicit emphasis was placed on the time needed to allow the clients to be fully consulted as to their views: 'Sometimes it comes out that the "yes" was not an agreement after all' (Fargion, 2003, p. 525). Client expressions of disagreement were seen by these particular social workers as a constructive part of clear and open communication that actually made things easier by providing opportunities for further discussion and re-negotiation. Characteristically, if something went wrong, these social workers went back to the agreement as the likely source of the problem, to explore whether the agreement had been only a formal one rather than a substantive one, and to make more room for the client's point of view in the attempt to re-negotiate it. In contrast, the social workers who saw structure and not agreement as primary, tended to regard failures as evidence of a lack of dependability on the part of the client.

In a later contribution to the literature, Fargion has juxtaposed the different policy orientations comprised by a child welfare approach to vulnerable families as against a more narrowly conceived child protection one. The latter approach frames the issue as that of rescuing the children from damaging parents; it rarely investigates whether there are existing strengths and resources in the family that can be adequately supported with services and more resources (Fargion, 2014).

What Fargion's research and Munro's review have both in their different ways laid bare is that the assumption implicit in the New Public Management's hegemony over public and corporate life – namely, that human concerns are to be solved by prescribed didactic instructions that can be widely disseminated – is not axiomatic (Fargion, 2003, 2014; Munro, 2011a, 2011b). Both have demonstrated that an alternative conception of social work method as process facilitation is clearly available. My aim here is to make a further contribution to that conception of process facilitation.

Theories and knowledge for social work: room for dialogue?

One aspect of the introduction of market principles into welfare is the tendency to commodify knowledge and skills, which become seen as so many packaged products competing for attention and funding in the marketplace. It is not a helpful basis for sorting out the relation between ideas.

This is true, for example, of strengths-based social work and solution-based social work placed in juxtaposition with psychodynamic social work. The recommendation to focus on strengths and solutions rather than on problems is a helpful and constructive reminder that where individuals and families are struggling under multiple burdens, an imaginative social work mind-set which actively notices, renders explicit and supports strengths that are there (including a stubbornly resistant capacity for sheer survival) and that concentrates on identifying risk factors and protective factors, may be all-important as an intervention that supports rather than crushes (Saleebey, 2006; Guo & Tsui, 2010). However, it is unfortunate that it is inclined to be presented as standing in *opposition* to psychodynamic social work, rather than a potentially helpful enhancement of it – especially when it misleadingly implies that the collaborative approach it endorses stands in contrast to the approach taken by those who employ a psychodynamic framework (e.g. Guo & Tsui, 2010, p. 234–235).

A second and different issue bears on the question of which theories are relevant to social work practice. Social work has always had to draw on other disciplines for some of its body of knowledge (Brekke, 2014). One reason for the variety of the theories that it draws on is that there is in the very nature of social work an inherent tension. Social need calls for redress at different levels that require different kinds of focus. Social work has therefore traditionally enumerated its four methods as casework, group work, community organisation (called in Britain community work) and social action (often now called political activism) (Hamilton, 1952). Sometimes all four methods draw on the same theoretical knowledge and practical skills, such as that the social worker's use of relationship can be crucial – including for community work and social action, as Jane Addams knew long ago and as community work practitioners now still attest (Murdach, 2007; Fook, 2002). Despite such overlap, the pool of theoretical knowledge and practical skills drawn on for one method will not be coterminous with that drawn on for another method. Tensions exist between the rival claims that different levels of need make on social work attention and between the claims for primacy of different theories that illuminate the need at one level or another and hence a method of redress at that level. Thus poverty, deprivation and other structurally caused strains that weigh on vulnerable individuals and families call for social action to achieve redress at a structural level, but there may be pressing immediacy of need, such as grave risk of harm to children in overburdened families, or suicidal depression in a life-term prisoner, where intervention cannot wait on structural redress but may need to be offered as casework (Kita, 2012). Sociological analysis (especially critical theory deriving from the tradition of the Frankfurt School) is an important part of the theory informing the call for structural intervention using the methods of community work and social action (Dominelli, 2002; Brookfield, 2009;), while casework is particularly indebted to theories that can assist relationship-based work, such as psychodynamic theory and recognition theory (John & Trevithick, 2012; Ruch, Turney & Ward, 2010; Houston, 2009).

Polarisation from the 1970s to the 1990s saw 1970s radical social work and the later anti-oppressive practice condemn psychodynamic casework as value-less or worse in the absence of its directly setting out to address structural ine-qualities (Bailey & Brake, 1975, Dominelli, 2002). The more recent discourse of critical theory and anti-oppressive social work, however, together with modern revisions of psychosocial theory and other developments, hold out the promise of dialogue and rapprochement, to which the theory of the introjected site may now contribute.

From anti-oppressive rhetoric to anti-oppressive practice

Whereas much writing on anti-oppressive practice is inclined to exhort rather than to demonstrate, a notable exception is the account of the endeavour by a group of Family Aid centres in Jerusalem to put anti-oppressive theory into practice in a concerted and thorough-going way. An early publication set out the way that, in this project, anti-oppressive principles were translated in a practical way into institutional terms (Strier & Binyamin, 2010). A later publication presents the progress of the project ten years after its beginning (Strier & Binyamin, 2014). I have found nothing to compare with this project in terms of determined alteration of institutional arrangements to meet client preferences and in terms of deter-minedly systematic, multi-level interventions in the situation of a poverty-stricken clientele entailing casework, group work and community work with advocacy. This development is evidently heir to the Israeli tradition, referred to in Chapter 8, of relating closely to perceived client need, including at the level of adaptations of institutional arrangements (Rosenfeld & Sykes, 1998).

The Jerusalem Family Aid project is said to have inspired other agencies in Israel (Strier & Binyamin, 2014). The practice of consulting clients on how ser-vices should be run is increasingly recognised as a principle of good practice, dubbed 'democratic professionalism' by Northdufter and Lorenz and seen as a possible way forward for social work generally (Northdufter & Lorenz, 2010; Houston, 2009). Naturally, a critical perspective remains important. There is all the difference in the world between consulting clients' viewpoints on institutional arrangements in a serious, respectful and sustained way, as has been done in the Jerusalem Family Aid centres, and doing so in a token manner: the rhetoric of anti-oppressive practice is as susceptible of being harnessed to a managerialist agenda as has been the language of 'partnership' and 'contract' (c.f. Fargion, 2003; McLoughlin, 2005; Stepney, 2010). At the same time, human ambivalence must be taken into account. In the Jerusalem project, an immense amount of work went into establishing client membership of the institution's new Steering Committee, but the client members eventually dropped out, and the social workers were too discouraged to undertake again the labour of recruiting and training other cli-ents to replace them (Strier & Binyamin, 2014). This situation calls to mind what Mattinson and Sinclair have written about the work with their deprived Social Services Department clientele, when they referred to the crucial requirement to bear with them, stay with them, stick with them – and, above all, to bear with their ambivalence (Mattinson & Sinclair, 1979). The ethos of critical theory, from the time of Adorno, has to do with being a subject and taking part in corporate life as a responsible citizen (Horkheimer & Adorno, 1987; Matthies, 2009). It is important to put this on offer to those who are clients of social work services. This requires preparedness to work patiently with human ambivalence, as the 1970s IMS social workers showed while they worked within a psychodynamic theoretical framework, and as the contemporary Jerusalem Family Aid social workers are showing while they work within an anti-oppressive theoretical framework (Mattinson & Sinclair, 1979; Strier & Binyamin, 2010, 2014).

Postmodern critical reflectivity vis-à-vis the theory of the introjected site

Discourse on critical practice, anti-oppressive practice and community work, once antagonistic to casework, tends now to be collaborative in tone, at least in some quarters. The contributions of Strier and Binyamin and their Israeli colleagues have themselves been notable in that respect, and so have those of Jan Fook. Fook has recalled that during the final year of her Australian social work training in the 1970s, her colleagues were opting to specialise in community work and were dismissive of casework, whereas she valued both approaches and went on to demonstrate in her first job that she could practise both (Fook, 2002). She was subsequently critical of the way that structural perspectives were being taught on post-qualification course, where the male sociology teachers, in her view, taught from a solely theoretical perspective drawn from sociology which was insistent on ideological conversion to ideals of empowerment and devalued the actual social work practice experience, and especially the 'micro-level' work, of the social work practitioners. There was, in her view, a disparity between empowerment ideals and people's lived experience. This is reminiscent of what was happening at that time in the British context, when the preaching of empowerment philosophy was dismissive of casework, whereas the lived experience of the clients of, for example, the IMS project workers (as described above) was that through the support of their caseworkers they gained confidence in various ways. This included learning how to negotiate for themselves with the various social agencies with which they had to deal; this *was* empowering (Mattinson & Sinclair, 1979).

There are other ways in which the more recent discourse of critical practice is much less far removed from the social work tradition with which I am concerned in this book than appearances might suggest. Anti-oppressive practice as expounded by authors such as Dominelli has generally been articulated in terms of facilitating corporate action by those identified as oppressed within certain group identities such as back, or female, or lesbian, gay, bisexual or transgender (LBGT). Dominelli herself came to acknowledge, however, criticisms of this propensity to treat clients as homogeneous objects or subjects seen as 'black', 'disabled', 'old' or 'gendered' rather than recognising them as complex individuals in complex situations (Healy, 2000; Dominelli, 2002, pp. 161–165). Authors such as Fook have pointed out, too, that there has been a tendency within anti-oppressive thinking to see clients as objects who do the bidding of powerful others rather than as having agency: and that since clients' lives are actually rooted in everyday interactions, they do not generally set out to change macro-level power relations (Pease & Fook, 2016). This is not to dismiss the potential importance of social workers forming tactical alliances with client groups and with others to set about achieving structural changes, but to point out that if the social worker's agenda on behalf of the client is not felt by the latter to be his own agenda, the ordinary, traditional social work procedure of stopping to listen to the client, and genuinely to negotiate with him, needs to come into play (Fargion, 2003, 2014). Meanwhile contemporary theorisation of the concept of the psycho-social has engaged with critical theory (Frost, 2008; Froggett, Ramvi & Davies, 2015).

Fook and her colleagues, from a critical theory perspective, emphasise the importance of listening to narratives of personal experience, which they define as an account of a life experience that explains the narrator's understanding of the world as part of the account (Fook & Gardiner, 2007, p. 11). This implies that listening closely has a functional importance. It is exactly this which I have been at pains to illustrate – for example, in Chapter 12, in the account of Mrs F's revealing narrative during the visit after her little girl's injuries had been found.

Above all, it is the inclusion of postmodernism within critical perspectives that opens the door to the possibility of dialogue between two social work traditions, that of critical practice and the particular casework tradition that became (as I am contending) all but lost from British social work soon after the end of the 1970s, before it had been fully theorised. A fine contribution by Fook entitled 'Critical reflectivity in education and practice' exemplifies this postmodern dimension in critical discourse (Fook, 1999). Fook observes that the two lucidly detailed examples with which her paper opens illustrate reflectivity as involving:

> The ability to locate oneself in a situation through the recognition of how actions and interpretations, social and cultural background and personal history, emotional aspects of experience, and personally held assumptions and values influence the situation.
>
> (Fook, 1999, p. 199)

She makes the important point, amongst others, that such reflectivity is potentially empowering: 'it is as if [they i.e. the authors of her two examples], in being able to recognise their own influence in the situation, *are able to locate a concrete site for change*' (Fook, 1999, p. 199; italics mine).

A comparable recognition of one's own influence in the situation, *and the potential for significant change that that act of recognition can have*, has been illustrated in the work with Miss M (Chapter 7), Mrs F (Chapter 12) and in the work with Michael (Chapters 10 & 11). In the case of Mrs F, for example, it started to become clear in retrospect (when I visited her after Ruth was found to be injured) that Mrs F had been trying to get help with a problem that she also felt she had to conceal – first by asking our agency to assign another social worker to her, and then by a fragmentary series of visits to Social Services. When I acknowledged to Mrs F that I had not understood her desperate attempts to get help, there was an immediate deepening of rapport, followed by her clear series of narratives with a single theme – she had contact with someone important to her, who subsequently died. This allowed me at last to understand her situation coherently, and to arrange to work in a purposeful way with her. In the case of Michael, it was when the social worker understood and acknowledged that her agreeing to stop working with the family had been unhelpful, and had played a part in Michael's escalating behaviour problems, that she was able to restore constructive working relations with Michael and his mother.

The same issue has been illustrated in the present chapter in the family casework of the IMS social workers in a Social Services Department (Mattinson & Sinclair, 1979). I have already given two examples of what enabled a concrete site for change to be identified. The earliest is one that occurred during the first few months of the visits to Mr and Mrs Whiteside, when, after a disagreement, the worker went along with the cessation of visits for a while, which she subsequently recognised as rejecting behaviour on her part towards the clients (who had been rejecting her). Her recognition and acknowledgement of her own rejecting behaviour appears to have been a highly significant factor in the renegotiation of a relationship and working contract with the couple, who soon confirmed that they wanted her visits to continue, even though they could not at first quite explain why.

As for the second example, it is striking that on looking back in a retrospective overview of all the families in the IMS project, it was recognised that the worker had sometimes joined the family in an unhelpful way of relating, and had only belatedly realised this. Where this had happened and had subsequently been recognised and admitted by the worker, in the context of clarifying the particular way of relating in which the family members and the worker had been implicated, this indeed became a site for significant change: it was *here* that the parental couple were able to change their way of relating to each other and to their children. The passage has been quoted in a previous chapter. Here it is again:

> The interpretations which apparently enabled them to relinquish or change their behaviour towards each other were few, remain etched on our minds and related to their relationship with us. *Those that seemed to have the most effect were often those in which we could include reference to our own behaviour in relation to them, when previously we had got drawn into their interactive strategy and then only belatedly become aware of what we were doing.*
>
> (Mattinson & Sinclair, 1979, p. 203; italics mine)

This phenomenon of becoming implicated in a way of being that is central also to the difficulties of the clients had been termed in an earlier book by Janet

Mattinson the 'reflection process' (Mattinson, 1975). This earlier book, together with the book about the IMS project in the Social Services Department, has been cited in Ferguson's incisive article on the *Laming Report*, as an example of the sophisticated psychological theory that modern child protection social work desperately needs (Ferguson, 2005; Mattinson, 1975; Mattinson & Sinclair, 1979). Psychoanalysts will recognise that the theory under discussion includes that of the countertransference.

Empowerment and agency, in critical theory and in the theory of the social work site

Other instances of such recognition by the social worker of her own influence on the situation, and the transforming effect of her acknowledgement of it, can be found in the work with Michael and Mrs F and also in the work with Miss M. For the present, the point from Fook's postmodern conception of reflectivity that I wish to pursue, is the issue of empowerment and agency.

Another social work critical theorist has also declared the issue of a sense of agency to be of crucial importance. In an article that applies the thought of the Frankfurt critical theorist Theodor Adorno to social work, Aila-Leena Matthies (2009) points out that the vital substance of Adorno's critical theory concerns the process of becoming a subject – meaning a fully autonomous, thinking, responsible citizen as opposed to a manipulated, systems-functioning one – and that the subjectivisation of those who use social work services is indispensable if the social work is to be effective. Now, a process of subjectivisation is exactly what I have shown, earlier in this book, to be a product of the introjection of the 'site' of social work practice. It could be seen particularly clearly, stage by stage, in the work with Miss M in Chapter 7. A capacity for subjectivised, highly individual exploitation of the resources of the social work itself, in a range of ways such as her play with the television license money, had preceded the marriage project which she called in to tell me about some time after the completion of our work together, and about which, as she told me, there was warm neighbourhood interest and approval. *That* was a project all her own! In a comparable fashion, the clients of the IMS project showed, at an advanced stage of the work with them, just such a capacity for subjectivised exploitation of the resources of their social work situation. I have cited just one example, that of the family who, very touchingly, asked their social worker to read them a story: and I have referred the reader to other highly individual examples (Mattinson & Sinclair, 1979, pp. 186, 205–214, 219–220, 235–239). Many of these clients were also empowered to conduct negotiations on their own behalf with external agencies such as utilities services, landlords, courts and the Department of Health and Social Security, when previously they had felt helpless in the face of doing so.

This phenomenon of the process of becoming a subject *as a direct result of the social work process* has not, to date, been adequately recognised. The issue of its recognition in theoretical terms is relevant here. In contemporary social work with marginalised families, a thoughtful Israeli social work manager volunteered to a researcher her observation that the social workers who have been most effectively engaged with marginalised families, over a period of time, tend to notice and speak of their sense of a *process* (Knei-Paz, 2009). Evidently this phenomenon of a process struck the social workers, and struck the manager, as significant. For further evidence about this question of a process, pathways for further research might include semi-structured interviews with social workers at intervals during their work with a sample of families, with a research focus on client engagement over a period of time, and might also include interrogation of existing research data already built into initiatives such as the Jerusalem Family Aid projects. Meanwhile, I infer that the process sensed by the Israeli social workers, and mentioned to Knei-Paz, amounted to the gradual introjection of the social work site that ushers in the discovery by the client of being an active agent in a working, functioning 'social work situation'. It is the theme of the whole of Part III of this book. Subjectivisation results from this process, and a greater empowerment accompanies it.

Note

1 The social worker here would be theoretically understood as being comparable to the mother whose distressed, angry and frightened baby attempts to expel his unmanageable feelings just as he expels unwanted products from his body; the responsive mother under the impact of his urgent crying receives his communications, 'metabolises' them in a process of maternal reverie and, through her response, returns them to the baby in a detoxified form that he is better able to manage (Bion, 1977).

References

Adams, R., Dominelli, L. & Payne, M. (2009) *Critical Practice in Social Work*. 2nd edition. Basingstoke, Palgrave Macmillan.

Addams, J. (1965) Democracy and social ethics. In: C. Lasch (ed.), *The Social Thought of Jane Addams*, pp. 28–43. Indianapolis, Bobbs-Merrill. Original work published 1902.

Bailey, R. & Brake, M. (eds.) (1975) *Radical Social Work*. London, Edward Arnold.

Bion, W. (1977) Learning from experience. In: W. Bion, *Seven Servants: Four Works by Wilfred R. Bion*, pp. 1–111. New York, Jason Aronson Inc.

Brekke, J. S. (2014) A science of social work, and social work as an integrative scientific discipline: Have we gone too far, or not far enough? *Research on Social Work Practice*. 24 (5), pp. 517–523.

Brookfield, S. (2009) The concept of critical reflection: Promises and contradictions. *European Journal of Social Work* 12 (3), pp. 293–304.

Burns, E. (1958) Social welfare is our commitment. In: National Conference on Social Welfare, *Official Proceedings of the Annual Meeting: 1958: The Presidential Address*. [Mistakenly headed in Contents: Social work is our commitment.] Available from: Quod.lib.umich.edu/n/ncosw/ACH8650.1958.001.

Chu, W. & Tsui, M. (2008) The nature of practice wisdom in social work revisited. *International Social Work* 51 (1), pp. 47–54.

Cohen, R. (n.d.) The history of Toynbee Hall – a timeline. Available from: www.toynbee
hall.org.uk/the-history-of-toynbee-hall-a-timeline-from-1884-2015- [Accessed 23rd
September 2017].

Cooper, A. & Lousada, J. (2005) *Borderline Welfare: Feeling and Fear of Feeling in
Modern Welfare*. London, Karnac.

Cornell, K. (2006) 'Person-in-situation': History, theory and new directions for social work
practice. *Praxis* 6, pp. 50–57.

Corrigan, P. & Leonard, P. (1978) *Social Work Practice under Capitalism: A Marxist
Approach*. London, Macmillan.

Davis, A. (2008) *Celebrating 100 Years of Social Work*. University of Birmingham.
Available from: www.birmingham.ac.uk/Documents/college-social-sciences/social-
policy/IASS/100-years-of-social-work.pdf.

Dominelli, L. (1996) Deprofessionalizing social work: Anti-oppressive practice, competencies and postmodernism. *British Journal of Social Work* 26 (2), pp. 153–175. Available
from: https://doi.org/101093/oxfordjournals.bjsw.a011077.

Dominelli, L. (2002) *Anti-Oppressive Social Work Theory and Practice*. Basingstoke,
Palgrave Macmillan.

Fargion, S. (2003) Images of contract: An empirical study of the use of theory in practice.
British Journal of Social Work 33 (4), pp. 517–534. Available from: DOI.org/10.1093/
bjsw/33.4.517.

Fargion, S. (2014) Synergies and tensions in child protection and parent support: Policy
lines and practitioners cultures. *Child & Family social Work* 19 (1), pp. 24–33. Available
from: DOI: 10.1111/j.1365-2206.2012.00877.x.

Ferguson, H. (2005) Working with violence, the emotions and the psycho-social dynamics
of child protection: Reflections on the Victoria Climbié case. *Social Work Education:
The International Journal* 24 (7), pp. 781–795.

Ferguson, I. & Woodward, R. (2009) *Radical Social Work: Making a Difference*. Bristol,
The Policy Press.

Fook, J. (1999) Critical reflectivity in education and practice. In: B. Pease and J. Fook (eds.)
Transforming Social Work Practice: Postmodern Critical Perspectives, pp. 195–208.
London, Routledge.

Fook, J. (2002) *Social Work: Critical Theory and Practice*. London, Sage.

Fook, J. & Gardiner, F. (2007) *Practising Critical Reflection: A Resource Handbook*.
Maidenhead, Open University Press.

Froggett, L., Ramvi, E. & Davies, L. (2015) Thinking from experience in psychosocial
practice: reclaiming and teaching 'use of self'. *Journal of Social Work Practice* 29 (2),
pp. 133–150. Available from: http://dx.doi.org/10.1080/02650533.2014.923389 [Accessed
1st May 2017].

Frost, L. (2008) Why teach social work students psychosocial studies? *Social Work
Education: The International Journal* 27 (3), pp. 243–261. Available from: DOI: 10.1080/
02615470701381426.

Goldstein, H. (1990) The knowledge base of social work practice: Theory, wisdom,
analogue or art? *Families in Society* 71 (1), pp. 32–43.

Golightly, M. & Hollway, M. (2015). Editorial. *British Journal of Social Work* 45 (6),
pp. 1653–1658.

Gray, M. & Fook, J. (2004) The quest for a universal social work: Some issues and implications. *Social Work Education* 23 (5), pp. 625–644.

Guo, W. & Tsui, M. (2010) From resilience to resistance: A reconstruction of the strengths perspective in social work practice. *International Social Work* 53 (2), pp. 233–245.

Hamilton, G. (1940) *Theory and Practice of Social Casework*. New York, Columbia University Press.

Hamilton, G. (1952) *Theory and Practice of Social Casework*. New York, Columbia University Press.

Healy, K. (2000) *Social Work Practices: Contemporary Perspectives on Change*. London, Sage.

Higgins, M. (2016) 'Cultivating our humanity' in child and family social work in England. *Social Work Education. The International Journal*. 35 (5), pp. 518–529. Available from: Doi.org/10.1080/02615479.2016.1181161 [Accessed 8th April 2017].

Hollis, F. (1964) *Casework: A Psychosocial Therapy*. New York, Columbia University Press.

Horkheimer, M. & Adorno, T. (1987) *Dialectic of Enlightenment (Cultural Memory in the Present)*. G. Schmid Noerr (ed.). Frankfurt, S. Fischer Verlag.

Houston, S. (2009) Communication, recognition and social work: Aligning the critical theories of Habermas and Honneth. *British Journal of Social Work* 39 (7), pp. 1274–1290. Available from: DOI: http://doi.org/10.1093/bjsw/bcn054 [Accessed 2nd May 2017].

Jordan, B. (1990) *Social Work in an Unjust Society*. Hemel Hempstead, Harvester Wheatsheaf.

Kita, E. (2012) Making it thinkable: A psychodynamic approach to the psychosocial problems of prisons and prisoners. In: J. Berzoff (ed.), *Falling through the Cracks: Psychodynamic Practice with Vulnerable and Oppressed Populations*. New York, Columbia University Press.

Knei-Paz, C. (2009) The central role of the therapeutic bond in a social agency setting. *Journal of Social Work* 9 (2), pp. 178–198.

Lymbery, M. (2005) The history and development of social work. In: M. Lymbery, *Social Work with Older People: Context, Policy and Practice*. London, Sage. Available from: DOI: http://dx.doi.org/10.4135/9781446211687.n3.

McLoughlin, K. (2005) From ridicule to institutionalization: Anti-oppression, the state and social work. *Critical Social Policy* 25 (3), pp. 283–305.

Matthies, A-L. (2009) The concept of subjectivisation by Adorno – applied in social work. *European Journal of Social Work* 12 (3), pp. 319–332.

Mattinson, J. (1975) *The Reflection Process in Casework Supervision*. London, Institute of Marital Studies, The Tavistock Institute of Human Relations.

Mattinson, J. & Sinclair, I. (1979) *Mate and Stalemate: Working with Marital Problems in a Social Services Department*. Oxford, Blackwell.

Maurice, E. (ed.) (1913) *The Life of Octavia Hill: As Told in Her Letters*. London, Cambridge University Press.

Munro, E. (2010) *The Munro Review of Child Protection. Part One: A Systems Analysis*. London, Department for Education. Available from: www.gov.uk/government/uploads/system/uploads/attachment_data/file/624949/TheMunroReview-Part_one.pdf.

Munro, E. (2011a) *The Munro Review Interim Report: 'The Child's Journey'*. London, Department for Education. Available from: www.trixonline.co.uk/website/news/pdf/policy_briefing_No-11.pdf.

Munro, E. (2011b) *The Munro Review of Child Protection. Final Report: A Child-Centred System*. London, Department for Education. Available from: www.gov.uk/government/uploads/system/uploads/attachment_data/file/175391/Munro-Review.pdf.

Murdach, A. (2007) Situational approaches to direct practice: Origin, decline and re-emergence. *Social Work* 52 (3), pp. 211–218. Available from: Doi.org/10.1093/sw/52.3.211.

Narey, M. (2014) Making the education of social workers consistently effective. Available from: www.gov.uk/government/uploads/system/uploads/attachment_data/file/278741/ Socialworker education report. PDF_.

O'Neill, S. (1999) Social work – a profession? *Journal of Social Work Practice* 13 (1), pp. 9–18.

Pease, B. & Fook, J. (eds.) (2016) *Transforming Social Work Practice: Postmodern Critical Perspectives*. Abingdon, Routledge.

Perlman, H. (1957) *Social Casework: A Problem-Solving Process*. Chicago, University of Chicago Press.

Richmond, M. (1917) *Social Diagnosis*. New York, Russell Sage Foundation.

Robinson, V. (1930) *A Changing Psychology in Social Casework*. Chapel Hill, University of North Carolina Press.

Ruch, G., Turney, D. & Ward, A. (2010) *Relationship-Based Social Work: Getting to the Heart of Practice*. London, Jessica Kingsley.

Saleeby, D. (1996) The strengths perspective in social work practice: Extensions and cautions. *Social Work* 41 (3), pp. 296–305. Available from: Doi.org/10.1093/sw/41.3.296.

Samson, P. (2015) Practice wisdom: The art and science of social work. *Journal of Social Work Practice: Psychotherapeutic Approaches in Health, Welfare and the Community*. 29 (2), pp. 119–131. Available from: DOI.10.1080/02650533.2014.922058.

Segal, N. (n.d.) Jane Addams of Hull House. Available from: http://scholastic.com/ browsw/article.jsp?id=4948 [Accessed 19th June 2017].

Stepney, P. (2010) Social Welfare at the crossroads: Evidence-based practice or critical practice? *International Journal of Interdisciplinary Social Sciences* 5 (5), pp. 105–119. Available from: www.SocialSciences-Journal.ISSN 1833–1882.

Stepney, P. (2012) An overview of the wider policy context. In: P. Stepney & D. Ford (eds.), *Social Work Models, Methods and Theories: A Framework for Practice*. 2nd edition. Lyme Regis, Russell House.

Stevenson, O. (2005) Foreword. In: M. Bower (ed.), *Psychoanalytic Theory for Social Work Practice: Thinking Under Fire*, pp. ix–xviii. London, Routledge.

Strier, R. & Binyamin, S. (2010) Developing anti-oppressive services for the poor: A theoretical and organisational rationale. *British Journal of Social Work* 40 (6), pp. 1908–1926. Available from: Doi.org/10.1093/bjsw/bcp122.

Strier, R. & Binyamin, S. (2014) Introducing anti-oppressive social work in public services: Rhetoric to practice. *British Journal of Social Work* 44 (8), pp. 2095–2112. Available from: Doi.org/10.1093/bjsw/bct049.

Taft, J. (1933) *The Dynamics of Therapy in a Controlled Relationship*. New York, Macmillan.

Trevithick, P. (2003) Effective relationship-based practice: A theoretical explanation. *Journal of Social Work Practice* 17 (2), pp. 163–176.

Winnicott, C. (2004) Casework techniques in the child care services. In: J. Kanter (ed.), *Face to Face with Children: The Life and Work of Clare Winnicott*, pp.145–165. London, Karnac.

Yelloly, M. (1980) *Social Work Theory and Psychoanalysis*. Wokingham, Van Nostrum Reinhold Company.

Part IV

Conclusion

Chapter 14

A differential theory of therapeutic engagement

This chapter offers a summing up and concluding comment on the book's differential theory of therapeutic engagement.

Freud's challenge or prophecy to psychoanalysts at the 1918 Budapest Congress was that psychoanalysis would one day be extended to the poor, in modified form, on a large scale (Freud, 1919). In Chapter 1 I drew attention to an inherent ambiguity in Freud's Congress paper that leaves it uncertain whether the practice that he envisaged being offered to the poor would be psychoanalysis, albeit a psychoanalysis somewhat modified into something we now call psychotherapy – or a different kind of practice altogether, comparable with psychoanalysis only by way of analogy in certain respects, and amounting to social work. This book has proceeded to look at both kinds of practice, psychotherapy and social work.

The book has identified, conceptualised and illustrated a process of therapeutic engagement that can take place in psychotherapy, and in social work (and indeed in other kinds of psychodynamic practice), no less than in the psychoanalysis for which it has already been theorised (Donnet, 2009). It shows in practice and on clear theoretical grounds why no ready-made 'psychological-mindedness' is required. Because the theory is differential, it also shows it to be appropriate that social work in which a therapeutic bond is forged concerns itself as much with the concrete practical problems with which poverty-stricken, multiply burdened individuals and families are beset as with their emotional needs (c.f. Knei-Paz, 2009).

It may be helpful at this point to remind ourselves of the theory. I will first state it in abstract form, modelled closely on Donnet's formulation of the theory of the analytic site and analysing situation (Donnet, 2001, 2009), but stated in differential terms. By way of further recapitulation, I will then draw attention to four issues: (i) the difference of the theory from the concept of the therapeutic alliance; (ii) the factor in free psychotherapy corresponding in function to the fee of private practice; (iii) the enhanced sense of subjective agency that results from introjection of the relevant site; and (iv) the quasi-autonomous character of the process that introjection of the site sets in motion.

The differential theory stated at a general level

The concept of 'site' simply refers to that which is placed at the disposal of the person who enters psychoanalysis, psychotherapy or social work respectively. (In what follows I will substitute the word 'person' for 'patient-or-client'.) That which is placed at the person's disposal consists of an ensemble of elements proper to the sphere of practice being undertaken. The elements exist in latent form, are potentially discoverable by the person if the site is adequately constructed, and constitute the resources of the site which he can discover and utilise or exploit, just as human beings find and exploit the resources in a geographical location.

The order in which the person discovers the elements in the site is determined by his unconscious options and takes place in a paradoxical manner which confers a quality of ambiguity on whether the person has *found* an element that had a prior existence or whether he has *created* it (Donnet, 2001; Winnicott, 1974). This paradoxical created/found quality of the experience plays an important part in the person's eventual acquisition of a firmer sense of being an autonomous subject. If the person's encounter with a given element of the site is adequate, he takes it in or introjects it. (Readers not familiar with psychoanalysis are reminded that by introjection is meant an *unconscious* fantasy of taking something into the inside of ourselves, just as food is taken from the outside into the inside of the body.) This process goes on, element by element, until a critical proportion of the elements of the site has been discovered and introjected. This is the point at which the person can be said to have introjected (taken in) the site as a whole, and at which he discovers himself to be in a functioning situation whose inherent logic, ethics and specificity he can sense – variously, the 'analysing situation' of psychoanalysis, the 'psychotherapeutic situation' of psychotherapy, or the 'social work situation' of social casework. At this point a quasi-autonomous process (variously, the analytic process, the psychotherapeutic process or the social work process) has been set in motion. It is this of which Freud wrote, in relation to psychoanalysis, that the analyst:

> sets in motion a process . . . He can supervise this process, further it, remove obstacles in its way, and he can undoubtedly vitiate much of it. But on the whole, once begun, it goes its own way, and does not allow either the direction it takes or the order in which it picks up its points to be prescribed for it.
>
> (Freud, 1913, p. 130).

The person is, by this point, fully engaged in the work being undertaken. He senses that there are, in this 'functioning situation', 'rules of the game' entailing logic, ethics and specificity that the professional person working with him relates to and respects, and towards which the person himself develops a trusting attachment. One product of the attachment to the site – transformed, now into a 'functioning situation' with its own rules of the game – is a greater capacity on the part of the person for three-term relations, together with a more tolerant, reflective and adaptive relation to reality.

All of the above can be true of therapeutic engagement not only in psycho-analysis and psychoanalytic psychotherapy, but also in social work. In terms of the theory, what differentiates them is that the ensemble of elements that is proper to each of the three sites differs one from the other.

Difference from the concept of therapeutic alliance: the role of introjection

The part played in this theory by the process of introjection differentiates it from the concept of a therapeutic alliance. The irreducible role played by introjection can mean that, at times, the person who may be angrily berating the practitioner, or who is testing the practitioner to the uttermost with challenging behaviour, may actually be cooperating very fully at an *unconscious* level with the therapeutic process. One particularly clear illustration of this has been the account in Chapter 12 of the social work with Mrs F during the exhaustingly difficult period *after* introjection of the social work site, when realistic plans about the child's temporary foster care had to be negotiated. Chapter 12 shows that Mrs F's oppositional behaviour in that period was an essential part of her working on the issue that underlay the risk to the child. The issue therefore had to be resolved; and Chapter 12 adduces evidence that, at a level below that of consciousness, the client sensed this.

The psychotherapy site and the factor corresponding to the fee

There is an important lesson to be gleaned from Freud with regard to psycho-therapy in a setting where the patient pays no fee. Freud's thought about the function of the fee was that it grounds the treatment in the world of reality and so performs a regulating function for the patient (Freud, 1913). Chapter 3 has illus-trated the way that patients in a psychotherapy for which no fee is charged to the patient, and which is open-ended (that is, where the duration of the therapy is to be eventually negotiated rather than fixed in advance), are very apt to investigate the therapist's capacity to be grounded in the real world by proposing or starting to practise non-attendance on a relatively large scale. This issue often comes into play when the patient's piecemeal introjection of elements of the site has almost but not quite reached a level that is critically transformative; it is as though the patient needs to verify whether, in an important respect, the therapist is sane and in touch with ordinary realities. Consequently, as Chapter 3 illustrates, adequate handling of this issue often has a decisive effect on the patient's subsequent engagement with a new seriousness in his or her psychotherapy.

Subjectivity: the role of created/found

What is it about the paradoxical created/found ambiguity that proves to so impor-tant for the person's development of a more secure subjectivity?

Winnicott proposed the idea of the paradox of created/found in relation to his concept of the transitional object – the teddy bear or comparable object to which the very small child becomes attached for its association with his experience of his mother (Winnicott, 1974). The reality of ordinary everyday separations from the actual mother challenge, painfully, the child's infantile illusion of omnipotent control of her, but possession of the transitional object can assist the child to manage the pain of these separations because the illusion of omnipotent control can be maintained in relation to the transitional object. The transitional object is not hallucinated or imaginary, and in that sense the child *finds* it as existing outside himself, yet in his use of it to further his illusion of being in omnipotent possession of mother, it is his *creation*. Winnicott regarded this phase-appropriate support for the child's illusion of omnipotence as vital for the child's gaining of confidence in his own capacities and sense of self.

The opportunities for created/found discovery of elements of the site, function in a comparable way to support the person's confident sense of being a subjective agent. Indeed, Donnet regards the created/found character of the analysand's encounter with the elements of the analytic site as so vital that he declares the most important role of the analyst, in relation to it, is *not to hinder it* (Donnet, 2001). In the realm of psychotherapy, we saw this gradual process of the development of subjectivity illustrated particularly lucidly in the case of Velia (Chapter 5), whose severe lack of a sense of agency, at the start of her treatment, was eventually quite markedly transformed, and in social work it was particularly striking in the case of Miss M (Chapter 7).

A quasi-autonomous process

A process that can surprise

What is meant by the process being a quasi-autonomous one? Let us recall, from Chapter 7, its vivid illustration in the social work with Miss M.

The point in time where the sense of an autonomous process was most striking of all was *after* I had seen evidence that the mourning for Miss M's lost mother, once so blocked, had been successfully accomplished. It was time, I thought, to bring the work with Miss M to a conclusion, and I expected to set about doing this. To my surprise, she began to tell me eagerly about her growing acquaintance with the man on the building site. There was a disjunction between my considered formulation of the social work task – to help Miss M to recover her functioning (including keeping a roof over her head through rent payment) by helping her to mourn and relinquish her dependence on her mother, a task I considered accomplished – and my astonished sense of being shown, by Miss M, that an autonomous process was *still* in train and *still* unfolding. I felt that in telling me about her new adventure Miss M knew what she was doing, albeit at a level that was less than conscious, and, although surprised, I stayed my hand and the work continued.

The paradox of 'created/found' was in action par excellence. Did work on a building site, with a boastfully leg-pulling joker amongst the building crew, chance to take place near Miss M's home just when she was ready to work out something in relation to a man? Or, by lingering so frequently to watch the men at work, did Miss M create the opportunity for him to 'chat her up' and take her out for coffee?

What was it all about? The episode of the man on the building site was an important dimension of Miss M's developing sense of becoming, and feeling herself to be, an autonomous subject (Donnet, 2001; Matthies, 2009). Expressed differently, in the language of anti-oppressive social work, it was an important part of the process of her empowerment. In relation to the mother she had mourned and relinquished, Miss M had always been something of a manipulated object: mother, perhaps because it was the only way that occurred to her of relating to a daughter with a congenital learning disability, had decided and managed everything. Mother had also referred to her husband with grim contempt as '*Him!!*' At the time of the episode of the man on the building site, I was experienced by Miss M as a mother figure. At a level below that of consciousness, Miss M needed to find out how much freedom she was henceforth to have in her life as an adult woman, including as a sexual woman. Would interest in a man arouse baleful maternal envy in the internalised imago of the mother in her mind, and lead to her feeling persecuted, frightened and depressed? She had discovered, by then, that this could be investigated in the context of the maternal transference. The evidence that this final phase of the casework further strengthened her subjectivity is to be found in her happily finding a husband (an entirely different man!) a year after my work with her had ended, and in her recruiting the warm interest and support of neighbourhood friends for her marriage project. Who would have thought it? When I had thought that our work was accomplished and should be terminated, Miss M had conveyed (by telling me so eagerly about the man on the building site) that a quasi-autonomous social work process was still unfolding. My trust in that process was the basis for the decision to continue the work.

The social work process not confined to avowedly psychodynamic work

The 'social work process', with its quasi-autonomous character, can only be set in train when the ensemble of elements *proper to social work practice* has been made available. The social work client, who arrives at the door of the agency, institution or public service which employs the social worker because he is faced with some psychosocial privation, difficulty or suffering, is entitled to expect that attention will be paid to the concrete practical aspects of his need for help no less than to his emotional needs.

It is no part of my argument that only social workers holding an explicitly psychodynamic frame of reference can find that a 'social work process', in the sense in which I have used the term, can be set in motion. Jan Fook and Fiona Gardner, from the theoretical perspective of critical practice, have emphasised the importance of listening to personal narratives (narratives that reveal the subject's view and experience of the world), and this implies that such listening has a functional importance (Fook & Gardner, 2007, p. 11). From a different theoretical point of departure, Joan Berzoff considers that Freud's 'evenly hovering attention' has much to teach the social worker about how to listen (Berzoff, 2012). I have mentioned, as a related element of social work practice, the *preparedness not to foreclose too quickly when judging what*, in the client's account of himself and his difficulties, *is relevant*. That preparedness has been beautifully illustrated in the work of some of the Italian social workers, and one in particular, in Silvia Fargion's study (Fargion, 2014, p. 29). Although I happen to see the client's 'apparent irrelevancies' as analogous to free association in psychoanalysis, these Italian social workers may not necessarily think of their theories as psychodynamic. Indeed, the 'social work process' was evident in the work of the Israeli social workers in Knei-Paz's study, who impressed on their manager their sense of a *process*; and what we know is that a therapeutic bond was formed when the clients felt that attention was paid both to their concrete practical needs and to their emotional needs (Knei-Paz, 2009). This is what matters, not whether the social workers did or did not think in terms of a psychodynamic framework. When the social worker pays careful attention to offering social work in a sustained and consistent way, the social work process follows of its own accord.

However, professors of social work, heads of social work services and senior social work advisors to policy makers do need to have a good working understanding of psychodynamic theory in general and of the significance of the social work process in particular. How else is there to be an informed recognition of the profound impact that an established social work process can have, a process vividly illustrated by authors other than myself? (Knei-Paz, 2009; Kita, 2012). An incontrovertible case can and must be made for the time, resources and professional autonomy that allows social workers to work in the manner of the Israeli social workers whose clients so resoundingly affirmed to Knei-Paz the importance of the work. That requires a clear grasp at very senior levels of the theoretical reasons why such work is transforming.

It is also true that while good, principled social work can get along without theory couched specifically in psychodynamic terms, the teaching of explicitly psychodynamic theory and practice to practitioners, at the various levels of basic practice, supervisory level, and specialist consultant, can be immensely helpful (Temperley & Himmel, 1986). I recommend, to anyone still doubtful of the humanity and transforming potential of a psychodynamic perspective, the reading of Elizabeth Kita's account of her work in an American state prison, and especially her profoundly moving work as a young intern with the life-sentence prisoner she calls Mr K (Kita, 2012).

The extraordinary potential power of the quasi-autonomous social work process

My own social work practice was greatly supported by an appreciation of the interface between the external world of reality and the internal world of psychic reality.

Is it paradoxical, given how firmly I have emphasised that the parameters of social work must be respected by the social worker, that a sentence in André Green's 'The dead mother' recalls my social work client, Miss M?

> But this meaning-in-waiting is only truly significant when it is re-awakened by a re-cathexis which takes place in an absolutely different context.
>
> (Green, 1986, p. 172)

Green was here writing about the re-living, in the course of psychoanalysis, of the drama of the primal scene. The bold thought has struck me that the sentence, taken in itself, is equally true of my former social work client, Miss M (Chapter 7).

Miss M rarely spoke of her father, yet the episode of the man on the building site represented, for Miss M, the re-awakening of a meaning-in-waiting: the re-experiencing, that is, of her oedipal attachment to her father, containing her capacity for emotional investment in a man, and the question of whether or not a price was to be exacted in the form of loss of her sense of her mother's love. Miss M was anxious about allowing her capacities to be noticed, by herself and by others – we can recall her insistence that she understood nothing about money while revealing, astonishingly, that she had been keeping an accurate record of her rent payments! I inferred that she was afraid of a baleful envy, originally on the part of her mother. In the context of the transference – a resource in the social work site that she had discovered and introjected – it was possible for the oedipal drama to be re-kindled in the immediate here-and-now of the present. She paradoxically found/created a situation in which a man lavished some attention on her, for as long as she needed for investigation of her unconscious question about whether there could be a benign maternal attitude to her emotional and libidinal needs. I infer that she felt the answer to this question to be satisfactory, since a year after the end of her treatment she called to tell me, happily, that she was to be married.

What a reward, to see her embracing life to such a degree! Such experiences as this are the basis of my belief that much of what Freud and von Freund hoped might be on offer to the poor may indeed be entailed in the social work process.

References

Berzoff, J. (2012) Why we need a biopsychosocial perspective with vulnerable, oppressed and at-risk clients. In: J. Berzoff (ed.), *Falling Through the Cracks: Psychodynamic Practice with Vulnerable and Oppressed Populations*, pp. 1–39. New York, Columbia University Press.

Donnet, J.-L. (2001) From the fundamental rule to the analysing situation. *International Journal of Psychoanalysis* 82 (1), pp. 129–140. Available from: DOI: 10.1516/3FUH-9WTT-E68B-WF70.

Donnet, J.-L. (2009) *The Analyzing Situation*. A. Weller (trans.). London, Karnac. Originally published in French as *La Situation Analysante*. Presses Universitaires de France, 2005.

Fargion, S. (2014) Synergies and tensions in child protection and parent support: Policy lines and practitioners cultures. *Child & Family social Work* 19 (1), pp. 24–33. Available from: DOI: 10.1111/j.1365-2206.2012.00877.x.

Fook, J. & Gardner, F. (2007) *Practising Critical Reflection: A Resource Handbook.* Maidenhead, Open University Press.

Freud, S. (1913) On beginning the treatment (further recommendations on the technique of psycho-analysis I). In: J. Strachey (ed. and trans.), *The Standard Edition of the Complete Psychological Works of Sigmund Freud* (Vol. 12), pp. 121–144. London, Hogarth Press.

Freud, S. (1919) Lines of advance in psycho-analytic therapy. In: J. Strachey (ed. and trans.), *The Standard Edition of the Complete Psychological Works of Sigmund Freud* (Vol. 17), pp. 157–168. London, Hogarth Press.

Green, A. (1986) The dead mother. K. Aubertin (trans.). In: A. Green, *On Private Madness*, pp. 142–173. London, Hogarth Press.

Kita, E. (2012) Making it thinkable: A psychodynamic approach to the psychosocial problems of prisons and prisoners. In: J. Berzoff (ed.), *Falling through the Cracks: Psychodynamic Practice with Vulnerable and Oppressed Populations.* New York, Columbia University Press.

Knei-Paz, C. (2009) The central role of the therapeutic bond in a social agency setting. *Journal of Social Work.* 9 (2), pp. 178–198.

Matthies, A-L. (2009) The concept of subjectivisation by Adorno – applied in social work. *European Journal of Social Work* 12 (3), pp. 319–332. Available from: DOI: 10.1111/cfs.12061.

Temperley, J. & Himmel, S. (1986) Training for psychodynamic social work. *Journal of Social Work Practice* 2 (3), pp. 4–14. Available from: DOI: 10.1080/02650538608414967.

Winnicott, D. (1974) Transitional objects and transitional phenomena. In: Winnicott, D. *Playing and Reality*, Chapter 1, pp. 1–30. Harmondsworth, Pelican Books.

Index

For Product Safety Concerns and Information please contact our EU
representative GPSR@taylorandfrancis.com
Taylor & Francis Verlag GmbH, Kaufingerstraße 24, 80331 München, Germany